In and Out of the Mind

GREEK IMAGES OF THE TRAGIC SELF

Ruth Padel

PRINCETON UNIVERSITY PRESS

PRINCETON, NEW JERSEY

The following publishers have generously given permission to use quotations
from copyrighted works: From "In Memory of Sigmund Freud," in *W. H.
Auden: Collected Poems* by W. H. Auden, edited by Edward Mendelson.
Copyright 1940 and renewed 1968 by W. H. Auden. Reprinted by
permission of Random House, Inc. and Faber & Faber Ltd. From "A Newly
Discovered 'Homeric Hymn' . . . ," in *The Distances* by Charles Olsen.
Copyright 1950, 1951, 1953 (c) 1960 Charles Olsen. Used by permission of
Grove Press, Inc. From "Snow," in *Collected Poems 1945–48* by Louis
MacNeice, © 1949, and from *Murder in the Cathedral* by T. S. Eliot, © 1963,
used by permission of Faber & Faber Ltd. Excerpts from *Murder in the
Cathedral* by T. S. Eliot, copyright 1953 by Harcourt Brace Jovanovich, Inc.
and renewed 1963 by T. S. Eliot. Reprinted by permission of the publisher.

Library of Congress Cataloging-in-Publication Data

Padel, Ruth.
In and out of the mind : Greek images of the tragic self / Ruth Padel.
p.   cm.
Includes bibliographical references and index.
1. Greek drama (Tragedy)—History and criticism.   2. Athens
(Greece)—Intellectual life.   3. Consciousness in literature.
4. Self in literature.   I. Title.
PA3136.P28   1992   882'.010916—dc20   91-5103

ISBN 0-691-07379-1

This book has been composed in Linotron Galliard

Princeton University Press books are printed on acid-free paper, and meet the
guidelines for permanence and durability of the Committee on Production
Guidelines for Book Longevity of the Council on Library Resources

Printed in the United States of America

3   5   7   9   10   8   6   4   2

For my parents, John and Hilda

With love

CONTENTS

PREFACE

THIS BOOK is about the manifestations of consciousness in Greek thought, specifically Athenian thought as expressed in the tragedies of the fifth century B.C. Its main brief is that the phenomena of consciousness are the phenomena of religion.

The extant tragedies have complex relations with many other manifestations of Greek culture. With early science, philosophy, and cult, with representations of plays by the vase-painters of contemporary Attica and of south Italy a century later, with the extensive scraps of lost plays, and, most complex of all, with the centuries of historical and literary research that put all this painstakingly together. As far as we are concerned, all this material must interact with modern disciplines of anthropology, psychology, history of science: with all the arts of reading in our time. The combination challenges us to respond for ourselves to tragedy's ideas of what moves the imaginary people whose interiors, and whose words, tragedy invents.

This is not strictly a literary study. Reading any play means weighing its language in its historical time, considering the resonances of the divinities who appear in it, understanding its life both in its political, social, and physical context, and during its aftergrowth, in its reception. Ideally, all these considerations should be brought to bear on every line and word. I take this aim of full reading for granted, but I am not doing it here, except occasionally, en route to other points. This book is concerned with drawing different sorts of connection together, as prolegomena to a reading of tragedy. I use the question of what tragedy thinks is inside people, to focus inquiry into fifth-century Athenian understanding of mind and of *daimōn*—which I take (see Chapters 6 and 7) to mean divinity as it interferes with human lives and minds. On the whole, the method is descriptive and phenomenological rather than analytic. Its material is literature, mainly but not only tragedy. It is only obliquely about tragedy. It uses tragedy as a lens through which to look at the mentality of tragedy's age, and in particular, Greek representations of consciousness and divinity. Of course it does this in the hope that tragedy may also be illumined by what it finds, but that is not its first objective.

I have transliterated and translated. I want to give readers who do not know Greek some feel for the texture and range of the words on which translations are based. The transliterations are not translated in the notes, where they are offered primarily as shorthand for scholars. I have marked long *ē* and *ō*, but not other vowels. Since the main points lie in the multiple connections between different ways of looking at specific thoughts, I have often worked by cross-referencing footnotes. I expect readers to refer to the discussions that the notes support.

Some of the points I make depend on three previous articles of mine (Padel 1981, 1983, 1990), which when they appeared were billed as coming from this book. In fact they do not. Their fuller versions should appear in future books.

London, December 1990

ACKNOWLEDGMENTS

THIS PROJECT was set in motion twenty years ago. Many friends and critics have read and commented on drafts. Some of the material that some of them read does not appear in this book, though I hope it will in others. I thank them all, for their gift of time as well as for what they said.

In particular, I thank the supervisors of my thesis, E. R. Dodds, H. Lloyd-Jones, R. Kassel, and J. de Romilly. The profound love of both scholarship and literature, and the friendship and encouragement based on this love and offered by Dodds and Lloyd-Jones through the seven years of my thesis, was a privilege for me to find, and has continued to support the work. I owe a great deal to John Gould for his inspiring teaching on tragedy, which accidentally but inevitably came into lessons on Greek verse composition years before I started the thesis. I owe much as well to W. G. Forrest. His assumption that part of the natural point of living one's own life is to use this world to understand new things about fifth-century Athens continues to be an inspiration, if he'll forgive the word. I am also grateful for the comments of my D.Phil. examiners, A. A. Long and, again, J. P. Gould.

Since the thesis I have been deeply indebted to the scrupulous, detailed, informed criticism and encouragement of C. Sourvinou-Inwood, T.C.W. Stinton, and G.E.R. Lloyd. It will always be a sadness that Tom Stinton is not around to read, give a slow smile, and disagree. I treasure his notes on earlier drafts. G.E.R. Lloyd reread, advised, and offered support with immeasurable generosity.

Other valued readers along the way may think I have forgotten the time and comments they gave, and the questions they patiently answered. I haven't. These readers include M. Argyle, Anne Barton, Robert Browning, P. Easterling, W. G. Forrest, Eric Handley, E. Hussey, Mary Lefkowitz, Godfrey Lienhardt, Charles Rycroft, Anthony Snodgrass, David Wiggins, and Froma Zeitlin. I find it hard to separate gratitude for their comments from my debts to their own work.

There are debts at many levels. Elaine Feinstein helped greatly by reading for flow and feel in my translations. Cheli Duran made me face the problem of what to call *splanchna* and came up with "innards." Oswyn Murray bumped into me crossing the road and told me to concentrate—I will never forget—on metaphor. John Bramble's daemonic readings of Roman poetry opened windows on worlds I did not know. In front of the Sphinx at Delphi, long before feminist readings of anything had appeared, Ken Ersser asked why Greek monsters were female. The support of Edward Fitzgerald and David Pears was particularly helpful. Raymond Asquith usefully commented on an early draft, "It sounds like a slaughterhouse," gave me the fruits of his research on root-magic, and introduced me to Maritain. Ewen Bowie let me loose on his pupils at Corpus Christi, even with the intricacies of Greek lyric. The way he entrusted me with the ins and outs of Alcman, the scholarship I absorbed on the way, and the many questions he answered patiently over the years have anchored and enriched my work. Writing in Michael Black's studio as he carved gargoyles, or in the quarry, and watching the way he looked at sculpture, taught me that it is impossible to make something well out of stone without feeling and following through its effect on other people.

Judith Higgins first took me in hand administratively, sorting out references in the early chapters, gentle, firm, generous, and indomitable. Jane Davies helped immeasurably over many years, with administrative assistance no one else could have given. I should like to put on record my thanks to Jo Kent, someone else who—sadly—is not around to read the finished book. She typed a massive draft of this and other books before I learned to use a word processor. Her pencilled reactions to what she was typing, and the fact that she went out and bought the Penguin *Odyssey* after copying a load of words about something she knew nothing of, were a source of warmth and pleasure from afar. I am also deeply grateful to Zara Steiner for lending me her college room in which to work.

I learned much from all the students I have taught, and am very grateful to the Classics Department, a much-loved institution, now also deceased, at Birkbeck College, London University, for its support. I must also thank the Craven Committee of Oxford University for paying me, via the Derby Fellowship, to leave England; and St. Cross College, Wadham College, and Wolfson College, for graduate fellowships and research fellowships. At all these places I benefitted from asking questions of people in other disciplines, especially in anthropology, and from having the precious time to learn things sideways as well as straight. I am infinitely grateful to the British School of Archaeology at Athens, not only for admitting me as a student, but for its collective surprise that I was not working on things you could hold in your hand, and its determination, for which I shall always thank it, that I should.

More recently, I am very grateful to Cambridge classics faculty, its atmosphere, and especially its librarians, for having admitted me as a maverick member and offered friendship, a key for a while, criticism, and help.

I also thank Joanna Hitchcock's team at Princeton University Press: the readers she found, who offered illuminating and useful reports; Sherry Wert, for her firm and thorough guidance through an intricate typescript; Joanna herself, for her calm and heartening voice on wires across the sea; and Froma, for introducing me to them all.

In my family, I have to thank my father John, who first taught me Greek and read Greek texts with me, for his psychoanalytic expertise and advice, especially in relation to literature; my brother Oliver, for help with Celtic things; and my brother Felix, for advice on anthropology and India. Also my mother, for carrying on supposing it was a good idea to write a book about those grim plays she never wants to see. She helped to make me see how very violent "the Greeks" are.

No words occur to me in which I can thank Myles Burnyeat, except (of course) his own. I thank him for very much midwifery. Only those who have had his comments, and the gift of his time spent on their work, know how valuable this is.

ABBREVIATIONS

AUTHORS, TEXTS, and periodicals appear here in alphabetical order. The point of this list is to enable those who do not know conventional abbreviations of classical scholarship to find references.

One kind of book I have not normally put in the bibliography, although apart from the texts and the lexicon it is the most important tool to a student of tragedy: editions and commentaries on the texts. These figure in the notes in two ways. Numbered fragments sometimes appear with the editor's name or initial after the number. "A. fr. 156R" means "Aeschylus, fragment 156 in Radt's edition." To find this in a library, start with "Aeschylus," then look for "fragments" edited by Radt. I also quote editors' comments on specific lines. "Jebb *ad OC* 1248," or "*OC* 1248 with Jebb *ad loc*.," means a comment by Jebb "on" (*ad*) the "place" (*loc*.), which is line 1248 of Sophocles' *Oedipus at Colonus*. Again, start in the library with the author, Sophocles, and find *OC* in Jebb's edition.

Referring to works of Aeschylus, Sophocles, Euripides, Homer, and Hesiod, I abbreviate title, not author (except for fragments, and for the four plays where titles overlap, S. *El.*, E. *El.*, A. *Supp.*, E. *Supp.*). The works of these authors form the basis of my book and appear in the following list alphabetically, not under the author's name.

Where Loeb volumes of Hippocratic works are available, I give the Loeb volume and page number in brackets; otherwise references are to Littré's edition. Only titles that I abbreviate appear in the following list. Some are in Latin, some in English. In popular reference to these works, a mixed bag of conventions operates. I have in mind readers who do not know Greek or Greek texts and want access to something I mention. How will they find it in the bookshop or library? The conventions I use are consistent to this book. I use them in the hope of letting people in, not keeping them out.

I cite pre-Socratics either by number in DK, or by number and page number in KRS, and occasionally KR.

If an author or publication (e.g., *Inscriptiones Graecae*) appears in this list without further documentation, the work will be found in the abbreviations lists at the beginning of LSJ.

A. = Aeschylus
Ael. *NA* = Aelian, *De natura animalium*
Aeschin. = Aeschines
Ag. = A. *Agamemnon*
Aj. = S. *Ajax*

Alc. = E. *Alcestis*
Anaxag. = Anaxagoras
Anc. Med. = Hp. *On Ancient Medicine*
Andr. = E. *Andromache*
Ant. = S. *Antigone*
AP = *Anthologia Palatina*
Aph. = Hp. *Aphorisms*
Apollod. = Apollodorus
Ap. Rh. = Apollonius Rhodius
Ar. = Aristophanes:
  Ach. = *Acharnians*
  Av. = *Birds*
  Eq. = *Knights*
  Lys. = *Lysistrata*
  Nub. = *Clouds*
  Pax = *Peace*
  Pl. = *Plutus*
  Ran. = *Frogs*
  Thesm. = *Thesmophoriazousae*
  V. = *Wasps*
Archil. = Archilochus
Arist. = Aristotle:
  De anim. = *De anima*
  GC = *De generatione et corruptione*
  De insom. = *De insomniis*
  De gen. an. = *De generatione animalium*
  De part. anim. = *De partibus animalium*
  EE = *Eudemian Ethics*
  EN = *Nicomachean Ethics*
  HA = *Historia animalium*
  Metaph. = *Metaphysica*
  Mir. = *Mirabilia*
  Poet. = *Poetics*
  Resp. = *De respiratione*
  Rh. = *Rhetoric*
  Top. = *Topics*
Artemid. = Artemidorus
Athen. = Athenaeus
Aug. *De div. daem.* = Augustine, *De divinatione daemonum*
AWP = Hp. *Airs, Waters, Places*
Ba. = E. *Bacchae*
Bacc. = Bacchylides
Call. = Callimachus

Cat. = Catullus
Cho. = A. *Choephoroe*
Cic. = Cicero:
  Acad. = *Academica*
  De div. = *On Divination*
  TD = *Tusculan Disputations*
Cord. = Hp. *On the Heart*
Corp. Herm. = *Hermetica*, ed. W. Scott (Oxford 1924)
Cyc. = E. *Cyclops*
Dem. = Demosthenes
Democrit. = Democritus
Diosc. = Dioscurides Medicus
DK = H. Diels and W. Kranz, *Die Fragmente der Vorsokratiker*, 6th ed., 3 vols. (Berlin 1951–52)
D.L. = Diogenes Laertius
DMS = Hp. *On the Sacred Disease*
E. = Euripides
El. = *Electra*
Emp. = Empedocles
Epic. *Ep. Men.* = Epicurus, *Epistle to Menoeceus*
Epich. = Epicharmus
Epid. I = Hp. *Epidemics I*
Epid. III = Hp. *Epidemics III*
Erg. = Hes. *Works and Days*
Et. Magn. = *Etymologicum Magnum*, ed. T. Gaisford (Oxford 1848)
Eum. = A. *Eumenides*
Farnell = L. R. Farnell, *Cults of the Greek States*, 5 vols. (Oxford 1896–1909)
Gal. = Galen, *Opera omnia*, ed. K. G. Kühn, 20 vols. (Leipzig 1821–23). Cited by volume and page number
Gal. *De plac. Hp. et Pl.* = *De placitis Hippocratis et Platonis*, ed. P. de Lacy, *Corpus medicorum Graecorum*, vol. 5 (Berlin 1984)
H. = Homer
h. Apoll. = H. *Hymn to Apollo*
h. Dem. = H. *Hymn to Demeter*
Hdt. = Herodotus
Hec. = E. *Hecuba*
Hel. = E. *Helen*
Heraclid. = E. *Heraclidae*
Hes. = Hesiod
Hesych. = Hesychius
HF = E. *Hercules furens*
Hipp. = E. *Hippolytus*

h. Merc. = H. *Hymn to Hermes*
Hor. = Horace:
  C. = *Odes*
  Ep. = *Epodes*
Hp. = Hippocratic author
Hum. = Hp. *Humors*
Hyps. = E. *Hypsipyle*
IA = E. *Iphigeneia at Aulis*
Ichn. = S. *Ichneutai* ("*Trackers*")
IG = *Inscriptiones Graecae*
Il. = H. *Iliad*
Ion = E. *Ion*
Isoc. = Isocrates
IT = E. *Iphigeneia among the Taurians*
KR = G. Kirk and J. E. Raven, *The Presocratic Philosophers* (Cambridge 1957)
KRS = G. Kirk, J. E. Raven, and M. Schofield, *The Presocratic Philosophers*, 2d ed. (Cambridge 1983)
Luc. *Phars.* = Lucan, *Pharsalia*
LSJ = H. G. Liddell, R. Scott, and H. S. Jones, *Greek-English Lexicon* (Oxford 1961)
Macrob. *Sat.* = Macrobius *Saturnalia*
Med. = E. *Medea*
Men. *Sam.* = Menander, *Samia*
Mimn. = Mimnermus
Nat. hom. = Hp. *De natura hominis*
OC = S. *Oedipus at Colonus*
OCT = *Oxford Classical Text*
Od. = H. *Odyssey*
Or. = E. *Orestes*
OT = S. *Oedipus Rex*
Parm. = Parmenides
Paus. = Pausanias
PCG = *Poetae Comici Fragmenta*, ed. R. Kassel and C. Austin, 4 vols. (Berlin and New York 1983–89)
Pers. = A. *The Persians*
Phil. = S. *Philoctetes*
Phoen. = E. *Phoenician Women*
Phot. = Photius:
  Lex. = *Lexicon*
  Bibl. = *Bibliotheca*
Pi. = Pindar:
  I. = *Isthmian Odes*

N. = *Nemean Odes*
O. = *Olympian Odes*
P. = *Pythian Odes*
Pl. = Plato:
  Alcib. I = *Alcibiades I*
  Charm. = *Charmides*
  Crat. = *Cratylus*
  Gorg. = *Gorgias*
  Euthyd. = *Euthydemus*
  Hipp. maj. = *Hippias major*
  Legg. = *Laws*
  Menex. = *Menexenus*
  Phd. = *Phaedo*
  Phdr. = *Phaedrus*
  Polit. = *Politicus*
  Rep. = *Republic*
  Symp. = *Symposium*
  Theaet. = *Theaetetus*
  Ti. = *Timaeus*
Pliny *NH* = Pliny *Natural History*
Plot. = Plotinus
Plu. = Plutarch:
  Alex. = *Alexander*
  De deis. = *De deisidaimonia*
  Mor. = *Moralia*
  Per. = *Pericles*
  Q. conv. = *Quaestiones conviviales*
  QR = *Quaestiones Romanae*
PMG = D. Page, *Poetae melici Graeci* (Oxford 1962)
Proclus *In Tim.* = Proclus, *In Platonis Timaeum Commentarii*, ed.
  H. Diehl (Leipzig 1903–6)
Progn. = Hp. *Prognostic*
PV = A. *Prometheus Bound*
RE = Pauly-Wissowa, *Real-Encyclopädie der klassischen Altertumswissen-schaft*
Reg. Acut. Dis. = Hp. *Regimen in Acute Diseases*
Reg. in Health = Hp. *Regimen in Health*
Rhes. = E. *Rhesus*
S. = Sophocles
Sept. = A. *Seven against Thebes*
schol. = scholia
Scut. = Hes. *Scutum Herculis*

SIG = *Sylloge inscriptionum Graecarum*, 3d ed., ed. W. Dittenberger (Leip-
zig 1915–24)
Sol. = Solon
Stat. *Theb.* = Statius, *Thebaid*
Supp. = *Suppliant Women*
SVF = *Stoicorum veterorum fragmenta*, ed. H. von Arnim, 4 vols. (Leipzig
1903–24)
Theb. = H. *Thebais* (lost Homeric epic)
Theoc. = Theocritus
Theog. = Hes. *Theogony*
Thgn. = Theognis
Th. = Thucydides
Thphr. = Theophrastus:
  Char. = *Characters*
  De lass. = *De lassitudine*
Trach. = S. *Women of Trachis*
Tro. = E. *Trojan Women*
V. = Virgil:
  Aen. = *Aeneid*
  Ec. = *Eclogues*
  Georg. = *Georgics*
Virg. = Hp. *On Virgins*
Xen. = Xenophon
  An. = *Anabasis*
  Cyr. = *Cyropaedia*
  Mem. = *Memorabilia*
  Symp. = *Symposium*
Xenoph. = Xenophanes

In and Out of the Mind

Chapter 1

INTRODUCTION: THE DIVINITY OF
INSIDE AND OUTSIDE

Hail and beware them, for they come from where you have not been,
they come from where you cannot have come, they come into life
by a different gate. They come from a place which is not easily known. . . .
—Charles Olson, *A Newly Discovered Homeric Hymn (for*
Jane Harrison, If She Were Alive)

THE CLASSICAL Athenians, like modern Hindus, had shrines throughout
their homes. At the house-door were shrines to Apollo Aguieus, lord of
roads, and to Hecate, mistress of crossroads, as well as an embodiment of
the god Hermes: the herm, a stone pillar with male head, genitals, and
erect penis.[1] Greek imagination divinized all kinds of things, activities, and
relationships between people. There was divinity in different moments of
relationships, different stages of life, different states of body and feeling.
Greeks found this a natural, and useful, way of being in the world. We find
it easy to disregard. "Worn-out and silly, like classical gods," says Sylvia
Plath's insomniac of sleeping pills that no longer work. But for the Greeks
of the fifth century B.C., there were gods—like electricity—at work all the
time, in their bodies, minds, homes, and cities. The divinities "of" (as we
put it) threshold tell us—we are very foreign observers—that Greek mentality saw something divine, with all the risk and exactingness of divinity,
in the act of entering and leaving, going from inside out and outside in.

This book uses the Greek tragedies to explore some aspects of what the
Athenians who wrote and watched them thought was outside and inside
human beings. What came in from outside? What came out from within?
What is inside and outside is seen in terms both biological (Chapters 2–5)
and daemonological (Chapters 6–8). These are not separate discourses.
Both biology and daemonology see what is outside as more aggressive,
more to be feared.

---

[1] Hecataia (e.g., Ar. *Ran.* 336, *V.* 804): see Kraus 1960; Thompson and Wycherley
1972:169. Aguieus (e.g., *Ion* 186, *Phoen.* 631, Ar. *Thesm.* 489): see McDowell *ad V.* 875;
Thompson and Wycherley 1972:169 n. 270; Fraenkel *ad Ag.* 1085–87. Herm resonances in
fifth-century Athens: see Osborne 1985.

It is often said that Greek tragedies distort their culture's outlook. Tragedy specializes in things going wrong. It does not show us, as for instance comedy and forensic rhetoric can, human nature functioning normally, people amused at gods and animals or manipulating them successfully. At most, tragedy only indicates Greek ideas about how human nature works under normal conditions, through fantasies of what happens when its systems break down. In tragedy, as in Greek medical writing, explanation (whether explicit or implied) is of something going wrong: in a relationship, body, life, or "house." Therefore, ideas about the mind derived from tragedy will overstress the Athenian culture's sense that the world is hostile to human beings.

Some of this argument is absurd. Things going wrong do tell us about what is normal. The Hippocratics formed ideas about how the healthy body functions by considering what happens when something goes wrong in it. Freud's ideas about normal mental functioning came through work on mental dysfunctioning. Work on illusion, the abnormal or paranormal, does tell us about reality and the normal.[2] The Hippocratics may have had some strange ideas about the body, but their approach—to normality through pathology—was sound.

Of course there are aspects of human existence and relationships that literature does not reveal. Faced with a study of early twentieth-century British and European life based on Joyce and Woolf, we might complain, what about images of life articulated in the music halls? Law Reports? *Times* leaders? But in fifth-century tragedy, there is a life we can legitimately talk about: imaginative life as experienced in, and illustrated by, tragedy. Evidence for the tone of this life, in particular for fear in the face of the environment's hostility, is not confined to tragedy. Cult speaks to it, and so, in different registers, do contemporary history, comedy, lyric, philosophy, and even science, as we shall see.

Further, fifth-century Athenian tragedy expresses contemporary imaginative life more soundly than Joyce and Woolf, in their élite genres, can express the inner world of early twentieth-century Britain and Ireland. Athenian tragedy was central to its community's life. The early twentieth-century British literary novel was not. Decorative arts of the 1930s would not have attracted many buyers with a scene from *To the Lighthouse*, but vase-painters from 470 B.C. onwards (roughly, from the earliest extant tragedies) often indicate that a mythic scene comes from a recent tragedy. When harpies, for instance, are labelled "Beautiful" in the masculine, they are not birdheaded women, but chorus men dressed as birdwomen. A woman at a tomb who is labelled "Beautiful" in the masculine is a male

---

[2] See W. James 1952: ch. 1.

actor playing Electra. The painter offers customers a picture of Aeschylus's handling of the myths, not of the myths themselves. Athenian society spent money on improving tragedy's setting, and even reputedly enabled poorer citizens to afford entrance by special grants.[3] Tragedy is Athens's central popular literary genre. It stages humanity's need to defend itself against the nonhuman (see Chapter 7). Human defenses are frail. The core hope is that something will survive nonhuman attacks. This tragic hope must have addressed something important in the popular imaginative appetite.

Of course there are problems in using tragedy as evidence for the values of its world. Some scholars stress the divide between tragedy and its world, and believe the worldview of comedy was more "familiar" to its audience.[4] But suppose we think of comedy as a genre deliberately anodyne at the daemonic level, offering, like television ads, Agatha Christie, or soap opera, a world that deals with fears by removing their real edge? Or does comedy testify to the possibility that by staging these intense and real anxieties, tragedy had brought its fifth-century audience through that fear, for a while? *Post tragoediam* laughter may sound a note of relief from real terror, rather than amusement at what is not normally taken seriously.

Listen to two scenes in which rules of living polytheism are treated as breakable, yet still serious. "Lycus," prays a lawsuit addict to the hero whose shrine adjoins the courts, "help me, and I'll never pee and fart by your wicker fence again." "This is the full-moon day of the goddess," says a wife. "How can I start cooking without taking a bath?" "Are you going to follow all those rules and waste time?" asks the husband. The first scene is from Aristophanes' vision of fifth-century Athens, the second from a modern short story set in the lived Hinduism of a village in modern Maharashtra.[5] In both, rules are important and serious, but people sometimes treat them as if they did not matter. Athenian comedy has bias, perhaps, towards those moments of "as if." But moments when the rules did matter were just as "familiar" to the audience.

Another argument against taking tragedy as evidence for the imagination of its society—one with which I have more sympathy—is to say it "challenged" assumptions of its audience: about, say, relations between men and women, old and young; about families, marriage, gods, laws. Therefore, what it says should not be taken to express what the culture normatively felt.

Sometimes this view is put excitingly, but it can become formulaic. One gets a picture of Sophocles sitting at his desk muttering, "What assump-

[3] See Trendall and Webster 1971: III, 1.2, 1.25; Plu. *Per.* 9.

[4] See, e.g., Parker 1983:13–15. *Contra*, see Humphreys 1983:71; Goldhill 1986:111 and passim.

[5] Ar. *V.* 394; Zelliot and Berntsen 1988:8.

tions shall I challenge today?" The aim of conscious challenge to current
values is shared by today's critics and scriptwriters, but was not, as far as
we know, on the dramatist's articulate agenda in fifth-century Athens. Nor
did the audience consciously expect it.

I would put it differently. The tragedians who wrote the plays were
drawn to focus on what was painful and precarious in contemporary imagination. Audiences shared this pain and precariousness. They were the people whose pain it was, and they were overpoweringly drawn to explore it
with their dramatists. Of course, there are areas of experience that tragedy
excludes, and there must be truths about the fifth-century psyche that tragedy does not reflect. Nonetheless, tragedy is the concentrated, intense
genre that its community prized, for which they shut up shop, came to
their uncomfortable theater, and sat still for days on end. Its ways of looking at human beings and human relations with the outside world must
have had some bearing on that community's inner life.

This book concentrates on fifth-century ideas of bodily interiority and
of what we invoke when we say "mind." A sub-theme is our own differences in these areas from fifth-century Greeks. The main project is to approach Greek images of the human interior from connections the Greeks
saw between inside and outside. The book works mainly by making its
own connections: between, for example, Greek scientists' theories about
perception and disease, and Greek tragedy's vision of passion. Both suggest a particular pattern of relationship between inside and outside.

Inside and outside: the god of the relationship between them is Hermes,
god of the door, of connection-making. He has many other names: Strophaios, "the Pivoter," divinity of the *stropheus*, "hinge," and Prothuraios,
"Before the Door." He is male, mobile, master of language and roads, of
heralds, messages, interpretation, communication and its ambiguities.[6] He
is god of doubleness in several aspects, signified by his staff, which holds
two snakes, one on each side, mirroring each other. He is lord of linguistic
illusion, giving voice to what is unseen, within, silent: to the dead, to innards. He translates thought, which is within, into its external manifestation, speech. He is the bringer-out. He brings the dead back, ambiguously,
to the light. He is "most helpful of gods," with "a lovely voice" of his own.[7]

---

[6] Prothuraios, Pronaos, Propulaios: Farnell, 5:19, 66 (nn. 20–24). Propulaios on the
Acropolis: Thompson and Wycherley 1972:228ff. Strophaios: see Ar. *Nub*. 450; schol. *ad*
Ar. *Pl*. 1153; Phot. *Lex*. s.v. Hermes *stropheus*; Herter 1976:219; Kassel 1983:7; Detienne
and Vernant 1978:41.

[7] Hermes gives voice to Pandora, Peace, the dead tortoise: *Erg*. 78; Ar. *Pax* 602–67; *h.
Merc*. 38, 54; S. *Ichn*. 286. See L. Kahn 1978. Helpful: see *Et. Magn*. s.v. *eriounios*; Ar. *Pax*
392; *Il*. 24.334–36. His voice: see *h. Merc*. 426; Vernant 1983:128–29; Pease *ad* V. *Aen*.
2.242.

The Athenians' familiarity with this divinity of the threshold illuminates the ways in which both their tragedy and contemporary Greek science relate the inside of a human being to the outside world. Hermes' most common manifestation, the pervasive erect herm, stood at each front door, on street corners and important inner-city boundaries. The streets must have bristled. He was an active, talkative presence. People spoke to him. He spoke back. A herm was expected to breathe intimate, practical advice. Relationship with Hermes was one of dialogue. In sacrificing, one offered him the tongue.[8]

As outsiders, we feel our way into the Greeks' perceptions of the world by looking at their gods. Religion was the Greeks' most vivid medium for expressing their sense of their world and their relationships. Each divinity specialized in a different range of experience and phenomena, and each goddess or god was "many-named" according to her or his different activities. As in Hinduism, the plural deities had pluralizing epithets.[9] We may not happen to think the titles and roles of a god are intrinsically connected. But in Greek mentality, each divine persona was a many-faced crystal through which specific spheres of activity and experience, mutually explicatory, touched. Artemis's role as "mistress of the animals" had meaning in relation to her involvement in childbirth, chastity, hunting, and women's death. As foreigners, we start from the basic fact of connectedness between these things.

With Hermes, therefore, we work from his compound persona, from the fact that Greek mentality connected the activities designated by his titles, toward Greek responses to each phenomenon or experience he ruled. The concrete images of Hermes' presence—the threshold, the pivoting door—tell us that the Greeks found divinity in the relating of an inside to an outside. One way to approach Greek ideas of this relation would be to add up Hermes' titles and find their common denominators. As messenger, patron of heralds, he connects the relation of inside to outside, to self's communication with other through language. He is in—or he is the "divineness" of—the act of voicing a message, of interpreting it. "I interpret" is *hermēneuō*. A seer is *hermēneutēs*, "interpreter." Hermes is the divinity of making and reading signs. When vase-painters begin to show reading scenes, the text, if recognizable, is usually a hymn to Hermes.[10] He is the

---

[8] Dialogue: see Kassel 1983; Dover *ad* Ar. *Nub.* 1478, 1508; Thompson and Wycherley 1972:169; Vernant 1983:158. Voicing a message: see Ar. *Pl.* 1111 with scholia and Rogers *ad loc.*; L. Kahn 1978:155–56; Farnell, 5:30, 74. Herm-types: see Lullies 1931.

[9] See Vernant 1980:93–99, 1983:329–30. *Poluōnumos* is a common divine epithet, e.g., *h. Dem.* 18; *Sept.* 320; *Ant.* 1115.

[10] Beazley 1948; see also Svenbro 1990. A seer is *hermeneutēs*, see Pl. *Polit.* 290C.

orators' patron, the divinity within the joining and separating of thought and language.

Since he is also god of commerce and competition, Hermes tells us that the relation of inside to outside was connected to the relation of what is mine and what is yours.[11] He is also Psychopompos, "Conductor of Souls," and Kataibatēs, "He Who Goes Down," and so connects to all his other activities the relation of upper world and lower world, the living and the dead. He leads both ways, from me to you, from the light to the dark, from waking to sleep, and back again.[12]

Hermes is two-way in all his roles, present in the change from silence to speech, and in the swivel back from language to silence. When people fall silent suddenly, "Hermes has come in." He shares with his brother Dionysus, god of theater, an interest in illusion, in things seeming to be other than they are. Dionysus is present in visual and mental illusion; Hermes controls linguistic illusion. All *logoi* (words, arguments) are *hermaikoi* (belonging to Hermes), says Proclus, the great commentator on Plato.[13] Language can pronounce true messages, and also say things that are otherwise. Its herald-god is patron of lies. Hermes' lies please Zeus. He endows Pandora with lies. He is Peisinous, "Persuader of the Mind." He embodies the double meaning, the dual possibilities, of utterance. He is god of the possibility that my meaning may not be your meaning, though the words sound the same.[14]

Hermes connects verbal communication with other experience. As divine messenger, he is one of the most sociable of gods. He approaches human beings and other gods. The joining of female with male is (among other things) a Hermes compound, Hermaphroditus, Hermes' union with Aphrodite.[15] He is present *with* other gods, at a wedding, a funeral.

All this suggests that in Greek culture, the contrast between inside and outside for which Hermes stands interpenetrates other basic contrasts, contrasts that anthropology knows well. Male and female, outside and inside, culture and nature: these pairings today provide obvious ways of ap-

---

[11] Empolaios: see Farnell, 5:26; Kassel 1983:7 n. 32. Enagōnios: see Farnell, 5:28–29, 70–73 (nn. 46–77); Herter 1976:229; L. Kahn 1978:14.

[12] Psychopompos, Kataibates: see Farnell, 5:12–15, 65–66. Hermes takes the dead suitors to Hades, *Od.* 24.12; is asked to send souls up from Hades, *Pers.* 629, *Cho.* 124–25; escorts out of the ground Persephone (Burkert 1979:184 n. 29) and perhaps Pandora (Trendall and Webster 1971:33 [II. 8–9], a painting c. 450 B.C. that may represent Sophocles' satyr-play *Pandora* or *The Hammerers*). See L. Kahn 1978:12, 45ff., 78.

[13] Plu. *De garrulitate* 502F; Proclus *In Tim.* 148.5–6 (Diehl).

[14] See *Od.* 19.396; *Phil.* 123–24; *h. Merc.* 389–90; cf. Ar. *V.* 562, 580; *Erg.* 57. Peisinous: see Farnell, 5:27. It was L. Kahn (1978) who first argued that Hermes stood for communication's ambiguity.

[15] See *Od.* 8.335–37; Detienne and Vernant 1978:285–86; Vernant 1983:163 n. 26; Delcourt 1961.

proaching another thought-world. This book has evolved over a time when anthropological interest in dual classification, like nature and culture, dead and living, left and right, has been enriched by cross-cultural thinking about women, and also by psychosocial and psychosexual studies of self and other.[16] It is obvious now, but it wasn't always, that Greek culture and language, and specifically the Athenian culture that these tragedies reflect, is male, and therefore reflects male views of everything: of self, of language, of contrasts like nature and culture, self and other, male and female; and also of mind. Hermes tells us we should add inside and outside to that list. Greek thought and language were intensely aware of oppositions.[17] For the Greek male worldview, anything female, dead, or wild is easily perceived as "other." Tragedy depends on tensions, old against young, woman against man, upper world against lower world. Physically, tragedy was itself a paradox of inside and outside, an open space making public that which was unseen, such as feelings, the past, the secrets of the "house." Conceptually and physically, therefore, tragedy stages relationships of inside and outside.[18] I shall suggest that Greek men also intermittently regarded as alien what was "within" themselves.

This book explores some implications of these contrasts and connections. One of its main themes is metaphor, key to all ideas of mind and self.

From the century following these tragedies, the West began two thousand years of comment on metaphor, comment vitalized and revolutionized in our own century. Because of this accumulated and self-critical comment, the role of metaphor is visible to us in a way it was not to fifth-century Greeks. As far as we are concerned, the Greeks expressed their ideas of mind through metaphor. But they would not have used the word *metaphora* to describe what they were doing. It first appears in the fourth century. Partly, but not only, because of that difference, the fifth-century metaphors held meaning for their contemporary listeners that they do not hold for us.

It has been argued for some time, in the context not of tragedy but of science, that fifth-century Greeks did not distinguish literal from metaphorical, or not in the way we do. The evidence starts with pre-Aristotelian scientists, who use an image as if the image explained the problematic phenomenon, rather than saying *it is as if*. Students of Greek poetry, and of its words for consciousness, have not yet faced the enormous implications of this argument for poetry's language of thinking and feeling. I shall not

---

[16] E.g., a reading of Needham 1973 is enriched by Rosaldo and Lamphere (1974), a pioneer collection of feminist perspectives in anthropology.

[17] For the importance of opposition and binary thinking in Greek thought, see Lloyd 1966, 1973; Vidal-Naquet 1986:129–56. For the general interdependence of different dual classifications cross-culturally, see Needham 1973:xvii–xxiv and passim.

[18] See Padel 1990.

argue it fully myself in this book.[19] But I touch on it in Chapters 2, 6, and 7, on words for the equipment of consciousness, on Greek images of emotion wounding the mind, and on the Greek personification of emotion.

A second theme is how difficult, but also how rewarding, it is for us in the late twentieth century to think of ancient Greeks as astoundingly alien from ourselves. At various points I shall go into reasons for this difficulty. One obvious reason is that our newer languages are layered over with post-Greek associations to Greek images, constantly re-used and remade by succeeding societies, and these shape the ways in which "we," whoever that means at any time, think and speak.

As I learned Greek, I was given along the way the conviction that ancient Greeks believed and assumed everything in the male, British, late Victorian mindset belonging to most editors (I am not talking about the great ones) of my school texts—everything about women, feelings, bodies, language, madness, and life that the editor, the establisher of the text, himself believed—but *they pretended not to*. And so any apparent differences made no difference. These Greek authors were the editor's friends, not mine, and shared a very clear common sense with him.

Dismantling this belief entails identifying attitudes that "we" have, and different ones that the Greeks may have had, toward metaphors of thought and feeling. They helped to form these metaphors in us. If we say someone had a "seizure" or "heart attack," or was "on fire with love," we connect ourselves to an extraordinarily complex train of physiological and religious imagery and scientific theory winding back through eighteenth-century medicine, Renaissance scholarship, mediaeval theology, Hellenistic philosophy, to Greek poetry and medicine. And, since tragic poetry is, after Homer, the largest and most public early body of poetry about feeling, very often to tragedy itself. But the origins of such phrases do not explain our use of them. On the contrary, the way we say them and what we mean by them has been changed by the very centuries that handed them on.

This change makes them difficult to read in "the original," at least if we want through our reading to understand what they might have meant to their original users. We need to think away, as well as to value, the accumulated resonance of intervening years. This feels like, and to some extent is, fighting our own thought. The impulse to recognize ourselves in tragedy's words is very strong. I do not want to do away with it. Tragedy is there for whoever wants to read or perform it. It is right and necessary, I believe, to interpret tragedy for whatever you want to get out of it.

But what I want to get out of it, in this book, is a sense of how its culture

---

[19] The scholar who has perceived and followed through this point is Lloyd; see 1966:228, 1987:172–210, 1990:14–28. Silk (1974:34 n. 1) is the first, so far as I know, to face its consequences for poetic texts.

represented mind and feeling. So my reading often challenges that hope of recognizing ourselves in others, and especially the belief that the Greeks had toward metaphor (specifically, toward metaphors of feeling and consciousness) the same stance as we do. I head instead for the possibility that phrases had different meanings then from the meanings we attach to them when we respond to them as "like" what we say. The way I present tragic images reflects the perspective from which I have come to see the texts. It is not neutral. I try to point out as I go assumptions that came with or produced this perspective.

If any god could have claimed the title in the fifth century, the Greek god of metaphor would be Hermes. Hermes, lord of language, silence, lies, rhetoric, signs, revelation, trickery—lord of the double edge—embodies metaphor's movement from one place to another, alien place, and the enrichment and risk that move entails. He is, you might say, what metaphor was before the Greeks thought about it. His existence reminds us that when tragic poets write about what is inside people, they are also writing about what is outside, as their culture represents it. Outside explains inside, and vice versa. The two-way connection between them is fluid, ambiguous, mercurial, transformative, and divine.

Chapter 2

INNARDS

A story is told of Heraclitus, that visitors came, wanting
to meet him, but hesitated when they saw him warming
himself at the stove in the kitchen. He told them to be
bold and enter, "For there are gods even here."
——Aristotle *De part. anim.* 645A20–22

ENTRAILS: LEARNING, FEELING, DIVIDING

GREEK TRAGEDY describes what happens inside human beings daemonically and biologically, in ways that read to us like metaphor. But their daemonology and biology are very different from ours, and play a role in
Greek ideas about the self that matches little in our experience. I shall start
with biology, although daemonology will creep in even here.[1]

Most cultures picture some inner place for the site and equipment of
consciousness. Our culture is as anomalous and inconsistent as any, though
we do put consciousness mainly in the head.[2] In the fifth century, a few
intellectuals imagined the brain might have something to do with consciousness, but this was eccentric. Socrates refers to a controversy, current
when he was young, about what part of the body we think with. This
intellectual controversy continued through the fifth century and on into
the next.[3] But in ordinary fifth-century life, when people wondered what

---

[1] Basic studies on the biology and its implications include Snell 1953 and 1978, Dodds
1951, Onians 1954, Claus 1981, Bremmer 1983, Sullivan 1988, and Caswell 1990. Jaynes
1976 is an important eccentric addition. "Daemon": see pp. 114, 138 below.

[2] Cf. Jaynes 1976:44–45. Philosophically, Wollheim (1974:41–53) argues that the concept of mind behind English usage is not fully spatial but "tinged with spatiality": that we
attribute shifting degrees of spatiality to mind, and the greater the degree of spatiality, the
more distorted and inhibited our intellectual activity becomes. Yet all "spatially tinged" conceptions of mind "derive ultimately from an assimilation of mental activity to bodily functioning. . . . We are at home in our mind somewhat as in a body. This is the mind's image of
itself."

[3] Pl. *Phd.* 96A. Alcmaeon of Croton, in the early fifth century, was probably the first to
think the brain was important, KRS p. 339 (cf. Pl. *Phd.* 96B). *DMS* 17 (Loeb 2:174) may
owe something also to Diogenes (*floruit*, 420s B.C.), KRS p. 449 n. 1. Philolaus fr. 13DK
seems to argue (in the late fifth century) that the *archē* of rationality is in the brain: "The head
is the *archē* of *noos*, the heart of *psuchē* and perception." Plato followed Philolaus in siting
intellect in the head (Pl. *Ti.* 44D, cf. perhaps the joke "no ears and brain" at Pl. *Hipp. maj.*

was going on inside someone, what mattered was that person's *splanchna*, "guts." It is easy to forget this and to fail to follow through the differences it makes. Psychology in tragedy's world has practically nothing to do with the head.[4]

Splanchna (singular *splanchnon*) are the innards, the general collection of heart, liver, lungs, gallbladder, and attendant blood vessels. English translations of *splanchna* depend on context. The lexicon reaches for words like "entrails" (in contexts of divination) and "bowels" (in contexts of emotion). "Feeling," "mood," "temper," or "mind" often seem more apt. *Splanchna* feel. They feel anxiety, fear, grief, and sometimes love and desire. In the New Testament, *splanchnizomai* is "I feel pity." *Splanchna* soften in worry. The bully Menelaus "will soften his *splanchna*" when his daughter is at risk.[5] But in vehement feeling they are hot and taut. A young man "has a stretched *splanchnon* and says foolish things."[6]

How physical is this word? Sometimes the physicality seems obvious. When the Erinyes have chased Orestes, their *splanchnon* "pants with many labors." But sometimes it is less obvious. The word can read like "character." It is unfair, for instance, to dislike someone before you "clearly learn their *splanchnon*."[7]

Rather than prejudge this word's concreteness or abstraction, let us

292D; this may be an example of Aristophanes' influence on Plato, see on *Nub.* 1726 below). By the end of the fourth century, the brain had some supporters as the center of consciousness, but still had some powerful opponents. For Chrysippus (judging by Galen's attack on him, *De plac. Hp. et Pl.* 4.1, 2), the brain was just one inner part to which people vaguely refer: everyone believes the psyche's government is in the heart. Galen sites intelligence in the brain, spirit in the heart, daring in the liver. This position was only possible after Plato. But even after Plato, Aristotle, the Stoics, and the Epicureans went on putting consciousness in the heart (see A. E. Taylor 1962:518–21). Galen shows us how the culture held to the heart's primacy long after empirical proof was available that the brain was the locus of perception and locomotion. Before Plato, in fifth-century Athens, it was very odd to call the brain the center of anything. The apparent exception, Ar. *Nub.* 1726, proves the point. Strepsiades puns on *ap'onou* and *apo nou*, then says Amynias "had his brain shaken" when he fell (an imaginary, tragic-parody fall) out of the chariot. Is something missing in the text? Line 1275 ends uncertainly. R, the best manuscript, omits the attribution to Strepsiades, and Starkie, having studied facsimiles (intro., p. lviii), suggests *ad loc.* that R omitted something. Working with the accustomed text, however, we can simply note that Strepsiades makes this comment after becoming an "intellectual." The first signs of change in him are "mind" jokes: eccentric nonsense about the brain.

[4] Schneider (1968) argues that in painting Ajax and Achilles playing draughts, Exekias makes a psychological point—the mental concentration of the players. Anachronistically, he assumes the head is "the biological origin of thought and therefore of concentration" (p. 386) for Exekias, as for himself.

[5] Anxiety, fear, grief: e.g., *Ag.* 995, *Cho.* 413, *Aj.* 995. Desire: Herodas 1.56, Theoc. 7.99. Softening: *Or.* 1201.

[6] Hot: Ar. *Ran.* 844, cf. 1006. Stretched: *Hipp.* 118.

[7] *Eum.* 249, *Med.* 221.

watch how the word behaves and what ideas it attracts to its neighborhood. *Splanchna* contain feeling, but also hide it. One may conceal feeling "under one's *splanchna*." The very inner thing that must be learned, if we want to know people, masks their feeling. Tragedy, especially Euripides, gives voice to a Greek sense of lack here. There is no "clear proof" by which to understand *phrenes* (which I take, for the moment, to mean "mind"). If good people lived twice, *then* "it would be possible to know the bad, the good." External judgment is confusing. "There is no clear boundary set by the gods between the good and bad." One cannot "judge" people by a "clear" outside token, there is no "accurate" test of their value.[8]

This thought is voiced increasingly through the fifth century. Only being with people helps us judge them. We cannot see into another's *splanchna*. Would it were possible, says a fifth-century drinking-song,

> to see what sort of man each person is,
> divide up (*dielonta*) his breast
> and look at his mind (*nous*), then close it again,
> and think with an undeceiving mind (*phrēn*)
> that he's your friend.[9]

The Byzantine scholar Eustathius aligned this song with an Aesopic fable that blamed Prometheus for placing *pulai*, "gates," in the human breast.[10] He interprets the *splanchna* here as gates of thought and feeling, gates we close against outsiders. We are doubly masked. Our innards in themselves are hard to see, and they mask the feelings they contain. Perhaps these are two ways of saying the same thing.

Gates to what we cannot see must be forced. Or else we try art: an art of understanding what we do not know. In another context, *splanchna* do have "clear marks," and are opened to disclose what is unknown. This is divination, an aspect of Greek life as normal to the tragic audience as electronics is to us. That drinking-song assumes familiarity with it. Extispicy, the art of divining the gods' will from animal entrails, was ingrained and ancient in Greek communities. From at least the Bronze Age onwards, their eastern neighbors read entrails. Clay models of livers and lungs, scratched to divide different patches from each other, have been found in a Bronze Age temple at Ras Shamra, the Ugarit site on the Syrian coast (where, on a clear day, you can see Cyprus), which has clear affinities with Minoan-Mycenaean art. Division and marking are central to *splanchna* in divination from the Mediterranean start.[11]

[8] *HF* 657–71, *Alc.* 1009; *Med.* 516–19, *Hipp.* 925–29, cf. *Ag.* 838–39.

[9] See Athen. 694E, E. *El.* 367–90, cf. *Ag.* 840. Tragic "opacity": see Pigeaud 1981:395.

[10] Eustathius 1574.16. On this song (*PMG* no. 889, p. 473), cf. Barrett *ad Hipp.* 925.

[11] The models, and the "liver of Piacenza": see Courtois 1969: figs. 6, 7–11, 14; Körte 1905; Beard and North 1990:68. See generally Pliny *NH* 7.203; Blecher 1905; Bouché-

Fifth-century Athenians accepted that divination was important, and knew the physical procedures for reading those markings. Herodotus, telling his Greek audience about Egyptian sacrifice, points out that Egyptians extract intestines, leaving the *splanchna* and fat:[12] the opposite of Greeks, who take out *splanchna* first.

In tragedy, sacrifice is a likely occasion for murder, and *splanchna*, like dreams, can tell more than the immediate interpreter can know. Aegisthus invites a stranger, Orestes in disguise, to share his sacrifice. He kills the beast, offers the stranger his sword to carve it, and Orestes slashes:

> Aegisthus gazed earnestly at the sacred parts
> taking them in his hands. There was no liver lobe
> to the *splanchna*! And the portal-vein
> and gallbladder showed evil visitations near
> to the person looking at them.

"Visitation," in the sense of "attack," is indeed near. Aegisthus admits he is afraid of Orestes and fears "a stranger's trick." Orestes tells him not to worry, demands a heavier axe, and cuts. Aegisthus seizes the *splanchna*. "Dividing them (*diairōn*), he gazed earnestly at them." As he gazes, Orestes splits his spine.[13]

One link between animal *splanchna* opened and inspected in divination, and other people's *splanchna* that we want to learn, is the wish to know something "accurately," "rightly": words important in both contexts. We go to divination for "things unmarked," *asēma*, without a sign, obscure: for "things we do not know clearly." Seers "foretell" things "by looking at fire and through the folds of *splanchna*, and bird omens." One "unfolds" *splanchna* as one unfolds a writing tablet. Neither can be read without unfolding. Their message is apparent when they are "opened," as a friendly character is "disclosed."[14]

Another linkage is "dividing" words. Aegisthus "divides" the *splanchna*.

Leclerq 1879, 1:171; Halliday 1913:189–90, 200. The liver's "landscape": see Durand and Lissarague 1979:92ff.

[12] Hdt. 2.40. No one at Athens in the mid-fifth century consistently rejected divination; see Beard and North 1990:84.

[13] E. *El.* 826–29 (Denniston *ad loc.* supplies *ousas* after *prosbolas*, assuming that liver and gallbladder have further bad signs, it is not merely that there is no liver lobe), 838–39.

[14] See E. *Supp.* 211–13. Cf. Cic. *De div.* 2.32, Plu. *Alex.* 73. *Ptuchas* for *splanchna* and *deltos*: E. *Supp.* 212, *IA* 112, *IT* 760. Tablets "hide" writing in folds. Cf. *diaptuchas* for the *delton*, *IT* 793. *Diaptussō* is "I open, spread out, disclose." The written charge against Hippolytus seems reasonable, but not if you "unfold" it, *Hipp.* 985. People who think they're the only ones to be right are empty when "opened up," *Ant.* 709. Galen (2:520) uses the word of "opening up" the abdomen. People (or what they have said) can be "revealed" as tablets are "loosened," "opened," *IA* 307, 321. Ideally, you "open the clear key" of your *phrenes* to friends (*Med.* 660), as you "disclose" your name (and therefore identity), A. *Supp.* 322.

Division is vital in sacrifice. Plato compares logical "division" to division practiced in sacrifice: "Let us divide them by their parts, like a sacrifice," he says. Division in sacrifice is a basic image, available for intellectual use. In sacrifice, the pieces are "parted": apportioned to human beings for eating, to gods for burning. *Splanchna* are the centerpiece of the sacrificial meal.[15] Sacrificial innards have a Hermes-like dual role. Humans eat them, gods mark them.[16] Gods are concerned with both their demarcating markings and their due division.

The verb "divide," used for "breaking apart" *splanchna*, has other meanings: "distribute" (as in "apportioning" shares of a sacrifice), but also "distinguish or demarcate" (as in Plato's "division" of the soul, or the "distinction" between logical categories), and "determine," "decide" (rights in a legal action, the true interpretation of a dream).[17] The word for physical division is also "discernment," assessment of the mind by the mind. "Telling" a person's true character, their *splanchna*, involves judging from obscure signs, "dividing" good and bad.[18]

In both contexts, therefore, innards join the desire to know what is obscure and within, to the dividing and distinguishing needed to get at it. Greek fantasies about *splanchna* point also towards that vital division between divine and human. *Splanchna* markings matter to gods. The gods may be "pleased" by them, may even have put them there. One tradition attributed the first extispicy to Prometheus, mediator between human and divine, often held responsible for the civilizing arts, of which extispicy is one. "Prometheus" seems to mean "Forethought," aptly for a figure involved in divination. Myth linked his theft of fire to his invention of sacrifice, which embodies human effort to communicate with gods.[19]

Consulting the entrails of a sacrifice expresses (among other things) a

[15] Eating *splanchna*: see Ar. *V.* 654; cf. *Il.* 1.464, Ar. *Av.* 984. Sometimes *splanchna* seems to *mean* "sacrifical feast," e.g., Ar. *Eq.* 410, *SIG* 1002.4 (fifth or fourth century, Miletus). Cf. Semonides 12(W): "Grasping *splanchna* like a kite" means stealing them from a sacrifice. The horror of the story of Thyestes, who unwittingly eats his own children's *splanchna* (*Ag.* 1222), lies partly in his eating the best bits, the bits where consciousness and life had been. Dividing and eating sacrifices: Hes. *Theog.* 554; *h. Merc.* 130; Burkert 1983:6 nn. 21, 22, 36 n. 8. "Dividing," as in sacrifice: Pl. *Polit.* 287C.

[16] See L. Kahn 1978:67.

[17] *Diaireō*: "I distribute" *splanchna*, *Il.* 1.464, *Od.* 3.9; "tear open" a hare, Hdt. 1.23 (cf. Pl. *Phdr.* 253C, Ar. *Nub.* 742); "determine" rights, *Eum.* 472, 488, 630; "decide" a dream's interpretation, Hdt. 7.19.

[18] See *dieidenai, Med.* 518; *diagnōsin phrenōn, Hipp.* 926.

[19] Rival claimants for the invention of sacrifice include Delphus (at Delphi, Parke 1967:72) and Hermes, who invents fire and prepares a sacrifice afterwards (*h. Merc.* 111, 120–33). Cf. Prometheus (Dodds 1973:31); "Pro-metheus" might recall *prophētēs* (but Fascher 1927 argued this should mean "spokesman *for* the supernatural" and does not necessarily entail *fore*-knowledge).

hope that gods communicate back. Aeschylus's Prometheus says he taught human beings to watch for

> the *splanchna*'s smoothness,
> what color a gall vessel should be to please gods;
> and the liver lobe's dappling symmetry.

Extispicy assumed that gods took an active interest in innards. Hegesander, a historian from Delphi of the second century B.C., records two Cypriot epithets of Zeus, "Companion-of-the-Banquet" and "*Splanchna*-Cutter," Splanchnotomos. In late antiquity, *theos*, "god," referred also to some part of the entrails. Long before, in the sixth century B.C., Theagenes of Rhegium offered allegorizing interpretations of Homer in terms of entrails as if gods and innards were intimately connected. Apollo represented the gall, Dionysus the spleen, Demeter the liver, and so on.[20] In historical times, King Agesilaus supposedly lured the Spartans into war by writing VICTORY on his hand and imprinting it on the liver of a sacrifice. *Splanchna* receive the image-impress of gods. They reflect what gods want to be. The thought seems to be that god, in some sense, is in the innards, or has at least reached in there to divide and mark them.[21]

Why? Animals were in many ways felt to be closer to gods than were human beings. It is tempting to explain this Greek use of animal innards by structuralist argument. Animal mediates between human and divine (see Chapter 7). But this is not enough. The use of animal *innards* in divination must be connected to the interest gods took in their human equivalent. Homeric gods put or throw ideas and feelings into human innards.[22] Homeric and tragic imagery of feeling embodies the idea that gods, or godlike feelings, strike and enter the innards (see Chapter 6). At one level, emotion or inspiration *is* divinity's active interest in the entrails.

Demarcated, observed by gods and humans, animal innards are a medium of communication between divinity and humanity, as human innards are between one person and another. Innards are both ambiguous and necessary in two operations where "clarity" of "distinguishing" is vital: finding out what gods intend for you, and how other people really feel (and what they intend) for you.

To us, these sacrificial anatomic overtones seem alien and irrelevant to

[20] *PV* 493–95; Athen. 174A; Hesych. s.v. *theos*, see Stanford 1939:119–20.

[21] Plu. *Mor.* 214E–F. Roman poets are influenced by Etruscan and Roman divination, both practice and concept (see Beard and North 1990:55–61), but also by Greek poetry and *its* assumptions about divining. A seer inspecting entrails to "find out the gods' anger" cries, "The infernal gods have entered the breast of the slaughtered bull," Luc. *Phars.* 1.633. Before the Lemnians are murdered, "They filled the shrines with incense smoke, but the fire on every altar was black, and in no entrails did *deus integer* breathe," Stat. *Theb.* 5. 176.

[22] *Od.* 19.10, *Il.* 3.139; cf. Snell 1978:57.

questions of "mind." How many of us hold a calf's entrails in our hands, realize the liver lobe is missing or how markings vary on the "portal vein," believe this matters, and apply words for what we are holding to the inner equipment with which we imagine we feel and think? But tragedy and its audiences were familiar, in intense, mystery-surrounded, physical experience absent from our own lives, with the stuff to which they attribute activity within themselves.

I believe this divinatory dimension of *splanchna* radically affected Greek assumptions about the innards' role in consciousness, and ensured that some concrete picture of examinable organs was alive in their thought when they spoke or heard the word *splanchna*, or any of the multiple words associated with *splanchna*. I shall argue the "concreteness" later. First I want to introduce the detailed words.

There are many of them. Words for equipment of consciousness have a pluralizing effect, like the "many names" of gods who so often affect the innards. There are several "organs," and even more words. From the start, multiplicity is a core condition of consciousness, as of religion, in Greek thought.[23]

Tragedy's language of consciousness rests on Homer, with whom Athenian poets thought and worked, and on the lyric poets of the seventh and sixth centuries B.C. But later use of the accumulated Greek language of consciousness also illuminates tragic usage. The important later sources here are the Hellenistic poets of other cities, and above all the Athenian Plato, born 429 B.C. (Plato was 14 years old when *The Trojan Women* was first performed, and tragedy profoundly influenced his writing.) There are some variations in how these words behave in different genres. But in general, tragedy rests on a basic and consistently Greek poetic core of expectations about innards.

HEART, LIVER, *PHRENES*, INNER LIQUIDS

There are three words for "heart": *kardia* (feminine), and *kear* (or *kēr*) and *ētor* (neuter). These all behave in the same sort of way. *Kardia* is excitable and mobile; it knocks, shakes, jumps, or "leaps from the breast" in panic. "Knocked" by emotion, it receives grief and courage. It suffers, endures, is "eager." One can become "full of heart," "love from the heart." It beats and swells with rage.[24] *Kēr*, too, moves, rejoices, or grieves in the breast and

---

[23] This is a positive way of putting what Snell 1953 put as an absence, arguing that Homer lacks a sense of psychic whole; see below, nn. 112–17; this view rested partly on Böhme 1929 and deeply influenced subsequent thinking (references in Sullivan 1988:14 n. 9; add Jaynes 1976, chs. 3–4).

[24] "Leaping": e.g., *Il.* 13.282, cf. Thgn. 1199. Detienne 1989:57–60 takes the heart's leaping as the "physiological mechanism fundamental to Dionysism." "Jumping"; e.g., *Il.* 10.94,

thumos ("spirit"). The common Homeric phrase *kēri*, "with heart," qualifies loving, honoring, being angry. A person is emotionally hurt in the *kear*.[25] *Ētor* also "beats up to the throat." You feel passion, laughter, and grief with it. It "shouts in grief." You are "struck" in it. It, too, is a center of impulse. In longing for her husband, Penelope "wastes away in her *ētor*." Sometimes there is intellectual as well as emotional activity in it. Achilles "ponders" in his *ētor*, divided. Zeus's *ētor* can be "persuaded by prayers." It was a popular idea in the fifth century that the heart was a center of thought and perception as well as feeling.[26]

The liver, *hēpar*, is center of divinatory attention.[27] It can be pierced by a sword and "approached by" emotional pain. One feels anger in it, and fear.[28] Commentators sometimes call it the "seat" of passions, especially anger, fear, lust. But we should watch our own metaphors. These passions do not sit on the *hēpar* but slash, tear, and eat it. Love is "a harsh god" who "gashes the liver within." The center of lust is eternally lacerated and consumed. The mythological embodiment of lust's action on the liver is Tityus, who sexually assaulted the goddess Leto, and whose fate after death is to be chained in Hades while two vultures tear forever at his liver. But the liver is also a receptacle. It should have *cholē*, "bile," in it. A coward's liver does not. The liver is emotional, an image receptor. In Plato's visionary anatomy, the worst part of the soul, the bit that has no reason, simply receives images and is influenced by them. This part is nearest the liver.[29]

Some words have an uncertain physiological meaning, but nevertheless connect intuitive, mental, and emotional experience to the body. *Prapides*

Pl. *Symp.* 215E (cf. Ar. *Nub.* 1391), A. *Supp.* 785. "Knocked" by feeling, receiving feeling that "comes upon" it: *Il.* 2.171, 21.546; *Od.* 17.489; Ar. *Ran.* 54. Suffering, loving, etc.: *Od.* 20.18, cf. E. *Or.* 466 (with *psuchē*); *Il.* 10.244; Ar. *Nub.* 86. Handley (1956:208) sees *kardia* as a physical organ and emotional center both in everyday fifth-century language, as reflected by Aristophanes, and in poetic language.

[25] *Kēr*: *Il.* 14.139, 6.523, 7.428; *Od.* 18.344, 7.82 (see further Webster 1957:151). *Kēri*: *Il.* 9.117, 13.430; *Od.* 5.36; *Il.* 13.119. Tragedy: e.g., *PV* 247, 392. Idea parodied: Ar. *Ach.* 5. See Webster 1957:152–53.

[26] *Il.* 22.452, 21.389, 9.9; *Pers.* 991; *Il.* 3.31, 5.250, 21.114; *Od.* 19.136. Grief "comes on" Achilles, "in his *ētor* in his shaggy breast he wondered, divided," whether to kill Agamemnon or not, *Il.* 1.188. Cf. Pi. *O.* 2.79. Jaynes (1976:267) dislikes the idea of more than one word for "heart," and suggests that *ētor* means the gastrointestinal tract. This approach denies Greek psychological language its multiplicity (see below, n. 111). For the heart as a thinking, perceiving organ, see below, n. 31.

[27] See E. *El.* 827, Pl. *Ti.* 71E, Luc. *Phars.* 1.633ff., Stat. *Theb.* 5.176ff.

[28] *Ag.* 432, 792; *Eum.* 135; E. *Supp.* 599; *Aj.* 938. Physicality: see, e.g., *Il.* 20.469; E. *Supp.* 919.

[29] See Theoc. 13.71, *Od.* 11.578–80; cf. Prometheus's eagle at A. fr. 193.13–17R, "On my fat liver he screams. . . . But when my gnawed liver swells, renewed in growth, he returns greedily to his terrible meal." For liver with bile in it, see Archil. 234W. Our divinatory faculty is put near the liver to compensate for our foolish part, "which has no share in reason or intelligence," Pl. *Ti.* 71D–E.

is a rare plural word, used in Homer and tragedy to mean "understanding," or "place of understanding," and also "place of desiring": in the old-fashioned English sense, one's "heart." The giants tell Zeus they "know his *prapides* and *noēma* [thought] are all-surpassing." Achilles' longing to grieve leaves his *prapides* and limbs. Once women exist, even a man whose wife "fits his *prapides*" has a difficult time. If you push something (the text does not say what) "under your crowded [or dense] *prapides* [i.e., thoughts], and attend to them constantly, all will be well," says Empedocles mysteriously. That "something" seems to mean understanding. It belongs under our *prapides*.[30]

Phrēn and its plural, *phrenes*, much argued-over words, are at the center of tragic language of mind. *Phrēn* is not used in early prose but is common in poetry. The heart kicks it, it delights in music, *thumos* gathers towards it, it raves in madness, a united community hates "with one *phrēn*," and Zeus's *phrēn* is "*turned.*" The plural, *phrenes*, however, is common in both poetry and prose.

Instead of introducing *phrēn* by argument and categorization, considering possible original meanings and possible changes in use, let me bring forward a doctor's polemic written around the end of the fifth century, by one of the few writers who thinks the brain has something to do with consciousness. He is arguing against the popular idea that *phrenes* have a key role in thinking and feeling. His attack reveals, therefore, what most people in his day believed *phrenes* did:

> The *phrenes* have an empty name. They acquired it by chance and convention, not because of reality and nature. I do not know, myself, what power *phrenes* have to think (*noein*) and to be intelligent (*phronein*), except that if someone is unexpectedly overjoyed or upset, they leap and make the person jump. This is because of their fine texture and very wide extension in the body. They do *not* have a cavity into which they receive anything (either good or bad) falling into them. They are disturbed by both [good and bad] things because of their weak nature. They do *not* perceive anything before the other parts of the body, but have that irrelevant name, and are reputedly the cause [of perception], like the parts by the heart called "ears," though they do not share in hearing at all. Some people say that it is the heart with which we think (*phronein*), and that it feels upset and anxiety. This is *not* true.

His negatives show how popular thought in his day could ascribe perception and sane thinking (*phronein*) to the heart, or to *phrenes*—etymologically connected to *phronein*—and how it saw *phrenes* as a receptacle into which things "fall."[31]

---

[30] *Prapides*: *Theog.* 656, 698; *Il.* 24.514; A. *Supp.* 87–90 (see p. 135); Emp. frr. 132.1, 129.2–4, 110.1DK (see Wright 1981:258–59).

[31] *DMS* 20 (Loeb 2:178–80; my emphasis). *Phrēn*: the one early prose use is Heraclitus fr. 104DK, "What *noos* or *phrēn* do they have?" See *PV* 881; *Il.* 9.186, 22.475; *Sept.* 484; *Eum.*

At the end of the fifth century, by the end of extant tragedy, most people assume that they think and perceive and feel with internal organs, often their *phrenes*. What, precisely, do they think these are? Let us watch how *phrēn* and *phrenes* behave as words in Homer and tragedy, without pre-judging their physical, intellectual, or metaphysical qualities, and keeping alive our own uncertainties about what exactly in our terms *phrenes* might be.

Phrēn's first feature seems to be responsiveness. It is acted upon, rather than initiating action. The heart kicks the *phrēn*. A *phrēn*, as we saw, can be "turned." "A sleeping *phrēn* is lit with eyes." The verbs make *phrēn* passive. It is the emotions that are active. Grief covers Hector's *phrenes*, *erōs* covers those of Paris. Fear "holds" *phrenes*. They receive and express emotion. Tears fall from the *phrēn*. The dead, except Teiresias, do not have *phrenes*.[32]

Like the heart, *phrenes* have receptor passivity, are acted on by feelings. Thinking or perceiving mingles with feeling. Hearts have "ears"; *phrenes* may have eyes. Gods "place" in *phrenes* practical ideas like calling an assembly. Their roles imply a vital question. From where does human knowledge come, from inside or outside, from human beings or gods? Hector "knows in his *phrenes*" that gods have abandoned him.[33] Something done "from the *phrēn*" is like something done "with the heart," done "sincerely." "I measured your *phrenes* and realized how great a bitterness you are to me, as my enemy," says Ion to his would-be murderer.[34] He thinks he has seen into, as we would say, her heart or mind. Either of these problematic words of ours would fit. We know, act, respond to ideas, with *phrenes*.

All this seems in line with popular ideas attacked by the Hippocratic doctor. *Phrenes* contain emotion, practical ideas, and knowledge. We ourselves think of these as qualitatively different things, but popular fifth-century thought did not. *Phrenes* are containers: they fill with *menos*, "anger," or *thumos*, "passion." They are essentially mobile, too, and they "tremble within."[35] They are the holding center, folding the heart, holding the liver. A thunderbolt striking "in the very *phrenes*" is an image of annihilation. You are struck, you know, understand, tremble, feel, or ponder in that responsive, compact, containing center.[36]

986; *Il.* 10.45. Important work on *phrēn* and *phrenes* includes von Fritz 1943; Snell 1953, 1978:53–60; Claus 1981 (esp. p. 16); Sullivan 1988 (cf. Darcus 1979).

[32] *Eum.* 104 (cf. *Corp. Herm.* 4.11, 7.2, "eyes of the heart"); *Il.* 8.124, 3.442; A. *Supp.* 379; *Sept.* 919; *Od.* 10.493.

[33] *Il.* 1.55, 13.55 (cf. "throw this in your *phrenes*," i.e., "attend, think hard about this," 1.297), 22.296; *Od.* 9.600, cf. 10.438; *Il.* 9.434, 2.301.

[34] *Cho.* 107 (*logos* from *phrēn*); *Sept.* 919 (pouring tears from *phrēn*); *Ag.* 1515 (from a friendly *phrēn*, cf. 805, *ap' akras phrenos*); *Ion* 1271. These suggest that what comes from *phrēn*, a *phrēn* seen properly, is true.

[35] *Il.* 1.103, cf. 13.487.

[36] *Il.* 16.481; *Od.* 9.301; *PV* 363, cf. *Eum.* 159 (reproach is a blow, striking under the

But sometimes *phrenes* are an active, initiating force. They "pilot" the *thumos*, "spirit." They can imagine the opposite of what is, create what is not, and deny what is said. A man "rich in respect of his *phrenes*" is only imagining his wealth. When Hippolytus considers breaking his vow, he appeals to the inner integrity of *phrēn*: "My tongue promised, my *phrēn* did not."[37] By the mid-fifth century, it is possible to oppose *phrenes* to the externally seen body. They are its conscious inwardness. The word *phrenes* becomes popular in tragedy for "mind." Aristophanes, who stretches to brilliant absurdity the surreal implications of intellectual and tragic language, parodies tragedy when he uses *phrenes*, especially when mocking the mandarin "mind" of an intellectual.[38] But the emotional dimension of *phrenes* continues. In an early tragedy, *phrēn* "raves with grief-cries." In a later one, Theseus cries with grief for the too well-intentioned *phrēn* of Hippolytus, who did not, after all, break that vow: "Alas for your *phrēn*, pious and good." People feel intense love and grief in *phrenes*.[39] *Phrenes* are actively, decisively emotional and imaginative.

Even in activity, *phrenes* are responsive, answerable, vulnerable. Tragedy favors the word *phrenes* in contexts of feeling and thinking. But the vulnerability of *phrenes* is also important. The emotional and intellectual activity whose center they are often wounds them. They are more often acted on than active. When someone's *phrenes* are struck and gashed by fear, or by gods, that person is paralyzed, incapable of action or judgment.[40] *Phrenes* also abandon a person, "stand away," get lost. One can lose one's hold on them, be no longer "in" them, be "struck out," "empty of *phrenes*," "no longer in one's *phrenes*."[41]

There are inconsistencies in this language. It would be odd if there were not, for the damage and loss of *phrenes* is also madness: a territory where even professional theories are full of contradiction. The language of tragedians working for the "mad god's" theater, whose genre is perpetually

---

phrenes); *Il.* 10.10 (trembling), 1.362 (grief approaches *phrenes*). Knowing, thinking, wondering, planning with *phrenes*: see Snell 1978:59ff.

[37] *Pers.* 767, *Erg.* 455, *Hipp.* 612.

[38] *Phrenes* opposed to body: e.g., Hdt. 3.134; E. *El.* 387 ("flesh empty of *phrenes*"). For the comic parody of tragic language taking *phrenes* as "mind," see Handley 1956:217–18, 220–23.

[39] *Phrēn* and feeling: *Sept.* 484; *Hipp.* 1454; *Med.* 143; *IA* 1434. See Claus 1981:54 for more references. For *phrenes* and feeling in later tragedy, see, e.g., *Hipp.* 256; *Med.* 55; see also Claus 1981:55.

[40] Charioteers "struck in *phrenes*," frightened when their warrior is killed, cannot drive away from danger, *Il.* 13.394, 16.403; cf. *Pers.* 115, *Ag.* 479. Gods "harm" *phrenes*, *Il.* 7.360, 15.724.

[41] "Keep your head" (as English might say) is "Don't stand out of your *phrenes*," *Phil.* 865. A man should not let a woman "throw him out of his *phrenes*," *Ant.* 648. When her brother is to be killed, Electra "stands out" of her *phrenes*, *Or.* 1021. "Are you not-in-your-*phrenes*?" is "Are you mad?" *Heraclid.* 709; cf. "Where are you in your *phrenes*?" S. *El.* 390. "Empty of *phrenes*": *Ant.* 754. When Io goes mad, her *phrenes* are "twisted aside," *PV* 673.

aware of the possibility of madness, is entitled to verbal inconsistencies about what passion does to *phrenes*.[42] Normally, one has *phrenes*, and is in them. These are two ways, seemingly (to us) contradictory, of evoking the same thing: safe sanity. To "have" *phrenes* is to be in control, be sane. *Sōphrōn*, "having a safe *phrēn*," means prudent, ideally controlled, sane, "in one's senses."[43] In tragedy, the acts and attitudes that precipitate the tragic action are precisely not *sōphrōn*. They could be *aphrōn*, "without *phrēn*," or *ekphrōn*, "out of *phrēn*." Like Xerxes' sacriligious attempt to invade Greece by chaining the sea, they are in some sense mad. Madness is a trembling, a battering, a confusion, a disease, or a loss, of *phrenes*. There are few tragedies that do not speak to the possibility that *phrenes* can be hurt, lost, damaged. And though *phrenes* return (tragedy, I believe, perceives madness as a temporary condition), this inward damage causes irrevocable damage in the outside world.[44] *Phrenes*, like *kardia*, receive both knowing and feeling. Accordingly, damage to them is emotional and intellectual and leads to madness. The possibility that they can be damaged or lost is central to the vision of human structures easily smashed, from and to which the tragedies speak. There is no *terra firma* in tragedy, especially not within.

These innards flow with emotions that behave like liquids. Blood is important here (see Chapter 8), but there are also other liquids, or liquid-looking words: *cholos, cholē, menos*.

Cholē, or *cholos*? Homer generally uses *cholos*, tragic poets and the Hippocratics use *cholē*. Both mean "gall," "bile." *Cholē* is normally "blonde," but when diseased is black. It is always bitter. Mothers smear it on the nipple to wean babies. There are vessels, gallbladders, to "hold" it, but it is stirred and moved, boils over, floods the heart. *Cholē* is also fury, or furious madness. The liquid's physical bitterness coheres with anger's emotionally bitter force. *Alastōr* (avenging daemon) is "bitter" too.[45] When Achilles stops his men from joining the Greeks, he is told, "Surely your mother raised you on *cholos*." The reproach would have suggested to fifth-century

---

[42] "*Mainomenos Dionysos*": *Il.* 6.132; see Padel 1981:110–14.

[43] *Sōphrōn*: see Pl. *Crat.* 411E; Arist. *EN* 1140B11. "*Sōphrōn* and in control of yourself": Pl. *Gorg.* 491D, sums up the general ideal; cf. *Ag.* 1664, *Cho.* 140, *Aj.* 132. "Having" *phrenes* and *nous*, Ar. *Ran.* 534, and being "in charge of *phrenes*," *Ant.* 492, mean being sane, being aware. *Emphrōn* is "sane," often as opposed to "mad" (*Cho.* 1026, *Aj.* 306, *PV* 848).

[44] See Snell 1978:55, 64–72, 76, on *aphrōn, diaphrōn, saophrōn, phrenes* trembling, raving. Mad grief is a trembling, madness a confusion, of *phrenes*: *Phoen.* 1285, *HF* 836. Xerxes' impious act was due to *nosos phrenōn, Pers.* 750. Tragic madness is a temporary episode of self-destructive, dangerous behavior, see Padel 1981:108–14.

[45] See *Anc. Med.* 19 (Loeb 1:48): "The bitter principle, which we call yellow *cholē* . . . ," cf. the color and processes described in Pl. *Ti.* 82E–83D. *Cholē* is cognate with German *gelb*, "yellow," and Latin *helvus*. Black, i.e., diseased: *Aph.* 4.23 (Loeb 4:140). Used in weaning: Diphilus 74 (Kock). *Cholē* is contained in the *cholai*, gallbladder, *Ant.* 1010; the "*dochai cholēs*," S. *El.* 828; cf. *PV* 495. *Cholades* are "bowels," "guts," *Il.* 4.526. *Thumos*, too, is bitter, *Cho.* 390 (see Chapter 4, n. 45), like *cholos, menos*, strife, and *alastōr* (*Ag.* 1501).

audiences a paradox: Achilles was nourished by what is used to turn a baby away.[46]

Cholē signifies bile, black fury. The principle here, which we shall meet in other contexts, is that when something goes wrong, things inside supposedly go black. When bile increases, when anger comes, this bile is black. The core verb, *cholaō*, "I fill with bile," means the same as *melancholaō*, "I fill with black bile." Both can mean "I am passionate" or "I am mad." Here is the basic ingredient of melancholia and its overpowering afterlife.[47] *Melancholia, melancholikos*: Greek medical writers use them of delirium or of anyone they think is full of black bile. The words begin to take on their extra tones of passion and madness in the late fifth century. Incorporated into Hippocratic humoral theory, they become psychological and ethical terms, moving towards that Renaissance vision of "melancholy" which compacts several categories of physiological, psychological, and moral damage.[48]

Cholos is "of the *phrenes*" that hold it. *Cholos* seizes you, sinks into you, conquers you, comes to you. You nurse, ripen, or quench it.[49] It has a close relation to *thumos* ("spirit"). *Cholos* "falls into," is thrown into, or is stored in *thumos*. Yet, like *thumos*, *cholos* can be roused, be moved, boil over.[50] The active verb *choloō* is "I make angry," that is, "I make full of bile." Its natural object is another person's *ētor*. It is more common in the passive voice, *choloomai*, "I am made angry" (i.e., I am angry) in my *phrenes*, heart, or *thumos*.[51]

Another closely related, but more diverse, liquid word for anger is *menos*. Odysseus says Achilles will not quench his *cholos* but "is filled even more with *menos*." These are not constant synonyms, though we can translate both as "anger." With *menos* we are not on such clear physical ground. It is a Homeric and tragic word, but no medical usage tells us what *menos* "is" or "is like," or if it is always liquid. Its function seems to be to fill things.

[46] Ar. *Lys.* 465; Dem. 25.27; Ar. *Ran.* 4, *Thesm.* 468, *V.* 403. At Ar. *Pax* 66, *cholē* seems to mean *mania*, see Platnauer *ad loc.*, Dover *ad Nub.* 833. *Cholē* floods heart in fury: *Cho.* 184. Achilles: see *Il.* 16.203.

[47] *Cholaō*: Ar. *Nub.* 833; *melancholaō*: Ar. *V.* 14, *Pl.* 12, 366, 903; Pl. *Phdr.* 268E; Dem. 48.56, Men. *Sam.* 218; and often in Galen. *Melancholikoi* means "dipped in black bile," of the arrows at *Trach.* 573. See Flashar 1966:11–49. The image of a "black sun" ruling the mind features in modern discussions of schizophrenia and melancholia, see Laing 1965:201–4; Kristeva 1989:151. Cf. the blackness of tragic madness, the absence of reason's image, light, Padel 1981:115, 125.

[48] See Klibansky, Panofsky, and Saxl 1964; Flashar 1966: chs. 3–8; Simon 1978:228–37.

[49] E.g., *Il.* 2.241, 15.122; Sol. 4.39 (West); *cholos* of a god: *Il.* 18.119; *Od.* 3.145; *h. Dem.* 350. Seizing, sinking in, etc.: *Med.* 1266; *Il.* 1.387, 4.23, 9.553, 18.119, 9.525. *Cholos*, nursed, ripened: *Il.* 4.513, 9.565 (cf. Arist. *EN* 1126A24, where it is softened and digested); should be quenched: *Il.* 9.678.

[50] *Il.* 9.436, 675, 14.50, 6.326; Pi. *P.* 11.23; *Med.* 99; *PV* 370. Black bile's later connection with laughter (the "smiling spleen"), see Pagel 1981:86.

[51] Active: *Theog.* 568; passive: *Il.* 16.61, 13.206, 16.585, 21.136, 1.217, 4.494.

When Agamemnon is angry, his "black *phrenes* fill around greatly with
menos." *Menos* fills *phrenes*, soul, and *thumos*. The *menos* of *thumos* "boils,"
like *cholē*. *Menos* is often coupled in these contexts with *thumos*, but their
relationship is mobile and inconsistent. Both can be taken as "anger" or as
"spirit," but one can act upon the other. *Menos* "seizes" and fills *thumos*.[52]

Menos can also more generally mean "energy." Wine "increases *menos* in
a weary man." *Menos* is "force," which is often "ferocity," as in a wild animal, the hot sun, fire, or stormy gales, or as in *atē*, that self-destructiveness
of mind.[53]

One can fantasize. Is blood, that obvious inner liquid, behind (in some
sense) this strong hot black strength filling the mind, which is increased by
wine and "lost" at death?

We should be clear about what this suggestion implies. It is true that
when *menos* has color it is black, that Greek often (not always) calls blood
"black," and that *menos* is said to flow away and be lost through a fatal
wound.[54] But if we say *menos* "is really" or "was once" blood, we impose
our own story patterns and assumptions about mind, and language, and
how we talk of mind, onto these Greek words. "Really" implies that the
physical is always present in, prior to, and more truthful than the abstract.
"Was once" implies a whole mythopoeic narrative behind Greek words for
"mind": that they "once" referred to physical organs "and then" developed
more abstract meanings.

I prefer to keep the uncertainty and variety of such a word alive in our
readings of it. It may be true both that these words mean real liquid in real
innards, and that they are anger and force. They may be more. Our own
categories are not the only ones to compare with Greek words. The Ilongot, for instance, a society of headhunters in the Philippines, have a word
liget, which suggests energy and anger. It rises in the heart. For them, "mo-
tions of the heart are emotions." Yet *liget* attaches not so much to selves as
to interactions. Chili pepper gives *liget* to a stew, ginger revitalizes *liget* in
a killer, winds have more *liget* when obstructed. *Liget* is engendered between things when they meet and confront each other. It is also revealed
in people when they pant and sweat. It flows inwardly and generates red-

---

[52] *Il.* 9.679, 1.104. *Menos* filling and boiling: *Il.* 1.103, 22.312; Arist. *Rh.* 1406A2; Ar. *V.*
424; cf. Pl. *Ti.* 70B. For further studies of *menos*, see Lindsay 1965:70–72; Nagy 1980. *Menos*
and *thumos*, *menos* seizing and filling *thumos*: see *Il.* 5.470, 23.468, 22.312.

[53] "Force" given by wine: *Il.* 6.261; *Reg. Acut. Dis.* 63 (Loeb 2:118, cf. *Anc. Med.* 9 [Loeb
1:26], effect of "the *menos* of fasting"). "Force" of sun, wind, rivers, fire: *Od.* 10.160; *Heraclid.* 428; *Il.* 12.18, 6.182; Ar. *Ach.* 665. Of *atē*: *Cho.* 1076. Claus (1981:25) comments that
menos compounds (like *dusmenēs*) underline the word's "power."

[54] Black blood flows from a wound: *Il.* 4.149. Blood is sometimes *chlōron*, e.g., *Trach.*
1055, but this is usually taken as "fresh." Cf. *melan menos*, *Aj.* 1412 (which might mean
gushing "life blood," but it is unclear; see Jebb on *phusai ad loc.*). At *Il.* 17.298, brain and
blood spurt out of a wound and *menos luthē*. *Menos* is often (e.g., *Il.* 5.296) "lost" with *psuchē*.
Onians (1954:46–51) sees *menos* as blood, but cf. pp. 89–91, and below, n. 56.

ness in the self. It is dynamic, organic, chaotic violence, and also the stuff of life.

The anthropologist who reports on the Ilongot at first simply translated *liget* as anger, but then saw that through the ways in which it worked, and the associations it held for the Ilongot, *liget* embodied a whole set of principles and connections underlying the entire way they conceptualized society, bodies, and world. Refraining from tying the word down to one kind of meaning, following it instead in its variety and implications, she found that this method yielded far richer insight into the Ilongot's understanding of self than she would have gained from the unthinking assumption that one English translation can always explain one word.[55]

So, rather than speak of *menos* as a liquid that "once" meant blood, or that by the time Homer uses it is only an abstract force, I would follow its diversity. In many places it behaves like blood, resonant with anger's blood connotations in the *Iliad*, that strongly male war-poem. But I think it unlikely that it ever *only* meant blood. The physical stuff belongs with the emotion. This is especially important because in other places *menos* behaves not as liquid but as breath. Homeric warriors "breathe *menea*" (the plural of *menos*). They are ready to attack and are "breathing fury."[56]

There are two points here. One, on the physiological side, is that in Greek anatomy, inner channels and vessels contain both breath (or air) and liquid. We shall meet this idea again later (Chapter 3). The other is a principle of approach. We do not have to say that *menos* "is" either breath or liquid. It acts now as one, now as another. In being now one, now another, it may also be other things, things that (in our terms) are more abstract. "Life force" has been suggested, for instance.[57] *Menos* in its diversity brings together three decisive Greek images: emotion's ferocious impact on innards, breath and liquid as interchangeable ways of describing this impact, and the flooding of the mind.[58]

Like the innards they fill, inner liquids are multiple. In Homer, *ichor* means the fluid gods have in their veins instead of blood. It seems pallid, blonde. In the fifth century and later, the word can mean putrified blood, occasionally ordinary blood, serum of blood or gall, or any pale discharge. Yellowish liquids in the innards seem to be identified not with anger, the blackening emotion, but with fear, like facial pallor.[59] Innards and their contents, like the meanings of these mind-words, are multiple and fluid.

[55] Rosaldo 1980:37–47.

[56] E.g., *Il.* 2.536, 3.8, 11.508. Onians (1954:49–58) argues that *menos* is conceived as liquid here. But *menos* seems to work sometimes as liquid, sometimes as breath (see pp. 89–91).

[57] Claus 1981:24–25, though cf. below, n. 66.

[58] See pp. 81–84 and 88.

[59] *Ichōr* in gods' veins: *Il.* 5.340. Pale liquid in human veins: *Cord.* 11 (Littré), *Nat. hom.* 12 (Loeb 4:34); cf. Pl. *Ti.* 83C; Arist. *Mir.* 845A8, *HA* 521B2, 630A6, 586B32. See Fraen-

"Spirit," "Soul," "Mind"

A word's meaning depends not so much on its linguistic
past but rather on the place the word occupies in relation to
the general system of the language at the period in question.
— J. P. Vernant, *Myth and Society in Ancient Greece*

Three final words, *thumos*, *psuchē*, and *nous*, raise new, more complicated
questions. Or perhaps they raise similar issues, but in more acute and complex ways. They have inspired argument throughout European philosophy. I introduce them here as "innards" because Greek is clear that they are
"in" us, and because they share profoundly in the learning, feeling, thinking, and dividing attributed to innards. In early Greek poetry, they share
the intermittent physicality of heart, *phrēn*, and *cholos*. They behave *like*
them.[60] The question is not what actual physical reference they might have,
but how the words behave. Homer and tragedy use them as if *thumos*, *nous*,
and *psuchē* are contained and move, like other innards, inside the body.
This must be the basis for our approach to them, as readers of the language
and poetry which pliantly express Greek assumptions about what is within
us.

Thumos derives from *thuō*, "I seethe," used of an angry man or sea. So
far, I have translated it as "spirit." "Soul" or "heart" work in some contexts,
"impulse," "desire," or "courage" in others. *Thumos* is notoriously difficult
to translate into English. It may be that other non-European languages—
Ilongot, for instance—would recognize and pinpoint its range better. In
action, *thumos* is appetitive, practical, urgent. It impels a person to satisfy
desire for food, drink, song. People wish in their *thumos*. It is energetic,
imperious. It "commands" people, stirs them up. It is often coupled with
menos in battle contexts ("energy and spirit," "force and courage"), but it
can be turned and persuaded, like the heart.[61]

---

kel *ad Ag*. 1480. *Krokou baphas* (*Ag.* 239) probably refers to the saffron-dyed dress (crocuses
make clothes "blossom with gold light," *Ion* 890). Blood flowing onto ground is usually dark,
Lloyd-Jones 1990 i. 303. *Krokou baphas*, from this fear-filled context, is echoed later: *kroko-
baphēs* qualifies a pale fearful inner liquid, *Ag.* 1121. Cf. *chlōron deima*, *Il.* 10.376; Sappho
31V; E. *Supp.* 599; Pi. fr. 123 (Snell-Maehler); and compare comic jokes about yellowing
oneself in fear, e.g., Ar. *Ran.* 308.

[60] Böhme (1929) projected modern distinctions between "physical" and "emotional," or
"psychological" onto his treatment of soul-words, as Snell (1931) said reviewing him. Snell's
own approach (1953, 1978) was to take psychic terms as "analogous to organs." He influenced Dodds 1951 and Fränkel 1975—he has influenced everybody—and this aspect of his
work is one basis of my approach. But I would stress that any "analogy" is in *our* minds, not
in Greek mentality, for to say that *Greek* imagination made an analogy between psychic and
physical would anachronistically imply that it drew that distinction.

[61] Ilongot: Rosaldo 1980:37–47. This example and this study illuminate Homeric mind-

A common practical but archaizing translation for *thumos* is "heart," as in "take heart," "heartening." Like *kardia*, *thumos* is a site of feeling. Fear "falls" into it. A person rejoices in or with it. It is glad in their breast. A friend is "dear to their *thumos*." Agamemnon cherished Briseis "from his *thumos*." Medea, seeing Jason, was "struck by desire in her *thumos*." *Thumos* suffers, endures. Immortal Apollo says mortals have an enduring *thumos*. In a sense, this tough *thumos* is independent of self. "You" can oppose your *thumos*. In a speech that grounds the fall of Troy in divine conflict—or self-conflict—Zeus expresses anger with Hera, who wants to abort the human truce. Hating Troy, she wants the war to go on to its destructive end. Zeus would rather save Troy. But he gives way, to avoid "conflict between us two." He gives ground "willingly but with an unwilling *thumos*."[62] War shall continue, based on conflict not between Zeus and his wife, but between Zeus and his own *thumos*.

Like *cholos* and *menos*, *thumos* is central to anger. When it is the subject of an active verb, it is often translated "anger." But people are also angry in or with their *thumos*. *Thumos* is "piercing," "stronger than reasoned plans." But, like *ētor*, it can also reason and consider. Words are thrown "into" it. One deliberates "in *phrenes* and *thumos*."[63] Yet *thumos* is "in" *phrenes*. It collects in them, increases there, fills a person. In this it seems to resemble *menos*. It is "breathed out" or flies off at death. The *thumos* of warring gods is "blown" in different directions. This range of usages suggests a liquid or

words profoundly. In her study of Homeric *thumos*, Caswell (1990) concentrates on its semantic associations and contexts, and sees *thumos* at the center of every internal experience. *Thumos* desiring, commanding: see *Il.* 8.301, 16.255; *Od.* 9.139; Pi. *O.* 3.25; *Il.* 10.220; S. *El.* 286. Cf. *Od.* 9.302, "but another *thumos* held me back." In everyday fifth-century vocabulary as reflected by Aristophanes, *thumos* often means "anger," "desire," or "instinct," Handley 1956:207–8. *Thumos* as "stronger than yourself": Dodds 1951:16. As "spirit": e.g., *Il.* 20.174; *Od.* 10.406 (cf. Sappho 42V). *Thumos* persuaded: *Il.* 15.94, *Od.* 9.33. Calypso's "is not made of iron but compassionate," *Od.* 5.191. Address to your own *thumos* or instruction by it: see Lloyd-Jones 1983:9, 14–20, 23, 38–39, 44; Darcus 1980.

[62] *Thumos* as "heart," enduring: e.g., *Il.* 14.156, 7.189, 24.49. Loving "from *thumos*": *Il.* 9.343. *Thumos* struck with desire: *Med.* 8. Locus of courage and endurance in Aristophanes: Handley 1956:216. *Thumos* declines in use after Homer; see Claus 1981:49; Darcus 1981. *Psuchē* replaces many innard-words in most fourth-century philosophy, but Plato brings back *thumos* for the divided soul in *Rep.* bk. 4. Under his influence (presumably), Aristotle reclaims this now old-fashioned-seeming word; see *EN* 1149A25–B2; Burnyeat 1980a:79, 84, 90 (see esp. nn. 17, 21). "Willing with unwilling *thumos*": *Il.* 4.38, 43.

[63] *Thumos* as sharp strong anger: *Il.* 1.429, 17.254, 9.496; *OC* 1193; *Med.* 1079. Site of "pondering": *Il.* 1.193, 2.409, 15.566; *PV* 706; Caswell 1990:2–3, 28, 35. S. *El.* 1347 seems to mean "I cannot even bring him [or memory of him] into my *thumos*." Electra cannot recognize or remember the man to whom she entrusted Orestes. Jebb (*ad loc.*) translates: "I cannot even bring [a conjecture] into my mind." Electra has just been asked, "Don't you understand what is going on?" She answers with *ge*: "No, and I don't even *es thumon pherō*." We should link this with *enthumoumai*, "I have in mind." *Thumos* is here expected to have an intellectual role.

breath, like *menos*, yet elsewhere *thumos* behaves more like a vessel or an object. Like *kardia*, *thumos* is "seized" by *menos* and beats in the breast. Like *phrēn*, it is "knocked" by *atē*. People "gnaw" it in anger.[64]

Clearly, the question "What is *thumos*?" must have a complex answer that allows it to be several kinds of thing. No single explanatory word, like "breath" or "agitation,"[65] "life force,"[66] or "faculty,"[67] will do. The "breath" element is important. The Latin equivalent of *thumos* is *spiritus*, related to "respiration." But *thumos* is also liquid, like *cholos*, which boils in and swells the innards. *Thumos* is a thing seized, struck, gnawed, a receptacle filled, a volatile, forceful breath or liquid, an emotion and impulse (passionate anger, desire), a *place* of emotion and inner debate ("heart," "mind"), and a

---

[64] *Thumos* in *phrenes*: *Od.* 20.38, *Il.* 13.280. Collects in the *phrēn*: *Il.* 22.475. Runs back into the breast: *Il.* 4.152. Caswell (1990) thinks it fundamental to Homeric *thumos* that it is contained in *phrenes*. Hector "increases the *thumos*" of his allies by food and gifts, *Il.* 17.226. *Thumoō*, like *choloō*, is "I make angry," presumably with a similar background picture, filling with angry liquid; cf. E. *Supp.* 581, *thumōsai phrenas*. The more common middle voice suggests, like *choloomai*, "I am filled with *thumos*," as with a liquid; cf. "filled" with *thumos*, e.g., Pl. *Rep.* 411C; Isoc. 12.81. It flies off, as if it were "spirit," at death, *Od.* 10.163, leaving the bones, *Il.* 12.386. Breathed out at death: *Il.* 13.654, 20.403. Blown different ways: *Il.* 21.386. *Menos* seizing, filling, thrown into *thumos*: *Il.* 23.468, 22.312, 17.451. *Thumos* "beats" in the breast in fear, hoping for victory: *Il.* 7.216, 23.370. Gashed in anger: *Il.* 1.243. Like *kradiē*, *thumos* "warms" in the breast, *Od.* 4.548. Grief "comes on" *thumos* and *kradiē* together, *Il.* 2.171. The obstinate, struggling *thumos* is struck by *atē*, *Ant.* 1097. Aristophanes parodies such passages: *Nub.* 1368–69, "My heart heaved, but biting my *thumos* I said . . ."; cf. above, n. 38. Bremmer (1983:54) takes *thumos* as an ego-soul that moves. He and Caswell (1990, who stresses the "wind-breath" view) do not make enough room for passages where *thumos* behaves as a vessel, as something beaten or gashed.

[65] Onians (1954:49–58) pioneered the concrete-to-abstract approach, took *thumos* as "breath," and collected rich material around this idea. Breath has been the strongest candidate in recent discussion; see Redfield 1975:174; and Caswell 1990:16, 62–63, who points out the qualities *thumos* has in common with winds and suggests it is "the human counterpart to winds." Jaynes (1976:69) calls *thumos* "simply motion or agitation." From the idea that a raging sea has *thumos*, he infers that *thumos* is "not really an organ and not always localized," not letting it be thought of in several ways at once.

[66] Claus (1981:22, 37–42) has the most useful analysis of possible approaches to this Greek material. Rosaldo (1980) suggests freer approaches to such words, perhaps because the language and society she studies are removed from the Greek tradition. Claus (p. 15) opposes the concrete-to-abstract reasoning of Onians (also reminding us, p. 25 n. 45, of the middle ground suggested by Nilsson). He identifies a core meaning "life force" in most "soul-words," which in my view weakens his clear-headed, skeptical approach. He analyzes (pp. 37–42) different "shadings" of *thumos* in different Homeric contexts, but his "anomalous uses" are those which do not fit his "life force" meaning. Like Jaynes (in this instance), he does not allow for fluctuations in ideas of *thumos*, which might behave in turn as a breath, an agent, an organ, a force, or as several (to us different) things at once.

[67] Sullivan (1988) takes the opposite corner from Onians. She rightly refuses to "limit each term to a particular range of meaning" (p. 36 n. 50). But in expounding soul-words, she substitutes "faculty indeterminately corporeal" for "organ" (pp. 8–9; see below, n. 86), and "faculty" in this context is equally loaded and anachronistic.

force or cast of mind: "spirit," "temper." We might compare it to a Greek
divine persona, and say that *thumos* "is" the principle that connects all these
different things in Greek mentality. Like the Ilongot's *liget*, *thumos* is either
the sum, or the common denominator, or both, of its possible activities, at
work in Greek imagination. Volatility is its own essence, and the essence
of how it is perceived.

A similar volatility marks the history and semantic field of *psuchē*. It, too,
behaves sometimes like breath,[68] sometimes like blood.[69] Sometimes it
means simply "life." You fight about it, risk it. You have only one, which
leaves you at death.[70] But *psuchē* is also the sensual, emotional, purposeful
self. It feels and endures. In battle you are "strong in hands and *psuchē*." In
this sense, it "dies" in you by faltering. You are struck in it, "overcome in
your *psuchē* by *erōs*." You please it by satisfying a desire.[71] *Psuchē* can be a
source of perception, can be coupled with "thought" and "reason" in an
intellectual and moral role. A *psuchē* can be "bad."[72]

[68] Breathlike, connected perhaps with *psuchō*, "I blow": see Snell 1953:9; Claus 1981:93 n.
3. It crosses your *herkos odontōn*, *Il.* 9.408. You gasp it away when you faint, *Il.* 22.467.
Psuchorrhageō is "I gasp out my life": *Alc.* 20, *HF* 324, *IT* 1466. For a critique of suggested
meanings (vital fluid, etc.), see Bremmer (1983:11, 13–17, 21 n. 21), who accepts the relation of *psuchē* with *psuchein*.

[69] Bloodlike as well as breathy (see Claus 1981:68), it gushes from a wound, *Il.* 14.518,
16.505. At moments of destruction it is linked with *menos*: see Böhme 1929:112; Claus
1981:61. Electra sucks the blood of her mother's *psuchē*, S. *El.* 786. Cf. Ar. *Nub.* 712, and
psuchopotēs (Hesych. s.v.). Onians (1954:94–122, 129ff.) associates it with brain-and-spinal
fluid, and semen. Claus reconsiders the "breath" view, starting from a usage that "implies
blood" (pp. 95–97). He elicits from the contradictory material a "relatively consistent life-
force identity" of *psuchē* in Homer. But again he loses the possibility that, like *menos*, the word
can mean something that is conceived in several ways at once. Bremmer (1983:5) points out
that the fact that *psuchē* may once have had a connection with breath does not necessarily
mean it has this meaning in Homer, nor that we should expect to find its use consistent.

[70] See *Od.* 3.74 (risking it), *Il.* 9.322, *Od.* 22.245 (fighting for it), *Il.* 21.569 (Achilles has
one, and men think him mortal). See Garland 1981; and for post-Homeric references, see
also Claus 1981:64 (with nn. 16–22). Struggle "about a *psuchē*" is about a "life" (often in
Euripides, e.g., *Heraclid.* 984 and *Or.* 847, but also in Aeschylus and Sophocles, e.g., *Eum.*
115, S. *El.* 1493, *Ant.* 559; cf. *OC* 999—a return to "life"). *Psuchē* can be coupled with *menos*,
aiōn (e.g., *Il.* 16.453), *biotos* (e.g., Thgn. 730 Bergk), and *thumos* (e.g., *Il.* 11.334), as if they
all meant "life." Things "dear as *psuchē*" are dear as life, *Erg.* 686. Your children are your
psuchē, *Andr.* 419 (see further Claus 1981:64 with n. 21). Claus (1981:93–102) discusses the
old view that *psuchē* developed from "shade" (of the dead) to "life," but he prefers to think
that even by Homer's time *psuchē* was absorbed into "life-force" words, and so behaved like
one itself. (His project is to elicit a model of patterns of usage for consciousness-words that
illuminates the presence of *psuchē* in classical Greek).

[71] Pi. *P.* 1.48; Ar. *Eq.* 457; Pi. *N.* 9.32, 39; S. *El.* 903 (the sight "impresses" my *psuchē*);
Hipp. 527, 505 (I have schooled my *psuchē* to endure *erōs*). Aristophanes reflects an everyday
usage of *psuchē* as courage, character, life, but a poetic usage of it as life, soul after life, the
enduring, emotional soul, according to Handley 1956:207, 212–15; cf. Webster 1957:150–
51.

[72] *Phil.* 1014; *Ant.* 176 (where it is coupled with *phronēma* and *gnōmē*); *OC* 499. In trag-

Psuchē was also used in a way that became historically crucial to us through Plato's speculation on it and subsequent usage in Christian Greek. Much Greek writing is lost. The first time in extant work that *psuchē* seems to mean soul, the essential "you," potentially immortal, is in Heraclitus in the late sixth century, followed by Pindar in the fifth century. This usage became important in prose in the fourth century, especially in philosophy, above all in Plato. Plato makes central the idea of *psuchē* as the important "you" in your life. He conceives of it in such a way that it makes sense to debate its immortality: does the important "you" survive death? *Psuchē* becomes the vehicle of personal identity between now and any possible afterlife.[73]

This meaning belongs with another early meaning of *psuchē*, common in Homer: "spirit" in the sense of "ghost." The *psuchai* of dying heroes go down to Hades, shrieking, while "they themselves" are left as carcasses on the field. *Psuchē* leaves the body in a faint, or at death, "when *thumos* first leaves the white bones, and *psuchē* takes wing and flies off like a dream." In Hades, the ghosts are *eidōla*, "images," insubstantial negatives of the bodies they once enlivened. Charon, like Hermes, is *psuchopompos*, "escort of souls." This *psuchē* is a flying thing: *psuchē* could mean "moth" in later prose.[74] As "ghost" or "immortal soul," *psuchē* is detachable from the physical self. Elsewhere, people address their own *psuchē*, or it speaks to them, as other innards do.[75]

Psuchē behaves differently, therefore, in different contexts. Like *thumos*, it can be breathlike or fluid, ebb from the body, fly or flutter overhead. But it also acts like an organ in the body. Like the heart, with which it is often coupled ("O my poor *psuchē* and heart"), it shakes in agitation. Like the *phrēn*, it "wanders" in madness. Dionysus is *psuchoplanēs*, "he who makes

edy, this usage appears most often in Sophocles. "Psychological" usage in Homer: Claus 1981:99–102. *Psuchē* associated with intelligence: Claus 1981:157–58.

[73] Pi. fr. 133 (Snell-Maehler), first used by Rohde to make his case for *psuchē* meaning "life"; see Hdt. 2.123; Pl. *Meno* 81B. For Heraclitus, see Snell 1953:17–19; C. Kahn 1979:126–30, 238–40, 311 (see esp. nn. 112–13); Claus 1981:125–38. Before Plato, the two issues (soul as the important "you," soul as immortal) should be treated separately. Heraclitus's *psuchē* may or may not be immortal, but it does already look like the essential "you"; see Nussbaum 1972.

[74] Soul distinguished from carcass-self: *Il.* 1.3. Soul flies off: *Od.* 11.221–22. Sarpedon's soul leaves him when the spear is pulled out. Mist covers his eyes, but he breathes again. Boreas's breath makes him live after he loses his *thumos*, *Il.* 5.696–99. *Psuchē* as soul flying off at death is rare in tragedy, but cf. *Or.* 676, and the images of flying things in the mind, the flying mind, pp. 96–97. Souls taken down to Styx and across it: *Od.* 11.37, 83. Hermes Psychopompos: Plu. *Mor.* 758B; *Od.* 24.1–10; see above, Chapter 1. Charon *psuchopompos*: *Alc.* 361. *Psuchē* as "shade": see Claus 1981:61, 66–68, 86–88. Nilsson (1955, 1:198 n. 53) connected the soul's departure with the first creatures settling on the corpse, as if early representations of the soul had the shape of flying insects. *Psuchē* as moth or butterfly: Arist. *HA* 551A14.

[75] Pi. *P.* 3.61; *Phil.* 712; *Ant.* 227; *Hipp.* 173. Internal dialogue: cf. above, n. 61.

souls wander."[76] *Psuchē* is appetitive, perceptive, mobile, intelligent, "life," "self," "mind," "soul," "ghost." When we choose a word to translate it, we tilt each passage with a particular load of *psuchē*'s semantic heritage, picking over the debris from centuries of reflection accumulated between the early Greeks and ourselves. As far as translation goes, different words fit different contexts. *Psuchē* escapes through wounds, continues an independent eternal existence outside the body, but keeps enough of its relationship with a particular self to resemble that self's body in Hades. If any inner human part is immortal, it is the *psuchē*. Yet even this is shadowily somatic.

Nous, no-os, is most often simply translated "mind." It is an essentially perceiving force: "intention," "sense." *Nous* sees and hears. People who act with *nous*, and "have" it, are sensible. People who do not are senseless, unwise, insane. When *nous* is directed towards an object it is something like "attention." But it is also emotional. People enjoy with their *nous*. *Nous* stays "unafraid in the breast."[77] It is intellect and intelligence: an *anoos kardia* is an "unintelligent heart." Or it is an act of intellect, a "thought," a "plan." The philosopher Anaxagoras uses it of the active cosmic principle, the blueprinting force behind the universe.[78]

No one has suggested any physical reference for *nous*, yet Greek poets often make it behave like *phrēn* or *kardia*. Verbally, it follows the pattern of heart, *phrēn, thumos*, suggesting a vessel, and an organ, and a force. In that drinking-song fantasy of carving the breast to see the mind, the aim is to see *nous*, and to know someone is your friend "with an undeceiving *phrēn*." This is a joke, of course, but what is it joking about? That *nous* and *phrēn* are hidden, like *splanchna*. If only we could see them and see into them.

---

[76] Ar. *Nub.* 319; *AP* 9.524.24; *Or.* 466. Cf. Pl. *Ti.* 69B–C, "Receiving the immortal *archēn psuchēs*, they framed round it a mortal body, and gave it the body as its vehicle, and housed in this another *eidos psuchēs*, the mortal one, which has terrible passions," a passage reflecting Plato's own "insight into the disunity" (see below, n. 115) of Greek soul-and-body language. Meissner (1951) documented *psuchē*'s organlike behavior in early Greek, suggesting that a distinction between organic and inorganic words begins to break down in Euripides, until *psuchē* is interchangeable with *kardia*.

[77] Intention and sense: *Il.* 5.461; Epich. 249; cf. *OT* 371; *Od.* 6.321; *Il.* 20.133; *OT* 550; *OC* 931; *Trach.* 553; *IA* 1139. Attending, enjoying: *Phoen.* 1418; *Or.* 1181; *Ion* 251; *Od.* 8.78; *Il.* 3.63. Handley (1956:208–9) looks at everyday fifth-century usage of *phrenes* and *nous* through Aristophanes: *nous* emerges as "attention, sense, intelligence, purpose, attitude."

[78] *Il.* 21.441; cf. Xenoph. fr. 25DK (KRS pp. 169–71 with n. 3). "The *phrēn* of *nous*": see Snell 1953:141, 316 n. 16. *Nous* with *mētis*: *Il.* 15.509; *Od.* 5.23; cf. *Il.* 23.149 (purpose, desire). See the crucial work of von Fritz 1943, 1945, and esp. 1946:30–31, which give the background to this usage (Anaxag. fr. 12DK). He concludes that usage of *nous* and *noein* changes after Parmenides. In early philosophy, the main function of *nous* and *noein* is to discover the "real" world. After Parmenides, *idein*'s range (used in Homer for thinking, realizing) is confined, while that of *noein* is enlarged. *Nous* appropriates the meanings of other words until it is used synonymously with *phrēn, mētis*, and *merimna*.

Thoughts are hidden "in" *nous*. *Cholos* swells it. Zeus's *noos* is "dense," "solid." People wish with their *nous* as well as with their tongue. Old age is "shed over" and damages their eyes and their *nous*. *Nous* suffers along with physical organs and faculties. Poets and philosophers treat it linguistically as they do the other innards. *Nous* pulls into itself a concreteness we associate with other innard-words.[79] The liver's associations show how gods are expected to signal their interest in innards. *Nous* shares this. Homer's Odysseus, a king disguised as a beggar, talks of human fortunes changing. When we are happy, we never expect to change. But "when gods decree trouble," a person

> bears this in his enduring *thumos*,
> for such is the *noos* of earth-born human beings,
> as is day, which the father of gods and men brings.

Our *nous* depends on the fortune and "day" that gods send, which change according to divine decision. These words reverberate throughout the Greek tradition, into and beyond the pre-Socratic idea that *nous* made the universe, yet *nous* is in us.[80] *Nous* brings out the thought that something inside human beings is divine, not (like *psuchē*) in the sense "immortal," but in the sense of sharing divine power or knowledge. Democritus speaks of *theios* (divine) *nous*. "*Nous* is to us in each of us a god" says Euripides in a contextless fragment of perfectly balanced ambiguity.[81]

METAPHOR AND "ANATOMICAL DETAILS"

We dissect nature along lines laid down by our native language.
—Benjamin Lee Whorf, *Language, Thought and Reality*

Heart, soul, mind, and spirit sharpen the issue of physical immediacy. I have brought up the question of whether the fifth century distinguished

---

[79] *Il.* 1.363, 9.554, 15.461; *OC* 936; Mimn. 5.8 (West). Zeus puts an *esthlos noos* in a man's breast, *Il.* 13.732. Sol. fr. 10 insults the Athenians by saying their *noos* is *chaunos*. Jaynes (1976:286) calls Solon on *noos* "the first real statement of the subjective conscious mind," but in fact Solon is of a piece with earlier and contemporary ideas of both *nous* and other innards. Aristotle is prepared to wonder whether *nous* has no essential connection with the body or any organ, *De anim.* 403A3–11, 429A24–27.

[80] *Od.* 18.136–37. *Ep'* is presumably separated from its verb, *ageisi*. *Ep' ēmar* is unlikely (*pace* Kelly 1979:227) to mean "each day." *Epi* with accusative of time means "throughout," "during." *Hoion* should go with *ēmar* and does not (unfortunately for ambiguity-prone translation) refer to *noos*. Archil. 131 (West—see Snell 1953:47, 313 n. 2) and Parm. fr. 16 (see Fränkel 1975:363 n. 37) both imitated the passage (see pp. 43 and 71 below). Cf. perhaps Heraclitus fr. 17DK (Fränkel 1975:372). *Nous* making the universe: see KRS pp. 362–66.

[81] Democrit. fr. 112DK; Arist. *De anim.* 404A28. With Euripides fr. 1018 (Nauck), cf. *Tro.* 884–88.

between literal and metaphorical. It is likely they did not, or not with the distinctions we make. Our distinctions rest on distinctions drawn first in the fourth century, in Aristotle's generation. Before Aristotle, scientists treat an image (the universe governed by justice, for example) as sufficient explanation of the phenomenon (that there is regularity and balance in the large-scale changes of the world). The image is not a vehicle for explanation. It *is* the explanation. Hippocratic writers, using figurative comparisons to state a theory about the body, often follow the "as" of the illustration by an emphatic "in this way," as if the comparison proved the theory. One Hippocratic writer explains how the body makes stones in the body by an image of "smelting." The image, a process similar to smelting, becomes the explanation. Its metaphorical status is not seen, or not as we perceive it. *We* take the Greek image of cosmic order as justice to be metaphor, an import from morality to cosmology, therefore not the *explanation* of cosmic order and relationships. Before Aristotle, to call it justice is to explain its working.[82]

The likelihood of a profound chasm here between "our" approach to metaphor and that of pre-Aristotelian Greeks has deep bearing on our response to tragic language of consciousness and feeling (Chapters 6 and 7). The words I have looked at either have a clear basic reference to a material organ or to breath or fluid ("heart," *cholos*), or behave intermittently as if they did (*phrēn, menos, thumos,* even *psuchē* and *nous*). We shall see that *theories* of the human interior assume that breath and fluid occupy the same channels of the body (Chapter 3). The poets do not put everything they say together at once as a "theory," to be "believed." They use their language and images flexibly, sometimes in what we receive as a metaphorical sense. We read phrases like "his *phrēn* was turned" as metaphors. We expect metaphors anyway in that type of context, since consciousness cannot be seen, and any account of "mind" and what happens to it must be framed in some metaphor or other. In our world, we knowingly substitute metaphor for observing that we cannot do.

Further, our own vocabulary, which we bring to these words and use in explaining them to ourselves, is not neutral. It incorporates centuries of philosophy in several languages, which began from, and then changed, these very words. Our sense of these Greek words as metaphors or as physical entities is invisibly but profoundly influenced by their semantic fortunes in major texts of philosophy and science from Plato onwards.

We often ignore the metaphorical status of apparently equivalent words. "Mind-blasting," we say. "Filled with fear." Or, more archaic, "heartsick." "Torn with grief." These are clichés so worn that they seem to describe. In

[82] See Chapter 1, n. 19; Lloyd 1966:357–58, 1990:23–24; Vlastos 1947. "Justice" in cosmic order first articulated by Anaximander: see C. Kahn 1979:19; Lloyd 1979:247, 1990:20.

fact, they are metaphors that imply specific images for what is inside us. *Phrēn, kardia, thumos*, nebulously vessel-like, fillable, tearable, recognizably Greek, lurk behind these phrases, having directed centuries of European imagery, but in our language they are unmeaning fossils that do not match what we now believe is inside us.

Here is another core difference between "us" and fifth-century Athenians. We tolerate extraordinary dissociations between what we think is inside us and what we imply is inside us when we speak of our feelings. We, not they, are the cultural oddity. We inherit Greek vocabulary and imagery about thought and feeling but do not share the ideas about innards that inform their usage in the fifth century. When we meet an image like "my heart leapt in fear," we translate it into terms of our own world, where it has a different life, metamorphosed by Christian, Roman, mediaeval, Renaissance, eighteenth-century, and later associations. There is no reason to think the Greeks tolerated similar dissociations. The Ilongot do not seem to. The Greeks did not have, as we do, theories and literature from many different cultures and languages behind their use of these words.

Our own dissociated condition has brought about rifts in scholars' approaches to Greek language of consciousness and feeling. At one point, for instance, Aeschylus speaks of the heart "circling" against the *phrēn*. Some scholars have argued against seeing any physical reference at all. "Anatomical details," says one very great scholar, "should not be dragged in: they would obscure the meaning." Others have taken the opposite line, defending purely physiological meaning over any abstract or metaphoric resonances. *Phrenes* only means lungs, and no more. This second approach can end in bizarre claims. In one passage, Aeschylus's chorus, faced with ambiguous prophecies of Agamemnon's death, sings of its hopeless, painful forebodings:

> My *kardia* would say all this,
> outrunning tongue, but as it is
> it mutters in the dark,
> hurt in the *thumos*, not hoping—
> though my *phrēn* is on fire—
> ever to unwind any useful plan.

What does this chorus mean? How should we respond to its talk of *thumos, kardia*, and *phrēn*? One physiologically-minded critic argues that gods must have prescribed a precise physical relationship between heart and tongue, which it was perilous to ignore.[83] But to take this at only a "concrete" level seems perverse.

[83] See Fraenkel *ad Ag*. 996; Barrett *ad Hipp*. 1464; *Ag*. 1028–30; Earp 1948:174; Lloyd-

I suspect that all fifth-century uses of these words have some somatic tinge, more or less strong in different contexts, but always available, in direct relationship (here the contrast with us is very strong) with what Greeks believed was inside people. It is always hard to know if we rightly distinguish literal from metaphorical senses in another culture's use of words. Our own language is a window through which *we* see the world and ourselves, and look at other languages.[84] If tragedy's contemporaries did not articulate the distinction that we draw between literal and metaphorical usage, what matters is the pattern of relationship and the associations with which they imbued these words. (We can call this their pattern of imagery, provided we remember that what looks like an "image" to us may have been truth for them.) This overall pattern—"heart," for example, is mobile, *thumos* rises and fills our *phrēn*—shapes explicit philosophical speculation after the fifth century and may reveal its own psychological assumptions. Faced with an ancient foreign language whose speakers are inaccessible, our business is to reach for as many implications as we can in the words they used for feeling and how it is felt. These implications must be grounded in their associations, not ours. But we need to be aware that the arm with which we reach exists in, and will go on being part of, the twentieth-century world. The way in which it grasps is ours.

It has traditionally been part of a philologist's job to prise apart a word's "shades" of meaning in a particular passage. It is against philology's grain to say that a Greek word has simultaneously an abstract or metaphorical as well as a literal and concrete sense. But the shades of meaning we find will always be directed by the relationship between Greek and the language or languages in which we ourselves think, and it may be that our own languages are not the best ones through which to approach these words and the picture of consciousness they enshrine. "Every language is a vast pattern-system, different from others, in which are culturally ordained the forms and categories by which the personality not only communicates, but also analyses nature, notices or neglects types of relationship and phenomena."[85]

Ordained? Maybe not. But our language does predispose us to make assumptions that impede objective observation of how Greek uses its con-

---

Jones 1990 i. 328. Webster (1957:152) merges different approaches by speaking of the physical concentrate of psychological stress.

[84] See Steiner 1972:877–88, 1975:49–108.

[85] Whorf 1956:252. He argues that each person's thought is controlled by specific patterns, "the unperceived systematizations" of their native language. Whorf's hypotheses are controversial, but the work he did in comparing language families has much to offer classicists, especially in this area of words for equipment of thinking and feeling (cf. our inheritance of "dark" discourse of mind, and the "flow of feeling," pp. 76 and 84). See further Dilthey 1972:232; Wicker 1975:74–75; Steiner 1975:88–89.

sciousness-words, and to take our own linguistic categories as the norm when we interpret theirs. Suppose that for Aeschylus, as for the Ilongot using their word *liget*, *phrēn* and *kardia* have a concrete force (like "tongue") *and* an abstract force simultaneously? Our word "abstract" comes from the Latin *ab-traho*, "I drag away." (In modern Greek, *aphairē-menos*, "taken away, removed," strikes the same note.) What if Aeschylus's thought-world does not feel, as we do, that the meaning of *phrēn* in one passage, where English translators say "mind," is "removed" or distanced in any way from its meaning in another, where translators find something like "diaphragm" more "natural"?

The same words appear in both kinds of context. Scholars have different affiliations. Some are drawn to ban "anatomical details" from emotion-filled passages or the word "organ" from explanations of *phrēn* or *thumos*. Others investigate the precise bloodlike or breathy or lunglike "origins" of specific words.[86] But both have turned for support to a favorite heuristic device, the story. Chronological explanation of these words, evolving in the early twentieth century under pressure from the nineteenth-century search for "origins," has an outline roughly as follows.[87] Once, in a time to which even Homer cannot carry us back, but which existed before his work, these words did have simple original concrete meanings. But society grew up, wrote literature, thought about its own thinking, and gave these words metaphoric, abstract meanings. Concrete, literal meaning "came first." More sophisticated meanings grew upon them.

This vision rests, so far as one can trust *its* origins, on the "myth of origins," a biographic approach to ideas and institutions. The claim is that if we could find the *beginning*, the original kernel of a belief, institution, rit-

---

[86] *Phrenes* as lungs, *menos* as blood, *psuchē* as breath, spinal fluid, semen, or blood: Onians 1954:24–51. Claus (1981:7) rightly (I think) rejects "the analysis of these words by etymology and identification with specific physical organs." Sullivan (1988:7–8) thinks one could argue the views of both Snell ("analogous to organs," 1953, 1978) and Onians (see references in Sullivan 1988:16 n. 29) that these words refer to specific organs. But because "psychic terms differ from physical organs," Sullivan (see above, n. 67) avoids the word "organ" because it stresses the "physical basis." Snell (1953:15) found it "hard" to use "organ" for *thumos*. Sullivan suggests that over time the psychic terms lost their mainly physical connotations and became what we call "faculties." Explicitly, she rejects the chronological model (that the words once designated something physical, then came to designate something psychological), reminding us that in Homer our distinction between material and immaterial is not made. But implicitly she does follow the model, though she pushes it further back to a pre-Homeric period. By calling innard-words "faculties indeterminately corporeal," she removes vivid somatic force from their usage; and an entire, complex, post-Greek philosophy lurks in her word "faculty."

[87] On the "genetic approach" of early anthropology in the context of the nineteenth-century search for "origins" (of law, religion, species, etc.), see Evans-Pritchard 1962:10, 1972:37. Böhme (1929:2–11) commented that attempts to explain the psychological weight of a word like *phrenes* from earlier physiological usage had not worked.

ual, or verbal meaning, this would adequately explain the meaning and function of the belief, institution, or word when later societies use it. A related assumption, also potent in early anthropology, is that evolutionary patterns move from the simple to the complex, from primitive literalness and concreteness to abstraction.

Nowadays none of this will do. It is clear that early things are not necessarily less complex than later ones. Ancient Greek is more complex than modern, for instance. Each case must be argued separately, in biology, anthropology, theology, or grammar. The "original meanings" or "genetic" approach to Greek words of consciousness is now part of history, to be seen in *its* context: an expression of the nineteenth century's desire to "explain the nearer by the farther."[88] Yet even if the nineteenth-century dream were true, and it were possible to find out what *phrēn*, for example, was or might have meant in some inaccessible Greek past, this does not explain what it is, at work in living systems like Homeric and tragic language.

The "original meanings" account also fitted assumptions behind the mythic narrative embodied in Freud's distinction between "primary" and "secondary" thought-processes. He distinguished between metaphoric, imaginative thought-processes, which he called "primary," and rational, analytic ones, which he called "secondary."[89] This implied that the European experience of a transition from magical to scientific thinking was universal, whereas in fact it seems to be unique and does not necessarily illustrate a general principle.[90] Today, most psychologists and psychoanalytic theorists reject the story pattern implicit in "primary" and "secondary," as well as the assumptions that these two modes of thought are in fact separate, that babies start with one and acquire the other. Historians of science accept that magical and rational modes of thought can operate simultaneously in the same society or individual—in Herodotus and the Hippocratics, for instance[91]—and that even scientific theories are influenced by story shapes of contemporary fiction. Darwin's theory of the origin of species, for example, seems to have been influenced by narratives and explanatory patterns in George Eliot. The nineteenth and early twentieth century perceived the world as "story-shaped" in a specific way,[92] to which the hid-

---

[88] Bloch 1954:29ff. Claus (1981:14) situates both Onians and Snell within this early anthropological belief that the evolutionary move is from simple to complex, concrete to abstract.

[89] Freud's "primary" and "secondary processes": see Laplanche and Pontalis 1973:37, 43, 102–10; Rycroft 1968:42–53. In the development of psychoanalytic theory, the "displacement" of meaning was always "from the physical to the psychical," E. Sharpe 1978:155–56.

[90] See Tambiah 1973:227–28.

[91] See Horton and Finnegan 1973:17–19; Lloyd 1979:5–7, 31, 49 (with reference to Herodotus and Hippocratic writers).

[92] See Wicker 1975; Beer 1983 (on the influence of George Eliot's narratives on the formation of Darwin's theories).

den fiction of Freud's "primary" and "secondary" thought-processes belonged.

A story outline for the "development" of Greek mind-words explained away any need to follow through significant differences between ourselves and ancient Greeks. "Once, *phrenes* meant lungs, *menos* blood, *psuchē* breath or semen. Then they developed, i.e., came to mean things more like what we recognize: abstract things, like mind, vigor, soul."

But it is too simple to claim that in one passage *kardia* has an original and literal sense, while in another it has a "developed," nonorganic metaphoric meaning. It ignores the labor that has gone into semantics, and interpretation, and the roles of metaphor in the history and philosophy of science in our own century. I would summarize tragic "innards" words, without story-shaped preconceptions, on the following lines. In tragedy, *phrēn, phrenes, kardia, hēpar, cholē, cholos*, and arguably *menos* refer to physical parts and substances that behave as physical parts and substances do behave (or as Greek mentality perceives them as behaving). Words whose physiological reference we cannot catch, like *thumos, psuchē, nous*, seem (to us at least) to pull this concreteness into their own behavioral range. *Menos, thumos, psuchē* all sometimes stream into or out of the body as breath or liquid. *Thumos* and *psuchē* also sometimes act like vessels filled by breath or fluid, that beat and knock and can be physically hurt by emotion. *Nous* never behaves as a fluid, but often behaves like a vessel receiving emotion or sensation. *Menos* and *cholos* are the only ones that are not occasionally treated as organs or vessels. No word has a total monopoly over thinking or feeling. Concrete physical inner organs belong with ideas of psychological agency. Intellectual activity is inseparable from emotional activity.

When I speak of innards, I mean all this equipment of feeling and thinking. The poets treat these words fluidly as organs, vessels, liquid, breath. But I am not suggesting that tragedians "blurred" distinctions we make between mind and body, or that these words were ambiguous, or that the psychological "overlapped" the physical in Greek thought. These critical metaphors of blur and overlap would imply that the Greeks perceived two different things to blur, two meanings to slip between. If the distinctions and meanings are ours, not theirs, then there were no two things for them to blur or be ambiguous about. It is not useful to project semantic fields of our own words, like heart, soul, mind, or spirit, or to talk in terms of slippage.[93]

Our own semantic fields, however, are what we have to work with. We

[93] Webster (1957) says that "a physical part of the body can be a psychological agent," that it is hard to distinguish mind from thinking or thinking from thought: "There is an overlap of meaning." Oosten (1973), Steiner (1975:92), and Bremmer (1983:4) warn, in widely different contexts, against the assumption that other cultures operate with the same "semantic fields" as our own.

might say that the essence of this Greek material is its contradictoriness and slipperiness *in our own eyes*. *We* can talk of overlap in meaning, because we find our categories climbing over each other like lobsters in the basket of each Greek word. A Dinka or Ilongot might find a quite different range of resonances in them (provided the mediating influence of English, French, or German lexica was absent). If scholars find inconsistencies and anomalies in the usage of these words, these may or may not bear upon inconsistencies in Greek thought and linguistic usage. We should not wish these away. They are a product of the relationship we create between our own culture and language and the one we want to understand. We should mark them, as scholars usefully do.[94] But we should remember that they belong to this *relationship* between our different languages and cultures, not necessarily to Greek itself. An Ilongot might find others.

It might be worth the effort to imagine a use of language in which both the abstract and the concrete coloring of each word are part of its sense, spoken into a world physically familiar with innards whose visible markings tell human beings things about divinity they could not otherwise see for themselves. This association alone warns us how far we are from fifth-century ideas of innards, and therefore from the tactile background to their use of those words in accounts of feeling and thinking.

CONCRETENESS OF THE INNARDS: *POROI* AND PRE-SOCRATICS

"Mind-words" have a strongly concrete sense in theorizing about the interior that is contemporary with tragedy: scientific thought whose starting point was popular ideas and poetic language. The fifth-century philosopher Diogenes thinks air is both *psuchē* and *noēsis* (intelligence). "That which has intelligence is what human beings call air. All people are steered by it; it has power over everything." We smell with "air around the brain." Aristophanes parodies these ideas, ascribing them, absurdly, not to Diogenes but to Socrates:

> I would never have found out rightly
> how things are above,
> except by hanging my *noēma* [intelligence]
> and mixing my rarified thought
> with air similar to it.

[94] Claus (1981:15, 28–46) argues that all Homeric "soul-words" (except *kradiē* and *psuchē*) designate one of three things. He tabulates their meanings, including a nomadic category of "anomalous instances." He rightly stresses that we should approach usage empirically, though I think he does not wipe the slate of our receptivity clean enough (cf. above, nn. 66–70). Caswell 1990, a "synchronic formulaic analysis," examines *thumos* in five categories of context.

Clearly such theories were known at Athens, though not necessarily un-
derstood.[95] Aristophanes loves mocking both philosophic and tragic language about mind and feeling. The tragic poets constantly use words for
the complexities of heart, soul, mind. When Aristophanes brings this vocabulary onto the comic stage, straining its concreteness into parody, the
audience knows he is mocking philosophy, or tragedy, or both.[96]

The writing of Anaxagoras, the fifth-century philosopher resident in
Athens, suggests a similar tangibility of soul or mind. *Nous* is "the purest of
all things." Heraclitus offers the thought that a "dry soul" is "best": when
drunk, you have a "moist soul" and do not know where you are going.[97]
He also has a topographic vision of the soul: "You would not find out the
boundaries of *psuchē*, even by travelling over every path, so deep an account
does it have." By "every path," he seems to suggest paths both outside in
the world and within the soul itself.[98]

By the late fifth century, a key word is *poroi*, "routes, channels, ways,
crossings": the word that gives us "pores." *Poroi* provide "ways" into,
within, and out of the body. In the fourth century, Aristotle will maintain
that the *splanchna* are situated on the "veiny *poroi*" (that is, those of the
"channels" which are veins). *Splanchna*, like mud from a running stream,
are deposited by the ooze of blood through veins. The great early pro-
moter of *poroi* was Empedocles, who invites his reader to think "wherever
there is a *poros* to understand." "Grasping with hands," he says (by which
he may mean "perceiving"), is the "greatest wagon-path of persuasion into
the *phrēn*":

> Observe with every grasp
> by whichever [sense] each thing is clear.
> Don't hold sight more trustworthy than hearing,
> or noisy hearing than the passages of the tongue.
> Don't keep from trusting any
> of the body's other parts,

[95] See Ar. *Nub.* 227–30; Diogenes, KRS 605, pp. 442–45; 612, pp. 447–49; cf. 616, pp.
451–52: *noēseis ginontai tou aeros sun tōi haimati to holon sōma katalambanontos dia tōn phlebōn.*

[96] Handley (1956:220–24) argues that "mind-words" in Aristophanes had little role in
everyday vocabulary but were words good to play with in comedy because of their usage in
serious poetry. This implies, however, that "serious poetry" addressed thinking and feeling
differently from ordinary language, and that we cannot know this "ordinary language" except
through the slippery evidence of the comedies themselves.

[97] KRS 476, pp. 362–64; Heraclitus, KRS 230–32, pp. 203–5. C. Kahn (1979:251)
thinks Heraclitus sees *psuchē* as "an atmospheric substance intermediate between water and
fire"; see his whole discussion, pp. 245–54. He suggests that *logon echei* (KRS 232) means
something like "has the right or capacity to speak."

[98] See C. Kahn 1979:128; cf. *OT* 67; *Ant.* 225–26; and Bachelard 1969:187–210 on the
poetics of internal routes, internal "immensity."

wherever there is a *poros* for understanding:
recognize each thing by whatever way it is clear.[99]

In his theory of respiration, *poroi* play a more precise role. "Bloodless pipes of flesh are stretched over the body's surface." Blood and "bubbling air" rush in and out of the body through these pipes. Perception happens, "when something fits into the *poroi* of any of the senses. One sense cannot judge the objects of another, since the passages of some are too wide, of others too narrow, for the object perceived." *Poroi* can also be used for arteries and veins or any inner ducts. Plutarch calls the lungs *poluporoi*, "many-holed": they are "like a sieve, for the sake of liquids and solids." *Poroi* offer entry into the body from outside, and channels within, through which liquid can move.[100]

The notion of concrete entry into body and mind was expressed also by the fifth-century "atomists" in their theory of vision. Something *comes into* the eye. Later reporters of their work, like Epicurus, say they thought *eidōla*, "images," caused vision. *Eidōla* "stream off from the objects of sight and fall into the eye." Plutarch says the atomists thought "that perception and thought happen when *eidōla* come in from outside." The atomists themselves may have spoken in different terms: of bits of air, imprinted by something coming from the eye, or by something emanating from the object seen. Thoughts, visions, and ideas come from, or actually are, "images," air-imprints. They infiltrate the mind. They travel in through the body's passages.[101] This pattern of inward flow is also central to Greek medical theory (see Chapter 3).

Empedocles insists on concreteness not only of the routes but of the substance of thinking. Learning "increases *phrenes*." "Blood around the heart is *noēma* [thought, intelligence] for human beings." It is "especially

[99] Arist. *De part. anim.* 647A35–B4; Emp. KRS 396, p. 312, KRS 343, pp. 284–85. (I take *pēi* and *hēi*, 9 and 13, together rather than taking *pēi* as an indirect question, so that both refer to the means by which one grasps each thing. *Noēsai* must mean more than "perceive" here.)

[100] KRS 453, p. 341 (fourth-century report, not a direct quotation), 391, pp. 309–10; cf. *suringes*, fr. 100.2DK. Empedocles also used the traditional *poros humnōn* image, e.g., KRS 360, p. 296. On concreteness in Empedocles' ideas about thinking, see Long 1966:266–73. *Poroi* as veins: Arist. *HA* 510A14; Ap. Rh. 4.1647; perhaps *Aj.* 1412. Cf. references in Onians (1954:28–29), who suggests Homeric *lasion kēr* refers not to a hairy chest but to thickly branching innards. *Poluporos* lung: Plu. *Q. conv.* 7.1, 699B.

[101] Some have argued that the atomists explain in this way only certain kinds of vision. But Burkert (1977) proposed that in Democritus's "effluences" theory (reported in KRS 587–90, pp. 428–29), images were imprinted on the air (the medium between seen object and seeing eye). This is now generally accepted; see Barnes 1979, 2:175–76. Inward flow is basic to the theory in any interpretation. Cf. the testimonium on Heraclitus, DK 22A16, "In sleep the passages of perception are shut, and so the *nous* in us is separated from its natural unity with the surrounding medium": see C. Kahn 1979:294.

with the blood" that you "think."[102] Central here is the assumption that we are made, body and mind, of the same stuff as the world outside us. Anaximenes argues that air, the substance that "holds together" the outside world, also constitutes human intelligence. Empedocles thinks all matter (including us and our inner equipment) "came from" the same things:

> From these things sprang all things
> that were and are and shall be:
> trees, men, women, beasts, birds,
> water-nourished fish, and the long-lived gods.

The earth has "come together with" fire, moisture and *aithēr* (upper air). "From these blood and the forms of flesh arose."[103]

Empedocles locates our intelligence and thought in our blood, formed from the same stuff as the world. The idea of being the same fabric as the world was around much earlier. Already in the sixth century, Xenophanes said, "We all come from earth and water," and "all things that come to be, that grow, are earth and water."[104] The idea that the equipment of *thought* is the same stuff as the world is essential to the concreteness with which Greek speaks of inner organs. In a much-discussed fragment, Parmenides, another philosopher-poet, echoes Odysseus's words comparing the human mind to the "day" that Zeus brings on. He echoes also the lyric poet Archilochus, who reworked these words. Parmenides says that thought varies "according to whether hot or cold prevails":

> For as each man has a mixture in his much-wandering limbs,
> so is *noos* present for human beings.
> For that is what thinks, the nature of limbs,
> for all and everyone. What there is more of,
> is thought (*noēma*).

This passage embodies the concreteness with which poetic and philosophic speculation approach what we call "mind." Mind is, or is in, or (a weaker version) is like, the body's limbs.[105]

I could quote many more illustrations from the pre-Socratics. I am not treating their work as theory, as the object of analysis, but listening to the imagery in the theories. Its concreteness resonates against the poets' language of mind and feeling. Both the theorists and the poets tell of a precise

---

[102] KRS 349, 394, 392, pp. 289, 311, 310.
[103] KRS 355, 373, pp. 392–94, 302. See Chapter 3, n. 4; Chapter 5, n. 10.
[104] KRS 373, 181–82, pp. 302, 175–76.
[105] There are alternative readings for Parm. fr. 16DK (e.g., *hekastote* for *hekastos*, *parestēken* for *paristatai*). This is my translation (cf. KRS 311, pp. 260–62). One alternative for lines 2–3 is, "the *phusis* of limbs is the same as what it thinks." For *Od.* 18.136 and Archil. 131 (West), see Fränkel 1975:123, above, n. 80.

pattern of relationship between the inside of the human being and the outside world. This pattern, I would say, is determined and disseminated by
their culture and language. I assume that the poets' imagery for inner experience indicates implicit beliefs abroad in the culture about what is in
people, how it gets there, and how it interacts with the world outside. Like
the early philosophers, the tragedians got these beliefs from and through
their language. It is not surprising that early theorizing about the world,
and human relations with it, works with the same pattern of imagery as the
poets, at a time when imagery is not a vehicle of explanation but embodies
it. Emotional and intellectual events are not merely describable in the same
terms as physical movement: they *are* physical movement. Aristotle attacks
the pre-Socratics for believing that thinking (*to noein*) is "somatic," like
perceiving (*to aisthanesthai*), and that "perceiving and thinking (*phronein*)
are alike." Aristotle does not agree. But he implies that this is the correct
interpretation of fifth-century views.[106]

Every writer has some story to tell or imply about mind and body. Languages outside the Western tradition also impel their users to think of self
and mind in terms of the body as their cultures perceive it.[107] I am stressing, as something in fifth-century Greece that is alien to us, how concretely
ideas about what we call mind are articulated. The pre-Socratics illustrate
this concreteness in just the area we might expect it to be dimmed or removed: in "abstract" speculation.

INSIGHT INTO DISUNITY

World is crazier and more of it than we think,
Incorrigibly plural.
                                        —Louis MacNeice, "Snow"

To this concrete Greek understanding of innards we now add their prophetic function. Innards are meaningfully marked and multiple. This concrete multiplicity, and its oddness in modern Western eyes, has inspired in
our century some magnetically alienating approaches to early Greek images
of self. The most influential approach compared early vase-painting, whose
human figures have limbs separated from trunk and no "middle part," to
both Homer's multiple words for the body in its different aspects and
Homer's lack of a single word corresponding to our "body." A Homeric
hero washes and puts armor on his "skin," moves his "limbs." Conclusion:

---

[106] See above, n. 82; Arist. *De anim.* 427A22–28, 427B6–7.

[107] See, e.g., Lienhardt 1980:76–79 on the bodily matrix in Dinka language of self; Rosaldo 1980:36–47 on Ilongot explanations of feeling and individuality through language of
heart and breath.

no "grasp of the body as a unit." The Homeric body-image is fragmented, a bunch of independent parts.[108]

This argument has been enormously important in discussions of Greek ideas about self and mind. We are all indebted to it. But new work on body images makes the body side of this approach look too simple, and the theory has long been challenged on other grounds.[109] Early vase-paintings may show no "middle part" to the body, but that part is horribly present in the *Iliad*. Shields cover it, spears pierce it, guts fall out of it. The body's unity is central in a war poem, much of which consists in body combat and disintegration. So often we hear a phrase like "that shield did not keep out the spear," followed by the penetration and destruction of yet another body. Homeric poetry stresses the body's variousness, the diversity of bodily experience, especially damage. On the linguistic side, we know that languages can display an ebullient variety of terms for multiple aspects of a central object in their cultures' lives. They depend on a concept of this core thing for which they have no single word. The Esquimaux have multiple words for different sorts of snow and no single word for it, but their culture does not lack the concept, snow.[110]

A more positive, less ethnocentric approach is to stress what Homeric language has, rather than to start from what "we" have and to talk of its absence in Homer. What Homeric language has, abundantly, is "unity in multiplicity." This is evident in its accounts of physical experience and the external world.[111]

The "unity in multiplicity" approach is useful in dealing with the further issue, not of "body" but of "self." Can we see in Homer ideas of a cohesive emotional and personal self that resemble ours? The "no unified body-image" argument says that this too is missing. Homer's different innards are just "separate organs." Homer reveals no experience of self, of emotional and intellectual processes, that is not similarly disjointed.[112] Witness the

---

[108] Snell 1953:5–8.

[109] Sullivan (1988:18 n. 46) documents attacks on Snell since the 1930s. Recent work on ancient body-images: see P. Brown 1988; duBois 1988.

[110] Cf. the rich Dinka vocabulary referring to the "almost innumerable" colorings and shadings in the cattle round which their life revolves, Lienhardt 1961:10–16. What is important in that thought-world is the variety of oxen and ox-colors, not the general concept "ox-color." Cf. Argentinian gauchos' 200 words for different patterns of horsehide, which is as "vital to their economy" (Steiner 1975:87) as are the woundable body's different parts to the poetic economy of the *Iliad*. Shields do not keep spears out, *Il.* 5.538. Arms are cut off, tongues are split, eyes fall out, fighters are wounded in precisely designated sites, like "the hip joint where the thigh rotates (men call it the socket)," 16.741; see 5.82, 292, 305–8.

[111] "Unity in multiplicity": see Austin 1975:81–107. He compares multiplicity in Homeric accounts of time and space to multiplicity in Homeric language of body.

[112] Snell 1953:8–14, 28. Böhme (1929) argued that there is no single word in Homer for "the whole mental equipment." Adkins (1970) argued that any touch of a "unitary self" in Homer is "so lightly expressed that *thumos*, *kradiē*, hands, feet, may be felt as springs of ac-

common Homeric phenomenon of internal dialogue in which someone talks to, or is talked to by, their *thumos* or heart.[113] Conclusion: internal fragmentation.

This argument should be seen in its own context of a century assimilating Freud, increasingly attracted to ideas of a divided self and "fractured" consciousness. Especially when it can attribute these to others, to the mad, to past cultures. But increasingly aware also, as it studies "others," of multiplicity, split, disunity in its own self-image and in its own images of consciousness.[114] It may be that consciousness is simply the kind of thing that is fragmented, and that the twentieth century is peculiarly able to perceive this as a truth. Now that the perception has been expressed, it is also attractive to attribute it to other people whose thinking is interestingly unlike ours. Or we could say that fragmented is what *we* would feel, if we had to use Homeric language to express ourselves, while accepting that the language expresses sufficiently to itself a sense of a unitary self. When trying to understand another culture's version of consciousness, what matters is (to use a word appropriate to innards) the particular pattern of demarcation: the specific lines of fracture in the culture's understanding of self and world.

This is where Homeric "unity in multiplicity" helps. If we add multiple innard-words to internal dialogue, we reach, not the absence of any consistent idea of self, but something far more positive: Homeric "insight into the disunity" of mental and emotional experience[115]: a unified vision of an inconsistent thing.

---

tion" (p. 45); that only fourth-century philosophy, with difficulty, reached a united (which, of course, implies "our own") idea of "human nature." Jaynes (1976) denies that any Greek word meant "consciousness." (His argument is towards a history of the brain's development, not part of debate within classical scholarship, though it enriches it.) He studies seven innard-words and claims, "The translation of any of these as mind or anything similar is entirely mistaken and without any warrant in the *Iliad*" (p. 257). This begs the question addressed by his book, that consciousness was acquired, and that the *Iliad* represents a time before it was acquired. In discussing innard-words (pp. 261–71), Jaynes rightly attends to the physical activity associated with each, but his prior assumption (p. 258) is that Homer's account of this physical activity marks a point in development when hallucinatory experience (stimulus experienced from outside) diminishes. He assumes that a culture finds its impulse to act *either* from outside *or* from within, allowing neither for multiple stimuli (e.g., causality from both directions at once) nor for self-conflict and insight into the disunity this implies. He depends on the *Iliad* for his "development" argument, but the *Iliad* does not represent a specific stage of development, since its language is composed of layers from many different societies (see Snodgrass 1974). Even if it had represented a real, homogeneous culture, it could have had multiple words for similar things.

[113] Snell 1953:14. "Dialogue with innards": see above, n. 61.

[114] See Laing 1965; and Martines 1983:416–59, historian of Renaissance Italy, on the "concussed sixteenth century" with its "fractured consciousness."

[115] This is the phrase of Dover 1974:151 (with n. 5), which works well with the notion of "unity in multiplicity" (Austin 1975:81–107).

Hector at bay is a telling example of emotional disunity. At first he is steadfast, a coiled snake watching "with unquenchable *menos*." Then he talks to his *thumos*, regretting his decision to camp outside the city. Why not sling his shield behind him, talk to Achilles, offer him Helen, negotiate peace? Then he is outraged: his own *thumos* is making craven suggestions like those he rejected from his parents. "Why does my own *thumos* talk to me like this?" Appalling, that the cowardly prompting should come finally from within. He stays where he is. Achilles approaches, flashing, deadly. "Trembling" seizes Hector. He runs off. The two men are falcon and dove, hound and fawn. Hector is like weak, cowardly creatures. Then he realizes: "The gods are calling me to death." He turns, faces Achilles, wants "not to perish ingloriously," draws his sword. He is an eagle rushing down on a lamb or hare. Before death, he recovers his aggressive animal nature. He was snake, then dove and fawn, then, at the last, eagle. Animal comparisons track his emotional movements in contradictory, inconsistent impulses from bravery to fear to final glory.[116]

The narrative shows us one man over a short time, not as a bunch of separate voices, but as someone experiencing disorientation, self-conflict. Disunity and multiplicity are part of the coherence with which Homer presents a human being.[117] They are essential to Homer's concretely multiple vision of persons and life, of body and its innards.

Tragedy uses Homeric insight into the diversity of bodily and emotional experience, but focusses it elsewhere. Tragedy speaks of battle but does not stage it. Translating the physical battleground of the *Iliad* into its own preoccupation with more inward conflict, tragedy explores scission within the domestic house, and the self that this house so often represents. If you sit on the hillside above the theater of Dionysus, you see why inward rather than external experience matters to tragedy. In the physical performance, crowded by the bodies of thousands of other people, peering a long way down to the stage, a spectator was distant from the actors' bodies, which were hidden in their tokens of representation, the mask, the long costume.

---

[116] *Il.* 22.96, 111–20, 38–91, 136, 138–40, 189, 217, 304, 306–10. Greek animal comparisons: see pp. 147–52 below.

[117] For the "strong appearance of coherence" in spirit and personality among Homeric heroes, see Lloyd-Jones 1983:9–10, 168 (esp. nn. 38, 42). Odysseus keeps alive his identity and intention through changing situations and disguises, in the face of the world's attempts to break his continuity with his past or his future (see *Od.* 5.136; 7.314; 9.30, 94, 369; 10.132, 317; 12.41), thereby becoming the West's favored icon for the survival of personal identity against long odds. When he, or any Homeric hero, is disorientated, it is often because something in the world has changed (e.g., *Il.* 6.201–2, 22.197–99, 17.631–50; *Od.* 10.190–92). Cf. "your own" *nostos*, which you "lose" if you die abroad, *Od.* 23.68. Your hope of *nostos* is part of "you" through battle and travel. The ancient idea that *nostos* was cognate with *nous* (see Frame 1978:28–33) speaks to the Homeric sense of identity it represents: a return to your place.

These bodies were very small. What the spectators received were the external and rhetorical trappings by which tragic language made apparent what they could not see: the stage figures' inwardness. "Insight into disunity" here is insight into the variety of inner experience, especially inner damage. In the *Iliad*, multiplicity, and damage, is a condition predominantly of the external body, but from Homer onward, the *innards'* damage is seen as madness. Tragedy, unlike Homer, specializes in insight into the disunity of, and damage done to, mind.[118]

If the multiple innards speak to tragic insight into the disunity of human inwardness, they also answer to a condition of the divine universe, which, in being multiple and potentially divided, resembles *splanchna*. Theagenes in the sixth century matched different gods to different bits of *splanchna*. *Splanchna* are made of the same fabric as the physical universe. They also match and mirror qualities of the divinity that runs and pervades that universe. This correspondence was articulated by the Greeks themselves.

In the *Iliad*, disunity among gods has a fatal effect on human bodies and lives. In tragedy, divine conflict has a fatal effect not only on bodies and lives, but also on minds. Heracles, Orestes, and Io go mad because they exist in a universe in which one divinity opposes another.[119] The outer multiplicity of divinity, when divided against itself, causes the inner multiplicity of innards to be damaged, go mad.

Greek mind-words, in fact, suggest a unity in multiplicity somewhat similar to that which preoccupied Greek philosophers from the beginning, as they set out to give an account of inner and outer worlds in terms of the same material. They did so knowing, in Thales' words, that "all things are full of gods."[120] Even in the natural philosophers, divinity is part of the fabric of the world and the self. The same explanatory patterns carry through from biological (see Chapters 3, 4) to daemonological understanding (Chapters 7, 8) of the world and human beings. Divinity, too, manifests "unity through multiplicity," and through its own self-conflict brings about self-conflicting damage in human innards. Rulers of tragedy's divine world make their disunity felt precisely in the human mind and its multiple pain.

[118] Madness as damaged *phrenes*, tragedy's interest in madness: see Padel 1981:106, 124–25. Greek theater's physical expression of interest in what cannot be seen, the inside of fictional persons: see Padel 1990:336, 361–65.

[119] See Padel 1981:110–11. Cf. Zeus's divided *thumos* when Hera breaks the truce, *Il.* 4.38–43. Theagenes of Rhegium: see Stanford 1936: 119–20.

[120] At least in the Aristotelian formulation of Thales' cosmology, *Metaph*. A3, 983B6 (though KRS p. 94 queries the normal view of Thales' supposed assertion that "all things are water"). "All things full of gods": KRS 91, p. 95.

Chapter 3

DISEASE AND DIVINATION: KNOWING THE CAUSES OF PAIN

EXTERNAL AND INTERNAL FORCES OF DISEASE

Pain is a natural and intended curse of the primal sin.
Any attempt to do away with it must be wrong.
—Zurich City Fathers, banning anesthesia

I ARGUED THAT in talking about what was inside them, fifth-century Greeks did not make a dissociation, as we do, between their imagery and what they really thought was inside. This argument has profound implications for their associations to the innards: above all, to their ideas about what goes wrong inside people, and why.

Suppose you are in the audience of *Equus*. What do you imagine is happening if suddenly, during the play, you feel violent inner pain? Appendix, dysentery, salmonella, heart? But suppose you are an original spectator of the *Hippolytus*, attacked by similar pain. What do you now think is happening? What relation is there in each case between the play, the way it represents causes of pain, and what you believe might be happening when you feel pain inside yourself?

Our own ideas about what is "really" in us are mostly based on reports of doctors and scientists. The equivalents for the tragic audience were doctors and diviners. These two groups were not distinct, as they are now. Spectators of the *Hippolytus* who found themselves in pain might have thought of daemonic sources, like the evil eye or an unpropitiated god. Something nonhuman had penetrated their innards. In the late fifth century ("Hippocratic" texts date from several centuries, but the earliest are probably from the late fifth century), doctors begin to offer explanations embodying more material, less animate relationships and causal sequences at work inside the body. But, though these mark the beginnings of an explanatory impulse that will eventually compete with the daemons, their underlying picture of innards in relation with the world and with the causes of disease is still propelled by divinatory arts and goes back to the *Iliad*.

Homer's heroes die from many kinds of wound, but innards are the first fear, like being "gut-shot." "Watch out, or as you run away, someone will catch you in the midriff with a spear." Pain of any kind is a stab through the vitals. Suffering is like a weapon. When spasms torture his ulcerated foot, Philoctetes tells his enemy,

> I wish this pain would come through you,
> through your breast.[1]

Pain in the foot provokes an image of a spear through the breast. The innards' vulnerability is central to explorations of pain. In the early Hippocratics, as in Homer, the pre-Socratics, and tragedy, the multiple innards are hurt by what comes in from outside. Doctors are as fascinated by pain and its causes as are epic and tragedy. They theorize about disease and hunt for causes of inner hurt. They have a newer genre, the prose treatise, in which to do this, but their language and imagery are directed by the same patterns of causality and express the same defensive bodily relation with the outside world as tragedy.

At most stages of the Western medical tradition, images inherited from earlier societies interact with contemporarily manufactured images, with local religious and social structures, to control descriptions of disease.[2] The earliest Greek medical writing is influenced by the pre-Socratics, especially Empedocles, and like them (see Chapter 2), it cannot escape a concrete language of outside and inside. One might think that, as doctors, the Hippocratics could have taken a more empirical attitude toward the body than poets or philosophers. But the doctors, too, are each telling their own story about human beings in the world and using popular belief and traditional imagery to do so. Criticism of popular belief and its imagery exists in their writing in a queer tension with their use of it. Some of the Hippocratics are clearly familiar with the body and disease, but most of them are writers first. Persuasion is everything. They need it to win clients. We distinguish between doctor and public debater; they do not. What matters is writerly coherence. "The art of writing is this: putting patterns (*schēmata*) together; signs of a human voice; power to remember things done in the past and to show what must be done."[3] If we want to understand tragic images of the human interior in its relation to the world, we should examine the Hippocratics' pattern of imagery, and the assumptions driving their causality

---

[1] *Phil.* 791–92, cf. *Il.* 8.95, 21.180 (someone stabbed in the navel): "All his *cholades* poured on the ground, darkness swamped his eyes as he lay gasping." Doctors and diviners: see Lloyd 1979:10–58.

[2] Cf. images of tuberculosis as "spiritualized" romantic consciousness, "aestheticized" death, and of cancer as an alien, mutant nonself in self. Each (argues Sontag 1979:29–31, 66–67, 20–21) expressed culturally determined fears, patterned by contemporary psychology and technology.

[3] Hp. *De victu I* 23 (Loeb 4:258). Importance of rhetoric and argument over empirical research in Hippocratic work, see Lloyd 1979:79–102, 138–68.

of disease, their vision of the body's interior interacting with the outside world.

Like pre-Socratic pictures of the human interior, Hippocratic images of inner ingredients and structures are based on and interact with Hippocratic readings of the external *kosmos*: of the "world," a word in which "order" merges with intentional "decoration." "When much air flows strongly," breaths (that is, winds) root up trees, swell the sea, and cause apoplexy: "for when they pass through the flesh and swell it, the parts of the body affected lose power of feeling. So if many breaths rush through the whole body, the patient is affected with apoplexy."[4] Air is both wind—breath in the world—and breath within a human being. It is part of the patterned system within and without.

All this exemplifies the basic anthropological observation that "the human body is the most readily available image of a system." Psychoanalysis reposes on this too. "Our imaginative apprehension of the external, not-self aspects of the world seems to be based on our capacity to perceive similarities between them and our own bodily organs, processes and sensations. There is a two-way imaginative traffic between our own body and its activities on the one hand, and objects in the external world on the other, so that each can supply metaphors to describe the other."[5]

Anthropology reminds us that, though bodies may be the same, perceptions of bodies vary infinitely across cultures. Body symbolism draws its power from a specific social life. Its significance depends on the way the culture classifies it, and the context in which this symbolism is set.[6] Everyone uses the outside world to speculate about an inner world, and vice versa. The significance of Greek ideas about the stuff and systems of body and *kosmos* is pinned down by context: by the use each writer makes of them, by the cultural context, by the writer's genre. In all classical Greek genres, and in the thought-world behind them, outer and inner worlds explain and influence each other. But in the fifth century, the dominant influence is not the inner world, as in our own Freud-framed era, but the outer.

---

[4] Hp. *Breaths* 3 and 13; cf. Chapter 2, nn. 103–4; Chapter 5, n. 10. *Nat. hom.* stresses that the body is made of the same elements as the world. Several treatises assume that the elements' alternation in the body matches the seasons' cycle, see Lloyd 1966:252 n. 1. Growth and moderation "are created when nothing forcibly predominates but *isomoiriē* prevails in every respect," *AWP* 12.10 (Loeb 1:166).

[5] M. Douglas 1970:xii; Rycroft 1979:72. Needham (1973) studies symbolic classification of experience and society based on distinguishing right from left.

[6] M. Douglas 1970:xiii; cf. R. Firth (*Times Literary Supplement*, Feb. 21, 1975, p. 191): "The importance of a symbolic classification [based on the human body] lies in this, that by analogy, it can apply widely to great areas of thought superficially far removed from its ostensible form. But the significance of such a classificatory scheme depends very much on what classifying is done in its terms, where and when."

The great cause of trouble in both is change. "It is changes that are chiefly responsible for disease, especially the greatest changes," the changing seasons. Change happens first in the environment. The prior cause of disease is outside. Doctors therefore record outside changes first. The itinerant author of *Epidemics* ("Stays Abroad") prefaces his descriptions of diseases with "situation," season, temperature, humidity, and prevailing wind:

> In Thasos, before and at the season of Arcturus, many violent rains, northerly winds. . . . Winter northerly, droughts, cold periods, violent winds, snow. Spring northerly, droughts, slight rains, periods of cold. . . . After the Dog Star, until Arcturus, hot summer. Great heat, not intermittent but continuous, severe. No rain. . . . In winter paralyses began. They attacked many. A few quickly died. . . . Early in spring burning fevers began. . . . When autumn and the rains came the cases were dangerous.

Changes of habit, such as a change in the color of the wine you drink, cause changes, maybe dangerous ones, in the body. Changing winds cause disease. Disease comes "from things that go in and come out, from cold and sun, and from *pneumatōn* [breaths] *metaballomenōn te kai oudepote atremizontōn* [changing and never not trembling]." "It is changes, most of all things, which rouse the *gnōmē* [mind] and do not let it stay still."[7] The main factors determining the diseases and moral character of people in a town may be prevailing wind, temperature, humidity:

> On arrival at a town . . . a doctor should examine its position with respect to the winds and the risings of the sun. . . . If he thinks all this belongs to meteorology, he will find, on second thoughts, that astronomy's contribution to medicine . . . is very great. Men's diseases, like their digestive organs, change with the seasons.[8]

Differences between societies are due to what comes into them, like diet and air. "What comes in," the environment, decides the moral as well as the physical makeup of human beings. Mild springlike rain cannot produce "courage, endurance, industry, and spirit." Its recipients "must be ruled by pleasure." This pattern of explanation has been part of European medicine since the fifth century. Outside terrain causes inner disease.[9]

Writers in the late fifth century often use medical imagery to explain

[7] *Epid. I* 13–14 (Loeb 1:164–65), *Hum.* 15 (Loeb 4:88), *Reg. Acut. Dis.* 37.26 (Loeb 2:92), *DMS* 21 (Loeb 2:182), *AWP* 16 (Loeb 1:114). Cf. winds as rapists, Chapter 6, n. 5.

[8] See *AWP* 1–2 (Loeb 1:70), *Epid. III* 2 (Loeb 1:238–40): *katastasis* always comes before the year's diseases and case histories.

[9] *AWP* 12.40 (Loeb 1:108). See Lloyd 1979:109 (with nn. 42–44). Modern aetiologies of disease continue to stress *katastasis*, e.g., the environment's role in creating psychosocial pressures; see Totman 1979.

moral and social change. Change in the body is an image for change in the body politic. Thucydides' parallel between the plague in book 2 of his *History* and *stasis*, "civil war," in book 3 rests on his culture's familiarity with this sort of comparison. His comment, "so *ōmē* [raw] did *stasis* become," introduces the symptoms and effects of *stasis*, summed up by *toiautai orgai*, "such angers," using for *stasis* an image of "rawness" applied in tragedy to *orgē, daimōn, phronēma*, "anger," daemon, and "(arrogant) thought." In tragedy, *ōmotēs* is "cruelty, savagery." In biology it appears as "indigestion." *Stasis* in book 3 behaves as an exterior overriding destroyer, like a disease or daemonic tragic passion. It gathers to itself the power of the plague in book 2, which "fell upon" Athens like an army, in an image of attack shared by passion and disease (see Chapter 6). "Harsher than human nature it attacked each man," affecting the mind, causing *athumia*, "despair," since those who got it "turned at once to despair in their *gnōmē* [mind]." The plague stimulated contempt of sacred and profane law and initiated wholesale *anomia*, "lawlessness," as moral and social principles are destroyed by *stasis* in book 3. The *nosēma*, sickness, is an alien intruder. It came from Ethiopia beyond Egypt, spreading through foreign lands (Egypt, Libya) and the home city, coming from outside to cause inner destruction, both in individual bodies and in relationships of the body politic. The image of *stasis* resonating against it adds a political dimension to the moral, physiological, and social disintegration possible in a Greek "body."[10]

This two-way traffic in medical and moral discourse directed European experience and European images of both plague and moral "pollution." Shakespeare uses imagery of disease (especially venereal) in *Troilus and Cressida* to delineate a sickening society. The "inflammations" of Mars and Venus, "wars and lechery," interact with each other. "Diseases" is the play's last word. Inflamed desire for lechery or love leads to "fight" within the soul, and syphilis. At one rhetorical extreme is Hector's image of an infected psyche, infected object of desire, infective lust to fight for a woman:

> The will dotes that is attributive
> To what infectiously itself affects.

At the other extreme is Thersites' infective curse: "Vengeance on the whole camp! or rather, the Neapolitan bone-ache! for that, methinks, is the curse depending on those that war for a placket." Thersites, main vehicle of the play's disease talk, has in the Greek camp the role of prose go-between that Pandarus plays in Troy. Diseases of Mars and Venus provide images of the

[10] Th. 3.82.1, 3.82.3–84, 3.85.1; A. *Supp.* 187; *OT* 828; *Sept.* 536; cf. *ōmophrōn*: *Cho.* 421; *Aj.* 930; *Trach.* 975; *Phil.* 194. *Ōmotēs*: *Ion* 47; Thphr. *De lass.* 4 (cf. the theory of coction, *Hum.* 1, Loeb 4:62). *Stasis*: see Th. 3.85. *Nosos*: see Th. 2.48.1, 50.1, 51.4, 52.3, 53.1; its source: Th. 2.48.1; its destructiveness in body and relationships: Th. 2.53.3–5.

other's activity. Odysseus images Achilles' martial pride as a plague, an infection of the blood:

> Imagin'd worth
> Holds in his blood such swol'n and hot discourse
> That 'twixt his mental and his active parts
> Kingdom'd Achilles in commotion rages,
> And batters down himself. What should I say?
> He is so plaguey proud that the death tokens of it
> Cry "No recovery."

Thersites says more "matter" would come from the inflamed Greeks' "general" if he were physically diseased: "How if he had boils . . . all over, generally?. . . And those boils did run. . . . Then there would come some matter from him; I see none now." The diseased matter of human passion and relationships is "all over" city and camp, lover and soldier, individual and "general."[11]

This intermingling of moral and physical corruption is essentially Greek, though different ages reuse it for their own purposes, with their own resonances. Disease is a staple Greek image for erotic obsession, and it pulls into erotic discourse resonances of battle and pollution. Illness in the Greek thought-world is inseparable from passion or pollution. Together they make an interlocking set of dangerous intrusions on life and self. When her husband falls in love elsewhere, Deianeira "does not know how to be angry with him." He is "very ill with this disease," which is also a divine adversary, whom no human can challenge. Phaedra, ashamed of desiring her stepson, says she has "a pollution in the *phrēn*."[12]

Even the professionals, the Hippocratics, use language of pollution for disease. Air "pollutes" blood. "It is *to theion* [the divine] that purifies, sanctifies, and cleanses us from the greatest and most unholy of our sins [*hamartēmata*]." Disease can be caused by pollution. Purification is asked to cope with both.[13]

Outside cause, therefore, is cardinal in Hippocratic nosology. Disease comes from *ta esionta*, "the things coming in," *exōthen*, "from outside." If you dream of "receiving something pure from a pure god," this shows you are healthy, "that *ta esionta* into the body are pure." If you dream the op-

---

[11] *Troilus and Cressida* 5.2.162–63, 195; 5.5.54. The "high blood chaf'd" for battle is spilled by wounds and gluts the sword (Prologue 2, 5.8.3, 5.2.145; 2.2.58–59; 2.3.17). Thersites' disease discourse: e.g., 5.1.16–22; 2.1.2–8. Odysseus on Achilles: 2.3.167–73.

[12] *Trach.* 544–45, 442; *Hipp.* 317; see Parker 1983:214.

[13] Hp. *Breaths* 14.48 (Loeb 2:250); *DMS* 4.53 (Loeb 4:148); see Parker 1983:220 (with n. 70). Sin and disease, pollution as cause of disease, Greek purification of disease, analogous roles of skin disease and madness in Greek myth: see Parker 1983:236ff., 216–18 (with n. 70). Burning, stinging, biting images, see Chapter 6.

posite, "that is bad, a sign that something diseased has entered the body." You are nourished, and can be sickened, by *esionta* like air and water. The writer may put this concretely even when the "coming-in things" are, we would think, abstract. "Into a human being creep parts of parts, wholes of wholes, with a mixture of fire and water, some entering to take, others to give."[14]

In all this terrain-aetiology, wind or breath is supreme. "South winds cause deafness, dimness of sight, headaches, heaviness. When such winds prevail, their characteristics extend to sufferers from disease." When many people have one disease, "It is clear the cause is not diet but what we breathe. Plainly it is charged with some diseased exhalation." Epidemic fever is *koinos*, "common" to all, because everyone draws in the same *pneuma*, "air, breath."[15] But season and "situation" matter, too. "Early in spring, at the same time as the cold snaps that occurred, were many malignant forms of erysipelas." "In winter occur pleurisy, pneumonia, lethargy, pains in the chest, headache, dizziness, apoplexy."[16]

When "something diseased" does enter, doctors "evict" it, by bloodletting, lancing, draining, encouraging sweating and exhalation, "that by the rapidest possible breathing the patient may evict *to parelthon* [the thing that has come in]." It is "excellent" if dysentery or dropsy follow "madness," presumably because innards swell and fill in passion and madness, and if liquid comes out, some inner swelling must be dying down. You "evict" sweat "through the skin" in a kind of *katharsis*, cleaning, that is *exō*, external. Its opposite is emetic, an *antispasis* (drawing-off) that is *eisō*, internal. One or other, or both, is prescribed for different diseases.[17]

Emetic, purging, is a key strategy, because "when the drug enters the body, it clears out first the part of the body that is most like itself, then it draws out and purges the other parts." Hellebore was a common purge. "Black hellebore causes better . . . evacuations than peplium; but peplium breaks flatulence better than black hellebore. Both stop pain. So do many other evacuants, but these are the best I know. Evacuants given in gruel help, if they are not too unpleasant because of bitterness or other unpleasant taste, or because of . . . some quality that rouses the patient's suspicion." At work here is the image of something inside causing pain. If everything is flushed out, the pain (or its source) may go too.[18] As in

[14] Hp. *De victu I* 6.1 (Loeb 4:238), cf. Hp. *Dreams* 89.100, 104 (Loeb 4:434).

[15] *Hum.* 14 (Loeb 4:86–88), *Nat. hom.* 9.46–47 (Loeb 4:26), Hp. *Breaths* 6.7 (Loeb 2:232). Cf. pp. 97–98.

[16] *Epid. III* 3 (Loeb 1:240), *Aph.* 3.22 (Loeb 1:130).

[17] *Aph.* 7.5 (Loeb 4:194), Hp. *Dreams* 89.25–40 (Loeb 4:428). Bloodletting: e.g., *Nat. hom.* 11 (Loeb 4:30); see Majno 1975:152–53. Lancing, draining: *Progn.* 23 (Loeb 2:48). Breathing: Hp. *Dreams* 89.110 (Loeb 4:434).

[18] *Nat. hom.* 6.24ff. (Loeb 4:16), cf. *Reg. in Health* 5 (Loeb 4:50), *Reg. Acut. Dis.* 23–24 (Loeb 2:82).

inflammation and swelling, something intrusive has filled you. The doctor must drain this fluid "fullness." Disturbance in the soul is caused "by some *plēsmonē* [fullness]." A healthy soul is "conquered neither by fullness nor by emptiness, nor by anything intrusive from outside."[19]

Here the martial imagery comes into practical play. Some factors in disease are more "hostile" to the body than others. Diseases "fall upon" the body, "attack," seize, possess, conquer it.[20] Fevers are "burnings," "sharp." They attack "wanderingly," like the "ills" set free from Pandora's jar to wander and harm the earth: a background image for Greek external causality of disease. Disease did not exist before. When Pandora lifted the lid, "ills" flew out. Thousands of bitter plagues now roam among human beings. Earth and sea are full of them. They come on us day and night, "flitting *automatoi* [of themselves] bringing evils to mortals."[21]

The doctor must "combat" the disease, setting himself "against" it. Either he or it will "prevail." He writes of sending "in" his forces, namely his purge, and a diet. Diet is all-important. Hippocratic writers specify diets for pages and pages, and are touchingly proud of them. One author introduces his by saying, "This discovery casts glory on me, its discoverer. And is useful to those who have learned it." Bodies depend on "coming-in things," like diet. If *esionta* are "diseased," the body sickens. One writer, discussing the beginning of medicine, explains the early physicians' approach to diet: the idea was "that from over-strong foods come pain, disease, and death, but from foods that can be assimilated come nourishment, growth, and health."[22]

Alongside this stress on external cause, however, one element of Hippocratic theory suggests that disease comes also from within, from the body's *dunameis*, "powers."[23] This thought emerges especially in the context of *apokrisis*, "separation," the theory that one of the body's innate "powers," grown stronger than the others, becomes "extreme" and isolated, too "strong" for the body to cope with:

[19] Hp. *Dreams* 88.15 (Loeb 4:424).

[20] E.g., *epipiptein*, Hp. *Breaths* 6.13 (Loeb 2:234); *prospiptein*, Hp. *Dreams* 89.10 (Loeb 4:424), cf. *empiptein*, Th. 2.49.4 (of *lunx*, "retching," which "attacked" most plague victims). *Epilambanein*, DMS 9.16 (Loeb 2:158), cf. *Nat. hom.* 9.15 (Loeb 4:24). *Katechein*, AWP 2.10 (Loeb 1:72). *Polemiōtata* factors in disease, DMS 21.18 (Loeb 2:182), Hp. *Breaths* 6.20 (Loeb 2:234). Cf. the "kletic conceit," below pp. 126–27.

[21] Hp. *Breaths* 6 (Loeb 2:232); *Erg.* 11, 90–104. Hippocratic words for fever include *kausoi, puretos, kausōdēs*. Irregular fevers are *planētēs*, wandering, *Epid. I* 6.18 (Loeb 1:156). Cf. Chapter 6, nn. 9, 60–63.

[22] *Nat. hom.* 9 (Loeb 4:24), Hp. *De victu II* 69.10 (Loeb 4:382), *Anc. Med.* 6 and 3.46 (Loeb 1:22, 18), cf. Hp. *De victu I—IV*, *Reg. Acut. Dis.* Food must be the chief *esionta* at *Hum.* 16 (Loeb 4:90): in winter "*esionta* are ripe and simple."

[23] A doctor must "know which *pathēmata* arise from *dunameis* and which from *schēmata*," *Anc. Med.* 12 (Loeb 1:56). Cf. DMS 5–6 (Loeb 2:149–51): "Its origin, as with other diseases, is *kata genos*," i.e., inherited.

The strongest part of the sweet is the sweetest, the strongest part of the bitter
is the bitterest . . . each of the things inside a human being has its extreme.
[Early physicians] saw that these things both reside within the human being,
and harm the human being. For in a human being is the salt, the bitter, the
sweet, the acid . . . and many other things that have all kinds of power. . . .
When mixed with each other they do not show, and do no harm. But when
one of them is separated off, and is isolated, then it does show; and it harms
the human being.[24]

Hippocratic *apokrisis* offers a compact allegorical comment on tragic passion and tragic society. As individuals, we contain all things within us. If
one thing in us, or in society, overrides others, it will be isolated in its
strength, and put us all in danger. There were obvious political parallels.
By the end of the fifth century, theories of balance in the universe interacted in Hippocratic imagery with a picture of health as a balance of forces
within the body, while political ideas increasingly articulated an image of
health in society and government as a balance of inner powers that may be
upset, either by the emergence of a single stronger power or by the intrusion of an alien, outside force.[25]

In tragedy, external and internal causalities shift against each other. Aphrodite is outside but also inside, for she works through Phaedra's own
equipment of feeling to cause her "disease." In Hippocratic theories, disease is caused by flow from outside (see Chapter 4), or from inside, or by
interaction between the two:

Apoplexy . . . is caused by breaths . . . the so-called sacred disease also has this
cause. . . . Nothing in the body contributes more to intelligence (*phronēsis*)
than blood. . . . The sacred disease is caused . . . when a lot of air weighs on
the thick, blood-filled veins . . . a disturbance of the air disturbs and pollutes

---

[24] *Anc. Med.* 14 (Loeb 1:36–38). *Apokrisis* as a cause of disease is implied by the *krasis*
theory of health. The clearest example is *Nat. hom.*, much influenced by Empedocles (e.g.,
KRS 355, pp. 292–93, cf. KRS 349, pp. 289–90). *Philotēs* causes harmony and *krēsis* of the
elements. *Nat. hom.* 4 (Loeb 4:12) uses *chōrizein* rather than *apokrinein*, but the doctrine is
clearly stated at 4.10ff. (Loeb 4:12): "when an element is separated and stands by itself, the
place it left becomes diseased, and the place where it stays in a flood causes pain and distress,
because of its excess." Cf. *Anc. Med.* 14.37–42 (Loeb 1:38), a treatise close to Anaxagoras,
who uses *apokrisis* and *apokrinesthai* in discussing creation, e.g., KRS 468, pp. 357–58. Cf.
Alcmaeon, n. 30 below.

[25] The interaction between political and medical explanation is so deep by Plato's time that
it is practically inextricable. Plato affirms their allegiance to each other, using—or creating—
a concept of mental health that is identical with justice (see "Mental Health in Plato's *Republic*," in Kenny 1973:1–23). Cf. Thomas Mann's use of tuberculosis and cholera in *The Magic
Mountain* and *Death in Venice* as an image of something wrong in the society within which
each self sickens. Sontag (1979:36, 71–85) analyzes changing use of diseases in nineteenth-
and twentieth-century political rhetoric.

the blood. . . . Breaths are clearly the most active agent in all diseases. Everything else is a secondary, subordinate cause.[26]

We see the two causes interacting in explanations of the seasons' influence. Doctors must know "in what seasons the humors flower, and what
nosēmata they create in each, and what *pathēmata* in each cause disease."
The disease "comes into being and grows from the *prosionta* [things coming toward] and the *apionta* [things coming away]." Seasons affect the humors and cause disease in them; but *pathēmata* in the humors also cause
disease.[27]

Interaction is also vital to Hippocratic use of *poroi* (Chapter 2), which
seem to have been Empedocles' invention or discovery. Hippocratic doctors seized on *poroi* for explanatory theory. In Empedocles, the body's
"channels" let in sensation and many other things:

> Narrow are the powers that are spread through the limbs,
> many the miseries that burst in and blunt thought.[28]

For the doctors, this explains why "souls" suffer "irascibility, idleness,
craftiness, simplicity." Why are souls "quarrelsome" or "benevolent"? Because of "the nature of the *poroi* through which the soul passes (*poreuetai*)."
Soul is affected by the "nature of the vessels through which it goes, the
nature of the objects it meets and with which it mixes." The Hippocratics
use *poroi* with zest. Sweating is caused by air in the body condensing when
it hits particular pores, flowing through them to reach the body's outer
surface. Dropsy occurs when breaths have dilated the *poroi* by passing
through the flesh; moisture follows the breaths into the *poroi*, the body
becomes sodden, the legs swell. In a sense, "all Greek medical theories are
about *poroi*. The human body is simply a system of *poroi*." *Poroi* begin Western medical portraiture of the infinitely penetrable body.[29]

Poroi serve perfectly the idea of an outside cause of disease. But they also
work for a more interactive causality. In his theory of perception,
Alcmaeon (one of the few who said the brain was concerned in conscious-

[26] Hp. *Breaths* 23–25 (Loeb 2:246–52, cf. Emp. KRS 392, p. 310); see *Hipp.* 205, 269,
294, 394, 405, 479, 512, 698, 730, 766, 1306.

[27] *Hum.* 8 (Loeb 4:78). Here, as sometimes elsewhere (e.g., *DMS* 16.43, 21 [Loeb 2:172,
182]), internal seems to balance external cause.

[28] Emp. KRS 342, p. 284; the word for "powers" here is *palamai*, "devices." *Stenōpoi*, "narrow," makes it clear that he is referring to *poroi*. "Miseries" come in through the *poroi*, cf. the
idea mentioned by Aristotle that action, passion, and perception are due to an agent "entering
in through certain pores," *GC* 324B27. Further, see KRS 391–92, pp. 309–10; Pl. *Meno*
76C, *porous di' hōn hai aporroai poreuontai*; and late accounts of atomist *eidōla*, Plu. *Mor.* 683A,
735A with Chapter 2, n. 101; Lloyd 1966:328–33.

[29] Hp. *De victu I* 36, Hp. *Breaths* 8.30, 12 (Loeb 2:238, 244–46). See Lonie 1965:128,
and Foucault's vision (1971:146–51) of eighteenth-century images of hysteria: the underlying idea is that hysteria involves some organic and moral penetration.

ness) stressed the inward flow of sensation along *poroi* to the brain. He also thought disease came in "from outside causes." But his influential theory of disease further described health politically, as an "equality of powers." Hence in Hippocratic writing on *apokrisis*, "separation," one of the body's own inward "powers" may grab the "monarchy" and cause disease from within.[30]

Tragedy offers similarly interactive explanations, not of disease but of destructive pain. We have powers in us. An external agent (say, Aphrodite) comes in and works on and through our inner material (say, Phaedra's feelings). The Hippocratics and tragedians are laying down the pattern of Western approaches to the question, Why pain? What goes wrong inside people and communities?

Though they move towards an interaction of outside and inside cause, however, tragic and medical writers do not keep interaction going all the time. Rather, they consistently suggest that there are more outside causes, more powerful, more likely to operate on their own, than anything within. Our innards are porous to suffering and interference. We do also carry in us things that hurt if they go wrong. But the heaviest danger is from things outside coming in.

CHANNELS TO THE SOUL: THE VULNERABILITY OF SIGHT AND HEARING

The same pattern of relationship between body-plus-mind on the one hand, and the universe on the other, governs contemporary images of perception. Vision is a two-way channel between the inner and outer worlds, whether the outside is seen in physical terms (as by the Hippocratics), daemonic terms (as by Phaedra, haunted by Aphrodite), or social terms.

The eye, for instance, is a source of something. In tragedy, people say they guess someone else's feelings from their eyes. The nurse fears for Medea's children because she has seen Medea's eyes on them:

> Don't bring them near their mother
> with her angry heart (*dusthumoumenēi*),
> for I saw her glare at them like a bull,
> as if she might do something to them.

---

[30] Alcmaeon's vision and language (*isonomia, monarchia*) were deeply influential. Health was *tēn isonomian tōn dunameōn*. *Monarchia* here created disease: "*nosos* happens directly through excess of heat or cold; indirectly though surfeit or deficiency of nourishment. . . . It sometimes comes . . . from external causes such as moisture or environment or fatigue or hardship or similar causes," KRS 310, p. 260. Alcmaeon and brain: see DK 24A5. "He stated that all the senses are connected somehow with the brain. So they are incapacitated when the brain moves or changes position. For it stops the *poroi* through which come the *aisthēseis*," KRS 284, p. 233; cf. *DMS* 6, 17, 20 (Loeb 2:152, 174, 178).

The eye is therefore an external sign of internal feeling. Phaedra fears Theseus will read what has happened from her eyes. A rolling, twisting, bloodshot eye is a sign of madness or (among doctors) delirium.[31]

Eyes ex-press. Something in comes out. In Homer, the glance of an angry man is "sharp" and flashes fire. In Democritus, an owl's eye flashes
cutting fire. In tragedy, the eyes of the matricide Orestes, like a snake's,
flash infectious lightnings.[32] In Empedocles, the eye is a lantern:

> Someone plans a journey through a stormy night
> and prepares a light, a beam of blazing fire,
> kindling a linen lantern for all kinds of wind.
> It scatters the breath of blowing winds,
> and the finer light leaps through, to the outside.
> It shines across the threshold with unyielding rays.
> So . . . [Aphrodite] gave birth to the round eye,
> fire confined in membranes and delicate cloths;
> these held back the deep water flowing round:
> but they let through the finer fire to outside.[33]

The light of intellect, of the inner eye, the "lamp" of consciousness: from
Homer onwards, seeing and light metaphors have governed ways of thinking about thought and understanding. The eye becomes a powerful image
of the soul it is felt to express. This idea, conveyed through images reused
in the West, is crystallized in Plato's theory of vision as an outward flow of
rays from the eye. It belongs with some core Greek notion that we have
fire in us, which flashes out through our eyes to illumine the world.[34]

Sometimes this fire seems to be part of our soul. A volume of fire and

[31] See *Med.* 90–93, *Hipp.* 280. Cf. *Alc.* 773 (*ti semnon kai pephrontikos blepeis?*), 778; *Phoen.*
1333 (*to men sēmeion eisorō tode / skuthrōpon omma kai prosōpon angelou*). A rolling, twisting
eye (*PV* 882, *HF* 868, *Ba.* 1123) is the first sign of madness or delirium (*Or.* 283; cf. *Progn.*
7 [Loeb 2:16]). Bloodshot eyes, sign of madness: Fraenkel *ad Ag.* 1428. Mad eyes are bloodshot, and roll, *HF* 933–34.

[32] *Ommata astraptonta, Iliu Persis* fr. 8 (H. *OCT* 5:139); see Snell 1953:2 on *oxutaton der-
ketai.* Fire in eye, streaming from it, see O'Brien 1968:111–13, 1970:140–46 (and owls' eyes
in Democritus, according to DK A157, see Burkert 1977:99–100). Cf. Bacc. 8.55, *Lemnian
phoinissan phloga,* and *noxii ocelli* of a snake or a wolf, Theoc. 14.18–19, Pliny *NH* 8.32–33
(cf. Chapter 6, n. 39). Orestes: *Or.* 480.

[33] Emp. fr. 84DK, KRS 389, p. 308. Arist. *De sensu* 437B–438A interprets Empedocles'
theory of seeing as emission of light from the eye. In KRS (p. 310 n. 1) the editors think
Aristotle was wrong, and that Theophrastus got Empedocles right: seeing was the *reception*
of effluences.

[34] Cf. images attributed to Heraclitus in the first century B.C., KRS 233–34, p. 205; see
C. Kahn 1979:213–16. On Plato's theory, *Ti.* 45B–46C, 67C–68D, see O'Brien 1968,
1970. Light or vision metaphors used later as model for thought: Harries 1979:83 (cf. Snell
1953:1–4 on Homeric verbs of seeing and thinking). Eye-image of soul: Bremmer 1983:40–
41 (esp. n. 74).

water, "which we call tears," says Plato, pours from the eye. The soul it-self—so runs the idea derived perhaps from Heraclitus—is made of fire and water. "Into man there enters a soul, which has a blend of fire and wa-ter. . . . The things that enter must contain all the parts. . . . Each grows in its own place. Nourishment is added from dry water and moist fire."[35]

Eyes are an outward-flowing channel for what is inside: soul, mind, feel-ings. Emotions stream from them. Eros "drips *pothos* [longing, yearning desire] from his eyes." The Erinyes threaten to "pour to the ground from the heart" a "drop" that is poisoned, a liquid blight. They drip loathsome blood and foul liquid from their eyes. This is the vehicle of the anger they breathe out and the other poisonous feelings they exist to express.[36] Eyes "flower" with fluid emotion, for overflowing is a kind of flowering. *Anthos*, "flower," is often used for the frothy surface of sea or wine.[37]

Fire, rays, or liquid, the eye's outflowing stream endangers others. The eyes of some animals, like Democritus's owl, held "noxious fire," which poisoned or petrified those who looked at them. In myth, the eyes of the Gorgon turned to stone those who saw her, an incarnation of the evil eye expressing (within a compacted nexus of meanings) the idea that one hu-man being can destroy another by looking, especially in envy.[38]

Evil eyes are dangerous because eyes are also receptive. They may send out liquid or fire, but they also receive. The world comes into them. Vul-nerable to incoming forces, like the innards, eyes receive harm from other eyes, from dangerous animals or polluted people. Heracles, seemingly afraid he will pollute Theseus, refuses to look at him. The atomists suppos-edly spoke of "images continually streaming off objects" that "impinge on the eye."[39]

Eyes, like *splanchna*, are involved in two-way traffic. From Homer to Plato, "subject and object meet through the body and its organs," espe-cially through the eye.[40] The eye's twin roles make it a symbol for reciproc-ity, the influence human beings have, for better or worse, on each other. Lovers' eyes are weapons or flames, thrown both ways. A generous host is

[35] Hp. *De victu I* 7 (Loeb 4:240); see Pl. *Ti.* 68E; KRS 232, p. 203.

[36] E.g., *Hipp.* 525–26, *Eum.* 781 (where Page obelizes), *Cho.* 1058, *Eum.* 54, 832.

[37] *Anthos*, of sea: *AP* 206; of wine: Gal. 11:628. Cf. the Homeric image, "crowning *kraters* of wine" (*Od.* 2.431, etc.). Even in antiquity it needed explaining, Athen. 673B–75A. Eyes flower with feeling: see *Ag.* 742; Lloyd-Jones 1990 i. 313.

[38] Evil eye: see *RE* s.v. *fascinum*; Fordyce *ad* Cat. 7.12; Deonna 1965:195–96; Eitrem 1953:531ff.; Walcot 1978. Gorgon: see Six 1885; Vernant 1985.

[39] *Noxii ocelli*: above, n. 32. Heracles: *HF* 1229–33; cf. *IT* 1212. Parker (1983:13–14) warns of problems in interpreting ideas expressed in literature as genuine historical beliefs about pollution, but the idea here is part of an overall pattern; cf. atomist theory of percep-tion, Chapter 2, n. 101.

[40] Burnyeat 1976:39–42, on the notion of seeing through (*dia*) the eye, and the spatiality of *dia*, in Plato's account of perception in *Theaet*.

"a just gaze [or 'regard'] to strangers." Clytemnestra offers welcome guests "baths and the intercourse of righteous eyes." Eye contact in one Platonic dialogue is used as an emblem of reciprocal love between like-minded friends.[41]

These symbolic roles for the eye are not exclusively Greek. Every culture uses eye contact in a complex set of biological and social symbolic associations. According to some modern research, we in our culture may be unconsciously directed in our evaluation of others by the degree of dilation in their pupils. In cultures where there is alert belief in the evil eye, as there was in fifth-century Greece, eye contact is a charged symbol of the relationship human beings make with the world about them, or which the world makes with them.[42] In twentieth-century Greek village life, the evil eye functions as "a symbol of the intense continuous judgement which villagers render on one another. It is through the eye that the villager watches the success . . . of others, which leads him to that envy which subverts the community. The eye . . . devours. It . . . would gain for oneself what others have."[43]

Eyes, therefore, have a key role in fifth-century language describing relations between a human being and the outside world, physical, social, or daemonic. Their social role is reflected in contemporary painting. At some point early in the century, the old convention of a single ground-line, by which painters related figures, was abandoned, probably by the innovative mural painters Polygnotus and Mikon. The way human beings looked at each other became a new method of relating them. Early fifth-century vase-painters followed these artists, in linking figures now freed from a single ground-line purely by a meeting gaze.[44] The development of tragedy—

[41] See Sappho 47V; A. *Supp.* 1004–5 (*ommatos thelktērion toxeum' epempsen*); *PV* 903 (*aphukton omma*). Pearson (1910:256–57 and *ad* S. fr. 474) collects references. "Fiery flashes" from the eyes reach the beloved's eye and are met by the beloved's responsive gaze. Cf. Malten 1961:17 n. 5. Host as "eye": Pi. *O.* 2.6, *opi* (or *opin*) *dikaion xenōn*. *Opis* is cognate with *opizomai* (in which looking is feeling, behaving, having an attitude toward), which denotes reverence to a visitor and means "regard with awe" (LSJ). Cf. *Cho.* 671, Pl. *Alcib. I* 133A–B.

[42] Modern research: see Hess 1965; Argyle 1976:58–59, 82–83. Evil eye in this context: see Argyle 1976:169.

[43] Blum and Blum 1970:221–41. Like many Levantine communities, rural Greece has been intensely alert to the evil eye. Lawson (1910:10) documents it for the early twentieth century. It is the devil's work, perverting human relations into jealous malice. The most common spell in rural Greece still is against "the eye": Du Boulay 1974:52, 66, 212.

[44] The meeting gaze: see, e.g., man and boy in the Paestum Tomb of the Diver (perhaps just pre-Polygnotus), Napoli 1970: fig. 6. The meeting gaze is found in early fifth-century vase-painting, possibly even in Exekias (third quarter of the sixth century), e.g., his Achilles and Penthesilea (see Robertson 1981:36, fig. 55). Schneider (1968) comments on the lines of gaze in Exekias's draught-game between Achilles and Ajax (above, Chapter 2, n. 4). In describing Polygnotus's now lost paintings at Delphi, Pausanias often comments on the direction of gaze. Ariadne looks at Phaedra, Pelias at Orpheus, Penthesilea at Paris (10.29.3,

human figures moving into and out of the audience's sight, acting with and against each other—is contemporary, therefore, with Western painting's first portrayal of human figures in free space, connected only by their eyes.

Though the eye goes two ways, Oedipus's explanation of why he blinded himself endorses the sense that the body is more vulnerable, through eyes, to inward-coming things than it is powerful in imposing itself on the outside world. He talks of his act as defense against invasion, against painful emotion and perception that would come at him through his eyes. He wanted to block the suffering this would bring:

> I do not know what eyes I could have seen with,
> to face my father when I came to Hades.
> Nor my poor mother. . . . The sight of my children then—
> would that be sweet for me to look at,
> born as they were? No, not for my eyes! . . .
> Having cursed myself, could I see these Thebans
> with upright eyes? No! If there'd been a way
> to block the source of hearing too,
> I wouldn't have hesitated to lock away my tortured body
> and be both blind and deaf. It's a precious thing
> for thought (*phrontida*) to live (*oikein*) outside griefs.

He blinded himself so that he would not see the city he polluted, his parents in Hades, or his children (whom he now knows to be his siblings). The pain he would feel on seeing them would arrive through the channel of his eyes. He "blocked" its route. If he could, he would block the "spring" or "source" of hearing, too.[45]

Here and elsewhere, tragedy expresses the same pattern as contemporary medical theory, which was abroad in fifth-century Athens. Tragedy clearly uses medical vocabulary.[46] Emotional suffering, like perception or disease, is due to intrusion. It wounds like a weapon, flows inward like *esionta*. As with innard-words, it is useful to think away our categories here: in this case, our tendency to distinguish emotion, sensation, disease, and pollution as things separate from each other and different in kind. Oedipus talks as if they were all part of the same thing. The pain he would feel on seeing his father would come in through his eyes, into his self, with the sight.

30.4, 31.8). Robertson (1981:78) suggests that Polygnotus and Mikon abandoned the single ground-line partly in order to make gaze the link between figures.

[45] *OT* 1369–90. Jebb takes *pēgē* as "the organ of hearing" and compares Pl. *Phdr.* 245C, *psuchē . . . pēgē kai archē kinēseōs* (but Lebeck [1973:269] relates this rather to the lover's "stream" of desire). Cf. "Are you bitten in the ears or in the soul?" and "the deed's doer hurts your *phrenes*, I hurt your ears," *Ant.* 317, 319. Ears are like *psuchē* and *phrenes*: vulnerable, receptive.

[46] See Collinge 1962; Lloyd-Jones and Wilson 1990: 172.

As Oedipus indicates, hearing is also vulnerable to the outside world, especially the social world. We are vulnerable through our ears to other people and their words. Pain enters, excites, wounds innards through words. The image embodies characteristic Greek alertness to the overwhelming power of language. When Hera enrages Zeus, her speech "hits" his "deep *phrēn*." Phaedra is horrified to hear a "voice within" the house. She realizes the nurse has betrayed her love to Hippolytus. The chorus heard nothing, and asks:

> What word terrifies you in your *phrenes*,
> rushing against you?

The sound of Hippolytus shouting: this is what rushed against her and terrorized her *phrenes* within.[47]

Hearing is intrusion from outside, through ears, into innards. Ears may be so dirtied and blocked they cannot hear, but words drill through them into the mind:[48]

> The slow assault in words comes hard
> through the dirtied [or bored-through] ear.[49]

The singers arousing Agamemnon's ghost say:

> Drill the speech through ears
> to [or with] the quiet *basis* of the *phrenes*.[50]

They want to excite his *basis phrenōn*, the "foundation of" his "*phrenes*." This has been "quiet." They want to goad it to action. A more interpretive translation might run,

[47] *Hipp.* 572–73, *Il.* 19.125. *Hipp.* 568, 577, 582.

[48] See D. West 1967:144 n. 23; Lloyd-Jones 1990 ii. 169. With "the ear's funnel," cf. smell entering a *tetrēmenēn rina* (a nose is wanted that is not "bored through, will not let in smell"), Ar. *Thesm.* 18, *Pax* 21.

[49] S. fr. 858. Radt follows Pearson in reading *rupomenou* (Meineke) for *trupoumenou*. Pearson's reason is that the present participle is properly applied to the progressive event, the continuing obstruction, the ear "that is growing dirty." He thinks the present would be awkward with *trupoumenou*. I disagree: the verb would repeat the idea of assault. Should a textual editor stay with the one image (assaulting, drilling) or accept both (drilling *and* blocked ears)? With Sophocles, who packs so much into each line, it is more likely to be both.

[50] *Cho.* 451–52. Page unhelpfully complains: *phrenōn basis quae sit nescio; etiam quaerendum est cur hoc loco hēsuchos esse debeat.* Like *stasis, basis* includes meanings so far apart they are near-opposites: a stationary foundation *and* movement. *Basis* as "step"—a stride, a movement—would not suit this context. Nobody's *phrenes* are moving, neither those of the singers nor those of Agamemnon. When tragedy talks of mobile *phrenes*, the context is violent, the movement not "quiet" (see Chapter 4). *Basis* as "step," like a doorstep—something to stand on, "foundation"—suits better. It is dative because *suntetrainō* can take the dative of that towards which the drilling moves (Hdt. 2.11), though its usual construction is *eis* plus accusative. The foundation of the *phrenes*, stable *phrenes*, in their normal state, is quiet before the song reaches in, disturbing it. The song must "move" the ghost (spoken of as if it had *phrenes*). "Calm" is *hēsuchos*, appropriate to an untroubled mind, see p. 88.

Drill the song through ears
to reach the mind's calm foundation.

If this is right, Aeschylus suggests here an image of the mind as something solid, normally unmoving but vulnerable, through the ear, to words. Words excite the mind to movement.

External influence, which enters through hearing, stirring and threatening the mind or self within, is realized in the Sirens. Their song offers knowledge of past and present. To hear it, for most people, is to be drawn to destruction. Odysseus blocks his companions' ears with wax, that even Sirens' words may not drill through. But he listens.[51] In Homer there are two Sirens: one for each ear, perhaps. They offer truly desirable knowledge. Their song is dangerous, not false. To modern imagination, its temptation might seem to lie in its beauty. In Greece this was inseparable from its intellectual content. The fact that the Sirens offer knowledge is the essence of their sensuous magnetism.

Sirens embody the Greek sense that what comes in through ears—poetry, words, music—is both supremely desirable, or treasurable, and lethal. Later philosophers turned Odysseus's encounter with them into moral allegory, reinterpreting it in the context of Plato's divine music. On earth, "a dim echo" of Sirens' music reaches us. It "appeals to our souls *dia logōn*," through words, reminding them of a previous existence. "But the ears of most souls are plastered over and blocked up, not with wax obstructions, but with blocks of the flesh and the affections." Only the moral hero, the true philosopher, keeps himself open to knowledge, and faces its attendant danger. Sirens, like Muses, are an image of utmost music that carries divine knowledge of the past (history), of hidden things in the present (science), or of the future (prophecy).[52] Sirens illustrate Greek ambivalence towards things that come into the mind. Innards can be damaged by what comes in through sight and hearing, wounded by emotion (Chapters 4, 6). But "what comes in" also stimulates, and gives innards skill and power. The innards' vulnerability is precious, and makes them a source of power and knowledge. "What comes in" moves them.

INNER MOVEMENT: SOURCE OF KNOWLEDGE, SIGN OF PAIN

Movement matters all over tragedy, in many different ways. Twists of plot are described in terms of "movement" by the critical vocabulary established by Aristotle. Tragic conflicts are movement. *Peripeteia*, "falling [or 'turning'] round," exemplifies *metabolē*, "wheel-about," "change," the aspect of

[51] See *Od.* 12.40, 189–91, 46, 177; on song's role generally in the poem, see 1.336; 8.522, 538. Sirens: see Pollard 1965.
[52] Plu. *Mor.* 745E-F. See further Chadwick 1942:14.

tragedy that "draws the soul most strongly."[53] Tragic performance is made of movement. Dancing while it sings, the chorus mirrors its own dance-figures in the musical, semantic patterning of its odes. The structures of the first stanza, the *strophē*, "turn," are duplicated in the *antistrophē*, "turn back." The actors' moves, entering and leaving the stage, pattern the structure and dynamics of the play.

These visible, tangible moves are the exterior analogue to the unseen, imaginary internal movement of passions within. They are flux and onslaught (Chapters 4, 6). Tragedy's crucial movement is emotion.

Fifth-century Athenians, like us, felt that emotion was central to tragedy. They valued emotionalism in performance. Actors developed specific visual and oral techniques, aiming for particular emotional responses.[54] They wanted, we would say, to "move" their audience. Tragic emotion is transitively "moving." "It is by *pathē* [emotions, sufferings] that men change their attitudes and judgments." And it is particularly the movements of emotion by which tragic poets move their audience. Passions cause "important" (Aristotle's word) "action."[55]

But contemporary culture also saw passion as movement in itself: inner movement, which led to inner conflict, inner hurt. The spectators do not see this. They behave as if they infer this from the outer movements of plot and dance and antagonism, which the actors put before them. In fact, what they see are pretended figures with actors inside them. In an important sense, the spectators create for themselves the moving feelings "of" Oedipus or Medea.[56]

In making unseen movement the center of their drama, tragedians were doing what writers with other preoccupations were doing in the same century. In one way or another, fifth-century philosophers, historians, and scientists are all concerned with conflicted, hurtful, important movement. Philosophers take movement, creative conflict, as necessary to the workings of the universe. "When Mind initiated motion," says Anaxagoras, "Mind was separated from all that moved; and as much as Mind moved was separated off." Mind begins movement. The movement it begins causes "separation" and sets cosmogony going. For Heraclitus, everything is movement. Plato plays in deliberately Heraclitean fashion with the idea that movement is the basis of change and life in the universe and human affairs. According to Aristotle, Heraclitus criticized Homer for saying, "Now let strife cease among gods and mortal men," since opposites are necessary to life. For Empedocles, strife is one of the two active principles by which the world continues.[57]

---

[53] Arist. *Poet.* 1452A22.
[54] See de Romilly 1958:134; Sansone 1975:75–76; Stanford 1983:1–10, 47–50.
[55] Arist. *Poet.* 1449B25, *Rh.* 1378A8.
[56] See Padel 1990:365.
[57] Anaxagoras: see KRS 477, pp. 371–73. Heraclitus: see KRS 218 (*tropai*), 219 (*anta-*

Thucydides expects history to focus on war. Homer took the Trojan War, Herodotus the Persian Wars. Thucydides takes the Peloponnesian War, calling it "the greatest *kinēsis* [movement] to happen among Greeks."[58] Medical writers infer inner movement from outer body movements. Restless kicking tells them that cold phlegm is flowing in the patient's body. The heart, like *phrenes*, is "convulsed" in anxiety and pain. It encloses veins from all over the body and so feels any *ponos*, suffering, that attacks it.[59] From outward movement, the doctor infers (or, it seems to us, imagines) some inward movement, which he takes to be the cause of disease. In tragedy, the audience infers (in fact, imagines) from the stage figures' outer movements (their acts and speech) the movements of mind and feeling that supposedly caused those acts.

The analogy between the known or seen and the unknown or unseen was common in and outside scientific debate: witness Anaxagoras's dictum *opsis tōn adēlōn ta phainomena*, "appearances are sight of the obscure," or Herodotus's claim that he concludes what is not known from what is known and clear.[60] "Men do not know how to perceive things that are obscure from things that are apparent," complains one Hippocratic writer, as if this was the proper thing to do.[61]

Greek doctors do not think that blood circulates. It moves a bit in a healthy body, but not much. When Plato speaks of blood moving strongly to all parts of the body, he does not mean circulation. His picture is more like the image (attributed to Heraclitus) of the soul moving in the body as a spider rushes to damaged parts of the web.[62] Greeks do not have our sense that perpetual movement within is normal. Inner surges signify passion and illness. Since breath and air are in the same inner sites, inner flux causes movement of air, inrushing air causes liquid flux. Outer movement may be caused by "a soul that is moved." Rapid breathing may be a sign of approaching apoplexy. Emotional movement (such as shivering caused by "excess of joy") has physical results.[63]

So in one context, movement—both outer movement and its accompanying, inferred inner movement—is a sign of something wrong. Its oppo-

---

moibē), pp. 193–94; Pl. *Theaet.* 152E, 153A–C; Arist. *EE* 1235A25; *Il.* 18.107. Empedocles: see KRS 348, 349, 359, 360, pp. 287, 289, 295–96.

[58] History: see Th. 1.1.2 (cf. n. 10 above).

[59] *DMS* 10.40, 20.20 (Loeb 2:160, 180); cf. *Hum.* 10 (Loeb 4:82). *Anc. Med.* infers what happens *inside* bodies from what is *exōthen* (24, Loeb 1:62). See further Lloyd 1979:148.

[60] Anaxag. fr. 21a DK; Hdt. 2.33, *toisi emphanesi ta mē ginōskomena tekmairomenos*.

[61] Hp. *De victu I* 11 (Loeb 4:248). See above, pp. 51–52 and 55–58; Lloyd 1966:341–44, 353–56; Padel 1990:336 n. 1.

[62] See Harris 1973:26, 40–43; Majno 1975:180–82, 197–98, 330–37; Pl. *Ti.* 70B; Heraclitus B 67a DK, see KRS p. 205 n. 2 (probably not Heraclitean in fact; see C. Kahn 1979:339).

[63] *DMS* 10.10 (Loeb 2:158); *Aph.* 7.30 (Loeb 4:220); Hp. *Breaths* 10, 13 (Loeb 2:240–49); *DMS* 10.20, and *DMS* 25 (Loeb 2:158, 180).

site is inner balance, a healthy stillness. The familiar and customary is safe. If people change (*metaballousi*) their habits, they suffer.[64] In fifth-century cosmogony, history, medicine, and tragedy, change is source of trouble in outer and inner worlds. And movement causes change.

But movement is also the source of being moved, of interest, intensity, excitement. External and internal movements are tragedy's, history's, philosophy's business. Movement is the focus of profound aesthetic and moral experience, as well as the sign and cause of pain. *Phrenes* are mobile in thought and feeling.[65] This is painful, but crucial to tragedy, as to political and personal life. Inner movement, the moving effect that "coming-in things" have on innards, is both destructive and essential. Like our receptivity to hearing and sight, our vulnerability is the source of treasured knowledge.

Black Prophetic Innards

Appearances are sight of the obscure.
—Anaxagoras

Greek culture also expresses ambivalence over the innards' vulnerability through images of obscurity and "darkness." Innards are hidden from other people, inaccessible, hard to interpret, "obscure." Tragic complaints that it is hard to see into another's mind (Chapter 2) interact with perceptions of innards as dark-colored.

There are fundamental problems in translating color words across languages and cultures. Greek uses "black," *melas*, of variously dark, indistinct things: blood ("black death-blood, fallen to earth before a man: who can call it back with a spell?"), *cholos*, and other bitter inner liquids.[66] Innards are "black" at moments of passion. In Agamemnon's anger, "his black *phrenes* filled around greatly with *menos*." Terrified tragic choruses sing, "My black-skinned heart is shaking," "my *phrēn* in its black tunic is gashed by fear."[67] Strong emotion blackens innards. Its dark liquids, especially anger and terror, swell the already dark-colored innards, and intensify their blackness. "My *splanchna* darken as I hear this speech." Later scholars of

---

[64] *Anc. Med.* 10 (Loeb 1:30). Change as source of trouble: see n. 7 above. *Metaballō* or *heteroō* often appear in aetiologies of disease, e.g., Hp. *Breaths* 14.8 (Loeb 2:248), *heteroioumenou . . . tou haimatos*.

[65] See Snell 1978:551.

[66] *Melas*, of blood: *Ag.* 1019, *Il.* 4.149, *Hec.* 536; of wine, waves: *Od.* 5.265, *Il.* 23.693. The fact that *melas* can qualify wine and waves does not mean that the Greeks called red, or blue, "black." It denotes tone rather than hue. Of voice, "indistinct" (or "deep"?): Arist. *Top.* 106A25. Inner bitter liquids: *Eum.* 832 (cf. "bitter" *menos*, *cholos*, *Il.* 18.322, *Od.* 24.319); see above, pp. 25–26.

[67] *Il.* 1.103, A. *Supp.* 785, *Pers.* 115.

antiquity, sensitive to this image, pointed out that the sea also "blackens when it is disturbed."[68]

Inward darkness, further blackened in passion: this image swept, via Aristotle, into later anatomy. In one series of mediaeval anatomic manuscripts, arteries originate in a "black grain" in the heart. We inherit the image through various routes. We feel it is natural, especially when passion is so extreme as to be mad. Madness, above all, darkens innards. *Melancholaō*, "I am filled with black bile," means "I am mad." Darkness repeatedly qualifies Greek madness.[69]

For madness, doctors prescribe "purges" of black hellebore. "Drink hellebore," says Xanthias to an old man dancing. For him, the dancing signals a change in his approach to life. For Xanthias, it is "the beginning of madness."[70] Black hellebore as treatment for madness may reflect homeopathic therapeutic principles important in Hippocratic thinking, for they worked along many magical lines. Hellebore is in fact a poison. It causes convulsive retching. It is dark and violent and therefore cures dark inner violence, madness.[71]

One title of Asclepius, the doctors' god, is Rizotomos, "Root-cutter." Root-magic supposedly spread from Persia and in Greece was associated with Hecate, goddess of night. Dark roots are gathered at Hecate's hour, in darkness, and used for both magical and medical purposes.[72] When

---

[68] *Cho.* 413. Onians (1954:23ff.) thinks the innards are black already; Irwin (1974:38) that *phrenes* are blackened by passion, specifically, by a smoking anger (cf. *Il.* 18.108, "anger swells like smoke in men's breasts"). Irwin thinks anger blackens innards because it is perceived as smoke. I think it is the other way round: smoke-images are apt in such contexts because of a pervasive belief that innards darken in passion; Onians should not be rejected, but built on. Innards are thought of as dark, *and* imagined to get darker in passion; cf. Chapter 4, n. 31.

[69] On the mediaeval idea of a *nigrum granum* in the heart, see Hill 1965:63. On the blackness of Greek madness, inherited by the West, see Padel 1981:125; pp. 24–25 above; cf. pp. 73 and 86 below.

[70] Ar. *V.* 1441, 1476, 1486. Black hellebore is prescribed after a fracture that brings fevers, "tremblings, hiccoughs, and upset *gnomē*," Hp. *On Fractures* 11.38, 58 (Loeb 3:124). See *helleboros, helleboriaō* ("I need hellebore," i.e., "I am mad"), *helleborizō* ("I dose with hellebore," i.e., make sane).

[71] Homeopathic principle in Greek material: Dodds 1951:98 (n. 100); Lloyd 1966:180–81. Overlap between medical and magical cures: Lloyd 1979:37–45. Melampus cured the Proetides' madness (symptomized by wild dancing) *with* dance, according to Apollodorus; see Dowden 1989:79, 85. Hellebore produced violent convulsions, then as now, *Aph.* 4.16 (Loeb 4:138); Majno 1975:188–89.

[72] Lucian *Dialogi deorum* 13. Epileptics should ward off fits (Galen believes) by wearing amulets made of a root, Lloyd 1979:42 (n. 169). On root-cutting in medicine and magic, see Lloyd 1983:119–35. One of Hecate's titles was *Kuno.* Many poisonous or pharmaceutic plants have the *kuno-* prefix, e.g., *kunozolon, kunokephalion, kunoktonos* (aconite), *kunomazon, kunomelon, kunomorion, kunomorphos, kunomuia, kunoprason, kunorodon, kunosbatos.* Patients who have nightly panics, or delirium, or rush out of bed, are being attacked by Hecate, *DMS* 4.30 (Loeb 2:148). Cf. Pliny *NH* 30.1–3.

something goes wrong within, there is darkness within. What is dark and comes from the dark, from earth (which is traditionally called "black"), may cure it. Roots can "bind" and darken the mind. In Homer, Hermes gives Odysseus a "good drug" to protect him, "black at the root, but with a flower like milk," "hard for mortal men to dig." Circe's "evil drugs" make the companions "forget their native land," transforming mind as well as body. Helen in Egypt learned "cunning drugs" that make men "forget all evils":

> Earth, the grain-giver, bears a great store of drugs.
> Many are healing when mixed, but many are harmful.[73]

What earth produces, what we "dig" from it, has power to change, often to harm and darken, human bodies and minds.

Sophocles wrote a tragedy called *Root-cutters* about Medea, which described her "cutting harmful plants" with head averted, so as not to be overcome by the drug. A few fragments survive. In one, the chorus (presumably the root-cutters) sings to Hecate "wreathed in oak and woven coils of savage snakes." A connection between female snake-twined divinities, magical "binding," and damage done to the mind is brought into focus by Aeschylus's Erinyes: their song is *desmios phrenōn*, "mind-binding."[74] These connections are supported by other root-cutting resonances. In the classical age, mandragora was used to stupefy, to put to sleep. Plato pictures mutineers "binding" the shipmaster "with mandragora or drink." *The Mandrake-Drugged Woman* was the title of a play by the comic dramatist Alexis. One name for mandragora was *mōrion*, cognate with *mōroomai* ("I am stupefied") and *mōros* ("stupid, foolish").[75]

Roots "bind" the mind. They come from chthonic female darkness. These connections, alive in fifth-century imagination, filtered through

[73] *Od.* 4.229–30, cf. 10.287, 304–6, 236. Our text is inconsistent. When Circe touches the companions, they have the heads, voice, bristles, and shape of pigs, but *nous ēn empedos, hōs to paros per*, 10.240. Different functions of different Odyssean drugs seem to merge here, cf. 4.221, 9.94–97 (they eat lotus *karpos*, not *riza*). Socrates mentions Circe's drug at Xen. *Mem.* 1.3.7: a fourth-century reference testifying to fifth-century awareness of the drug. "Black earth": e.g., *Il.* 2.699.

[74] *Eum.* 332. Cf. Macrob. *Sat.* 5.19, S. fr. 534–36 (Radt). Pearson (1917, 2:172–77) collects what is known about *Rizotomoi* (cf. p. 101). Euripides took its theme, Medea persuading Pelias's daughters to cause their father's death, for his *Peliades*, E. frr. 601–16N.

[75] See Pl. *Rep.* 488C. Mandragora puts you to sleep, Xen. *Symp.* 2.24. See Lloyd 1983:130 for its range of classical uses. One of Aphrodite's titles is Mandragoritis (Hesych. s.v.). In Pliny *NH* 25.150, and Apuleius *De magia* 32 (cf. Tertullian *De spectaculis* 27), black hellebore is linked closely with mandragora. Hellebore can cause or cure madness. So, apparently, can mandragora. *Mōrios* = (male) mandragora: Diosc. 4.75.2; Pliny *NH* 25.148. *Mōrios* is not linked explicitly with hellebore, but there is overlap between *mōrios*, mandragora, hellebore. *Mōroomai* appears in medical texts, e.g., of the heart, *Virg.* 1 (Littré). *Mōros* is "dull, foolish," *Ant.* 229; cf. *mōra phronein*, *Aj.* 594.

to the Renaissance. *Macbeth*'s witches are "bubbles of the earth," "secret black and midnight hags." Hecate commends them. Banquo, seeing them, asks,

> Have we eaten on the insane root
> That takes the reason prisoner?[76]

European ideas of witchcraft assume that dark roots, grown and gathered in darkness, have power to cure or cause darkness in the mind.

As in other cultures, darkness is dangerous, maybe evil. Clytemnestra has a "black *phrēn*" when she kills her husband. Some doctors told epileptics not to wear black. Darkness at sea means danger: storms darken waves. Inward turbulence is dark, dangerous.[77] The innards' blackness interacts with a maze of dangerous associations to darkness. We are afraid of what is in us and what we cannot see. The earth covers the dead, engenders roots and chthonic divinities, like Erinyes, who threaten human beings, especially their minds. What is in us is obscure, like earth.

But earth-darkness and night also enable seeing and a knowing that is impossible in the light. The earliest Greek oracles are earth shrines. "Night" is an ancient goddess. She has a "terrible house" in Hesiod and, in Homer, great power. Sleep flees from Zeus, but even he avoids annoying "swift Night." Night had an oracle at Megara. Orphic tradition, too, connects her with oracles.[78]

It is apparently from a goddess in the house of Night that Parmenides claims he learned to know.[79] We have seen how he reworks Homer's picture of *noos* dependent on Zeus's "day." Parmenides says *noos*, like everything in the universe, is composed of night and light. "According to [their] balance within us, so is our *noos*."[80] This may be a dismissive comment on

---

[76] *Macbeth* 1.3.79; 4.1.47, 39; 1.3.84.

[77] *Eum.* 459. Clytemnestra acts out of resentment (cf. Thgn. 1199, where the heart is "black" with resentment, and Van Groningen's parallels *ad loc.*). She also acts evilly. Her "darkness" is overdetermined. Black clothes: *DMS* 2.23 (Loeb 2:142). In the Pythagorean table of opposites, light and dark are contrasted. The idea that black is evil has Pythagorean authority (D.L. 8.34). Burkert (1972:295) argues that this table is from the late fifth century. Cf. blackening sea and inner "storm," Chapter 4.

[78] Early earth-oracles: Bouché-Leclerq 1882, 2:250–60; Parke 1967:26–27. House of Night: *Theog.* 726–30, 736–38, 744–45. Oracles of Night: Paus. 1.40.6; Wilamowitz 1931–32, 2:194 (n. 3); M. L. West 1983:70–71, 101, 116. In one tradition, Night held Delphi before Themis and Apollo, schol. Pi. *P.* 2, p. 2.6 (Drachmann). Zeus and Night: *Il.* 14.259–61.

[79] According to Burkert's now well-established interpretation of the *Proem*, Parm. fr. 1DK, see KRS 288, p. 242.

[80] See *Od.* 18.136 (and Chapter 2, n. 80). "Such, Glaucus, is *thumos* for mortal, human beings . . . as is the day Zeus brings on. And they think such things as are the things they meet," Archil. fr. 131 (West). On the influence of this, see Fränkel 1975:133–36, 151, 363 (nn. 51, 37), 372. Parm. fr. 16 brings back Homer's word *noos*. From the context (fr. 28DK,

the shifty fragility of mortal opinions. But it also sites within us the dark and light of the outer world. What is in us is like earth, like night.

Earth is the first prophetic power at Delphi in most traditions. Many prophetic shrines were chthonic centers. Consulting them often involved subterranean journeys. At Trophonius's oracle, clients underwent a ghost-train descent in an underground cave.[81] Inquirers at oracles also encountered darkness through sleep. Healing shrines set up "incubation," "sleeping in." Sleeping in the temple, patients found cures in their dreams. In one comic account of incubation at Asclepius's temple, the patient (who was supposed to put out the light) peeps. He sees the god making his rounds like a doctor. Professional medical writers also take dreams as a guide to diagnosis. What is dark and within can "indicate" what is wrong.[82] In darkness we see what we cannot see in light.

Darkness is the unknown. Heraclitus, the enigmatic, the obscure, is *skoteinos*, "dark." Darkness is where we are most likely to encounter gods.[83] And where we meet their prophets. Caves are associated with prophecy early in the Greek world, as elsewhere. Zeus's prophetic oracle was associated with the darkness of shadowy trees.[84] The Greek seer is characteristically "dark." The name of the *Iliad*'s Greek seer, Calchas, means "Dark." Seers often work from a *muchos*, "recess," or are blind. Blindness is linked to prophecy in the myths of Teiresias, the Theban seer, and many others.[85]

Thphr. *De sensu* 1), we know the "mixture" must be that of night and light: "He said . . . there were two elements and that knowledge depends on the excess of one or the other." On his night and light, see KRS, pp. 255–59.

[81] Earth's Delphic shrine: e.g., *IT* 1247–69. Trophonius: see Ar. *Nub.* 508 ("afraid to go down, as if to see Trophonius"); *Ion* 300–301; Paus. 9.39, 4, who consulted the oracle in the second century A.D. Underground consultation is central to it from the start: see Papathanassiou 1935; Kouretas 1960:10; Parke 1967:126–29.

[82] Incubation: see Deubner 1899; Hamilton 1906; Edelstein and Edelstein 1945, 2:145–46; Dodds 1951:110–16; Ar. *Pl.* 653–747. Some doctors think dreams "show" what is wrong within, see Lloyd 1979:43.

[83] [Arist.] *De mundo* 396B20; see C. Kahn 1979:95. Meeting god in the dark, and the *abaton* of a possessed mind: see Padel 1983:8.

[84] On Dodona, see Chapter 6, n. 75. Amphiaraus's cave: *Sept.* 587–88. Rhesus after death will inhabit caves "like Bacchus's prophet," *Rhes.* 970–73. Parke (1967:27) explains the Greek association of caves and prophecy through early Earth cults, Bronze Age cave-worship. We cannot ignore parallels from other cultures entirely. The earth, like the human body, is available to any culture (perhaps ours less than most) to invest with their particular strategies of mystery. "Because I am dark and always will be, let the book also be dark and mysterious in those places where I will not show myself," says Merlin in the thirteenth-century fragment of his life by Robert de Boron (see Nitze 1927: App.; Jung and von Franz 1971:351). Tolstoy (1985) claims to have found the historical Merlin's real cave, and documents his literary cave. Dark Merlin, dark prophecies; dark cave.

[85] "Calchas": Jebb *ad Ant.* 20. Teiresias: Brisson 1976:73–77, 108–9. Buxton (1980:27–29) compares Ophioneus, Evenius, Phormion, and Phineus. Apollo's Delphic shrine is called

Fundamental to Greek ideas of prophecy, and of the mind, is the idea that knowledge can be found in, and from, darkness. In tragedy, and the myths it explores, alternative ways of seeing may be (but need not be) "truer" than normal vision. Madness and intense passion blacken innards. In several tragedies, mad figures see things other people cannot see, and the poet validates their vision in his play. The mad see "otherwise" but sometimes more truly.[86] Alternative consciousness is uncontrollable, not *sōphrōn*, "having a safe *phrēn*," but dark, with darkness's danger. But it is also a source of insight. Like the Sirens' song, passion is destructive but illuminating.

This feature of the tragic background, the image of innards prophesying, unseen within the human being, interacts with the practice of divination through animal entrails (Chapter 2). Innards have power to remember, compose, and prophesy: activities closely associated with each other in early Greek thought. Frightened anger sings, within, a song that belongs to divinity:

> The *thumos* from inside sings, without a lyre,
> *autodidaktos* [self-taught], Erinys's song.

Heart has power to see, understand, speak. *Phrēn* sings. "*Thumos* prophesies, leaping from within."[87]

Innards are especially knowledgeable or prophetic at moments of intense emotion, when they pulse and twist:

> The *splanchna* do not speak in vain,
> heart circling beside the truthful *phrenes*
> in prophetic spirals.

Human innards spoke prophetically in several ways. Prophetic voices came from the stomach at the command of *engastromuthoi*, "belly-speakers." The best-known (or, on another interpretation, the only one there ever was) was someone called Eurycles. As Socrates says in the *Phaedrus*, touching many registers of irony and perceived truth at once, "What a prophetic thing the soul is!" Innards are things to be "consulted," as in Homeric internal dialogue.[88] Like oracles and prophets, they are consulted because they are an enigmatic but possibly divinely connected source of knowing.

Innards are dark-skinned and, like the seer, "in the dark":

---

mantikoi muchoi and *muchos chthonos*, *Eum*. 180, *Cho*. 954. *Muchos* is applied to its inner shrine: *Eum*. 39, 170; cf. Chapter 5, n. 5.

[86] See Padel 1981:126–29.

[87] *Ag*. 990–91; A. fr. 176N; Terpander 697P; Webster 1957:152–53.

[88] *Ag*. 995–97; Pl. *Phdr*. 242C. *Engastromuthoi*: see Dodds 1951:71; Macdowell *ad* Ar. *V*. 1019. Inner dialogue: Chapter 2, n. 61.

> Heart would tell all this, outrunning tongue,
> but as things are it mutters in the dark.

Innards know, "see," "tell," in the body's dark and in the dark of sleep. "The sleeping *phrēn* is illuminated with eyes." Dreams are prophetic.[89] *Muchos*, a seer's "cave," can also mean the "cave" of Hades, a storeroom, the women's (inmost) quarters of a house, or a hollow in the body. A wicked soul peers out at the world from a hiding-place, "through *muchoi*."[90] Caves, dark hollow places, are good for prophecy. Innards inhabit dark inner recesses, like prophets. In some strands of Greek thought, the soul "begins and becomes" in a cave. In the Neoplatonist myth, the soul is born in a cave, like the cave of Plato's *Republic*, or the cave of the Ithacan nymphs. Throughout Greek thought, caves are good places for important births.[91]

Muchos is the source of Clytemnestra's nightmare of punishment. The chorus hears a cry at night:

> Shrill, standing the hair on end,
> a dream-interpreter of the house,
> breathing anger from sleep,
> howled out in fear at night,
> a cry from *muchos*.

Grammar and text here are confused. (Aeschylus's own oracular ambiguity has often caused manuscript distortion.) Was it Clytemnestra who cried? Or a daemon? Or the prophetic dream itself?[92] The cry came *muchothen*, "from the *muchos*." This may mean "from the women's quarters," but might also imply a dark "prophetic *muchos*," the darkened consciousness of the dreamer, whose ghost will appear as a dream at an equivalent early stage in the following play and will say that a sleeping *phrēn* is illumined with eyes.

---

[89] *Ag.* 1028–30, *Eum.* 104.

[90] See Emp. fr. 100.23DK; Arist. *Resp.* 7.473B9. Blood surges through limbs, rushing back and in (*muchonde*), Emp. KR, p. 341 (KRS 471, pp. 359–60 quotes only 1–21). The soul "peers forth through the obscurity of the secret places from which it watches," *Phil.* 1013 (following Jebb). *Muchos* as "women's quarters," see Padel 1983:8.

[91] See *Od.* 13.109 (cf. Pl. *Rep.* 514A). The cave has two entrances, one for gods, one for mortals, a symbolism used later for divine and mortal access to the soul; see Buffière 1973:457ff. Porphyry (*De antro nympharum* 13) seemingly found these words (*muchoi, bothroi, antra, thurai, pulai*) and thoughts already in Pherecydes (KRS 51, p. 59): "Through these he speaks, riddling, of the becomings and deceases of souls." Other cave-births: see *h. Merc.* 6, 23; *Ion* 949.

[92] *Cho.* 32–35. *Phoibos* appears before *orthothrix* in M, the famous Medicean manuscript at Florence. This may be a gloss, or a distortion of *phobos* (original subject of *pneōn* and *elake*). Alternatively, *domōn* (genitive) could be a distortion of *daimōn*. But this would be unusually explicit. I would take *oneiromantis* as a noun, and *domōn* with it; cf. *Ag.* 409, *prophētai domōn*. Cf. the ambiguity at *Ag.* 1127, "apposite to oracular utterance, in which riddles are to be expected," Stinton 1990:112, and further Lloyd-Jones 1990 i. 353–54.

The *Oresteia* has a dense texture of divination, beginning with Calchas, the "army-seer."[93] There are traditional types of diviners, but the one who most resembles the innards is the *oneiropolos*, "dream-interpreter." As Achilles says in the *Iliad* when he asks for one, "Dream (*onar*) is also from Zeus."[94] Clytemnestra's prophetic dream emerges from *muchos*: the darkness of the house and of her guilt.

These, then, are the three main contributory images in tragic portaiture of prophetic, articulate innards: animal entrails in divination, internal dialogue, and the seer, a blind, "dark" speaker from a cave.

DISCOURSE OF DARKNESS

The notion that the stage is a place where the invisible
can appear has a deep hold on our thoughts.
—Peter Brook, *The Empty Space*

Through multiple resonances of divination, Greek mentality associates the innards' darkness with their status both as the physical center of life and consciousness and as the source of potential knowledge. They are consulted, like gods and prophets. They "speak," but not necessarily truthfully. Gods, too, often deceive. The first dream of Greek poetry is both god-sent and a lie.[95] Innards command and advise, as gods do. Their power, their knowledge, may or may not derive from gods. They are the internal human center of divine attention and activity.

Darkness is the condition and color of innards. From our point of view, we see this as metaphor, and say that the physiological background to Greek mind-words, however confusing we find it, helps us understand Greek patterns of belief about emotion and thought, as they are reflected in their (to us) metaphorical contexts. Metaphors charge the object to which they are applied with associations from their other applications. Activity that the Greek language attributes to innards therefore "comes from" Greek attitudes toward other things, such as prophecy, animals, gods, women, caves.

---

[93] *Ag*. 122. In *Ag*., no *mantis* is blamed (185), yet *mantis* urged Agamemnon into action (201), and his *technai* were *ouk akrantoi* (185, 201, 249). The chorus asks if Clytemnestra reverences dreams. They disbelieve her news, are skeptical when they hear Cassandra's prophecies, yet "interpret" Clytemnestra's deceptive words "clearly" themselves (274, 268, 1130–34, 616). *Prophētai domōn* cried out after Helen's departure. *Ag*. signals its interest in signs, truth, and proof, well before it brings on Cassandra in a central scene showing that interpretation is both needed and fallible (409, 268–72, 475–92, 681–85, 1083–1285). *Cho*. begins with Clytemnestra's anxiety about her dream, interpreted by "judges of dreams," and with this dream's true *mantis* and fulfiller, Orestes (*Cho*. 37–41, 541–50). He says that her "*phobos* from dreams" was *mantis* (887, 929): his last words to her fulfil the *muchothen* cry.

[94] Achilles asks for a *mantis*, *hiereus*, or *oneiropolos*, *Il*. 1.62–63.

[95] *Il*. 2.6. Internal dialogue: Chapter 2, n. 61.

But this "comes from" is fictive. We cannot get back, psychically, to a time before Homer. It is more valuable to forget our own preconceptions (including our distinction between literal and metaphorical), and say that innards' darkness had many simultaneous aspects and functions in fifth-century mentality. Multiplicity, concreteness, darkness: these core attributes of the human equipment of thinking, feeling, and knowing illuminate, and are illumined by, Greek use of these same innards in sacrificial animals. Divination raises the question: Does a human mind's knowledge come originally from outside? Have gods written on the *splanchna*? Or do they have knowledge from within? Are the *splanchna*'s markings and divisions, their disunity, their own? Or is all this divinely directed? These questions lie at the root of tragedy's vision of what people are and do. Memory is knowledge that can seem to come from outside, yet is also part of "mind." Information can be "written on" innards. You remember by inscribing "inside your *phrenes*," "on the tablets of your *phrenes*."[96] Has this knowledge come from outside, or was it partly there to start with?

These associations of darkness, which underpin Greek discourse of inner experience, are part of our own inheritance. They have directed European languages and thought. We cannot escape feeling they are "natural" in writing about the mind. Freud, who urged us, in Auden's words, "to be enthusiastic over the night," called the id "the dark, inaccessible part of our personality":

> For about him till the very end were still
> those he had studied, the fauna of the night.

For the theologian Maritain, speaking of "the nocturnal kingdom of the mind," the human spirit is most susceptible to myth and magic when "ideas of the world" become "things of the night, bound up with the fluid and twilight life of the imagination." This imagery runs so deep in our linguistic and imaginative inheritance that it is hard to hold oneself to the fifth-century perceptions that fed it.[97] Greek perceptions, Greek fantasies invented or discovered the Western discourse of darkness for the mind. These fantasies were fuelled by experience deeply alien to us; and yet later historical accident makes this discourse feel homegrown to us. To study it in ancient texts, we must look at it bifocally, as it were: as something that has formed our own discourse of inwardness (and therefore makes us feel we share it, it is part of ourselves), and as something absolutely foreign and outside us.

[96] *Cho.* 450, *Eum.* 275, *PV* 789, Pi. *O.* 10.3, *Trach.* 683, *Phil.* 1325. Cf. Pl. *Theaet.* 191D (memory as a block of wax). Muses as "daughters of Memory": documented by Murray 1981:94–95.

[97] See Auden, "In Memory of Sigmund Freud"; Freud [1932] 1933:73; Maritain 1943:201–2.

Tragedy's language stresses that whatever is within us is obscure, many-faceted, impossible to see. Performance gave this question of what is within a physical force. The spectators were far away from the performers, on that hill above the theater. At the center of their vision was a small hut, into which they could not see. The physical action presented to their attention was violent but mostly unseen. They inferred it, as they inferred inner movement, from words spoken by figures whose entrances and exits into and out of the visible space patterned the play. They saw its results when that facade opened to reveal a dead body. This genre, with its dialectics of seen and unseen, inside and outside, exit and entrance,[98] was a simultaneously internal and external, intellectual and somatic expression of contemporary questions about the inward sources of harm, knowledge, power, and darkness.

[98] See Padel 1990:336–37, 345, 363–64. Taplin's first project (1977, 1982) was to explore the tragedians' dramatics through their use of exit and entrance. "Dialectics of inside and outside": see Bachelard 1969:229.

Chapter 4

THE FLUX OF FEELING

DEATH, SLEEP, DREAMS, AND UNDERGROUND RIVERS

THE "DARK" OF CONSCIOUSNESS brings us, paradoxically, to images of losing consciousness. When people faint or die in Homer, "black night" or darkness "covers their eyes," is "poured," "shed" over them, or over their eyes. A "dark cloud of death" covers them. Unconsciousness is a night, a mist, black as death. Sleep is Death's brother, also a son of Night. Death is "bronze sleep."[1] What makes one lose consciousness is a fluid nonseeing, a pouring, covering dark.

Death is a dark covering. Those who die enter the covered underworld, a darkness. Dying souls "leave the light," enter "dark lifetime" on "dark plains." Tartarus is bordered by a bronze fence, a three-lapped necklace of night "shed" round it. The Titans are "hidden" there "under misty dark" where "are the springs and termini of dark earth and misty Tartarus." Here is the "terrible home of dark Night, covered in dark clouds."[2]

The underworld's dark is overdetermined. Earth is "dark." To bury someone is to "cover" them in earth; to kill them is to "cover them in night." When Theseus hears Phaedra is dead, he prays

> to inhabit the darkness under earth
> by dying in darkness.[3]

"Black earth" drinks the blood of the dying. In funeral speeches and epitaphs, the dead "return to the dark from which they came." A dead man is laid "in the earth in which he was nourished."[4] The darkness and closure of earth and the grave are one ingredient of Hades' dark; danger, death, and unconsciousness are others.

The fluid dark of nonconsciousness, of consciousness ending, is reified

[1] Black night, darkness, and "end of death" cover the dying and their eyes: *Il.* 13.580, 14.439, 4.461, 5.535 (cf. "dark cloud of death," Bacc. 17.64). Sleep: *Il.* 16.672, *Theog.* 212, *Il.* 11.241. Sleep "poured" over eyes: *Il.* 14.165, *Od.* 19.590; death's darkness, or death, "poured" over eyes, over you: *Il.* 5.696, 13.544; dark mist "poured" over eyes: *Il.* 20.321.

[2] *Phoen.* 1484, *Rhes.* 962, cf. *OC* 1681. Ghost leaving Hades by "gates of darkness": *Hec.* 1. House of Night: *Theog.* 726–45; Chapter 3, n. 78. House of Hades: see Sourvinou-Inwood 1981.

[3] *Hipp.* 836. Burying: *PV* 582, *Ant.* 28, *Phoen.* 1633 (cf. grave's darkness, Lattimore 1962:161–63); killing: *Il.* 13.425.

[4] See Chapter 5, n. 7; Alexiou 1974:9, 209 n. 51.

in Hades by underground rivers. In Homer, the dead souls appear near where "Periphlegethon and Cocytus flow into Acheron, which is a branch of the water of the Styx; there is a boulder, and the confluence of two roaring rivers." The Styx is "downward-flowing." In Hesiod, it trickles from a high rock. In Euripides, it is a "black-skinned ferry of Hades." In Plato, souls drink the water of Lethe. The topography of Hades developed through antiquity and is not fixed, but there are always rivers in it. Fourth-century Orphic gold wafers from Thessaly and south Italy urge the thirsting soul to drink from one spring rather than another:

> You will reach the well-built mansions of Hades. There on the right is a spring near a lovely cypress, to which the souls of the dead come down for refreshment. Do not approach this spring! Further on you'll find fresh water from Mnemosyne's lake. Say . . . "I am parched with thirst and dying; give me at once fresh water from Mnemosyne's lake."[5]

Underground rivers, rivers of the place that hides the dead, resonate against perceptions of the hidden, conscious innards, which blacken and fill with liquid in passion. In tragic imagery, emotion is often liquid, as this chapter will show. But even liquid can be personified. River Styx is a goddess in Hesiod.[6]

The darkness and fluidity of the living impassioned mind belongs, therefore, in a mentality that depicts the underworld in similar terms, imaging the equipment of consciousness through a darkness that also images its opposite. This paradox sits easily beside images of the darkened or blind seer, of black innards that are unseen and yet see (Chapter 3). We might wonder if passion itself is not felt to be a kind of loss of consciousness. Passion and madness share the darkness of death, fainting, sleep. In Greek mentality, mind and underworld have significant links. Both are a dark home to daemon. Earth is the home and provenance of chthonic divinities. Creatures called "children of Night," or Earth, dwell in Hades. Their function is to disturb human innards. Lyssa is "Madness." The Erinyes' persecution is also madness. "Dark" creatures, "born" from Night, rise from earth to distract and bind the mind.[7] The mind in its activity and pain is as dark as its own negation.

Dreams come from the dark of night and earth to affect the mind. They too are "children" of Night or Earth. Earth "engenders visions of dreams."

---

[5] *Od.* 10.513–15, *Il.* 15.37, *Od.* 5.185; *Theog.* 786–92; *Hec.* 1104; Pl. *Rep.* 621A–B. These words on a *lamella* c. 400 B.C. (from Hipponion) are repeated in others, e.g., one c. 350 B.C. from Petelia; see Breslin n.d.:6–7. Topography of Hades: see Garland 1985:49–51.

[6] *Theog.* 383–85. Emotion personified, especially as female: see below, pp. 157–61.

[7] *HF* 834; *Eum.* 322, 332, 343.

Dreams are her "black-winged children" rising from "lightless places."[8] Their origin is outside the dreamer. Dreams "come," in the dark of night and sleep. Hecate is mistress of "night-wandering dreams." Dreams roam the earth like Pandora's "diseases." Ghosts of the unburied appear as dreams, emerging through "Hades' gates," those "gates of darkness where Hades dwells." The place of dreams is somewhere on the way to death, near "gates" of the sun en route to Hades. Ghosts and dreams are released into our world from some dark "gate." The staff of Hermes, gate-keeper, lord of the hinge, master of inside and outside, touches us into sleep and wakes us from it. Hermes leads dying souls to Hades, summons dead souls from it;[9] he leads into and out of the dark.

Hecuba in Euripides is upset by what we ourselves would call "her" dream. She rightly sees it as a true vision of an external reality. The audience in fact sees it first. Dreams come from the ground, are sent by gods. But they may also be "the opinion of a sleeping *phrēn*."[10] In this they resemble other underworld emissaries. Erinyes, like Lyssa, come from somewhere else, yet take up habitation in human innards. Lyssa, "child of dusky Night," rushes "into Heracles' breast." The Erinys in Sophocles' *Electra* hides "in terrible ambush-places," a phrase suggesting parallels between the underworld and the house of Atreus, between the underworld and the minds of the curse-ridden family. Erinys "hides" in them all, especially in Electra, who is, as one critic says, "at once the victim and the agent of the Furies."[11] At the end of the *Oresteia*, the Erinyes will benefit their new habitat, the city of Athens, from "under primeval hiding-places of earth." But they will also be at work in the minds and feelings of Athens's citizens. Athene asks them not to incite civil war, saying,

> Do not hurl bloodied whetstones in my places,
> harm to the young men's *splanchna*.[12]

The Erinyes "are in" two places, the Athenians' *splanchna* and their own dwelling-place within the land. Both are "my places" to Athens's patron goddess.

Underworld and mind are parallel habitats, therefore, of Madness,

---

[8] *Hec.* 68–75, *IT* 1263 (cf. A. *Supp.* 888). Ar. *Ran.* 1332–35 parodies Euripides' dream-iconography: "O dark-lit Night, what . . . dream do you send *ex aphanous*, a servant of Hades, an awful terrible *opsin, melanonekuoeimona*?"

[9] See *Il.* 23.62–71; *Od.* 19.562, 24.12.

[10] *Hec.* 71, *Ag.* 275.

[11] Winnington-Ingram 1980:228 (and 218–25 on the relevance of this "hiding Erinys" to Electra's argument with her mother). See S. *El.* 490 (*lochois*), *HF* 863, *Ant.* 603 (*erinus phrenōn*), with Chapter 8, n. 61.

[12] *Eum.* 858–89, 1036, 976–87, cf. 518–19. Calling Erinyes *mnēmones* expresses the daemonic force of individual conscience, according to Winnington-Ingram 1980:208 n. 13. See, in more detail, below, Chapter 8, nn. 23–26.

Erinyes, black dreams. One is their provenance, the other their target. If we short-circuit the symbolism, we find innards disturbed by things—Erinyes, dreams, madness—that come from the place that symbolizes innards themselves. "Mind" is disturbed by what it has itself (as we would say) engendered.

FLOW AND STORM

> And who is not . . . moved in foul weather . . . ? . . . The
> air works on all men, more or less, but especially on such
> as are melancholy, or inclined to it.
> —Robert Burton, *Anatomy of Melancholy*

There are other connections between inner world and underworld. That in the mind which answers to Hades' rivers is the dark inner flow of passion. Tragedy often suggests that thought, feeling, or any inner change (such as disease) is a moving liquid, something swelling, flowing within. Greek philosophers and medical writers illustrate what tragic imagery implies: that thought and feeling are at work in the blood. Empedocles says the heart lives "in seas of blood that rush to and fro." Sleep is accompanied by a flux of blood. Aristotle thinks blood "boils" in emotion. Even the *psuchē*, in Plato, "boils."[13]

"Boiling" happens particularly in anger. Not just blood, but also other inner liquids, *cholos*, *thumos*, *menos*: black, bitter, raging, they rise in the innards like waves.[14] Hippocratics, who see inner moisture as dangerous, tend to attribute abnormality to inner flux. Flux of phlegm supposedly causes epileptic attacks. *Pneuma* upsetting the body in fever "condenses and flows as water": compare the Heraclitean comments that a dry soul is best, that it is death for a soul to become water.[15]

"Flux" causes or signifies harm. To dream that the earth is flooded signifies disease, "as there is much moisture in the body." *On the Sacred Disease* attributes epilepsy to flux from the brain. It causes "a diseased head, full of noise." The phlegm's flow causes palpitations, speechlessness, choking, according to what part of the body it flows into. The disease is caused in the first place by a failure in the embryo's head. The brain should be "purged" while the child is still in the womb. "If the flux from all the brain is too

---

[13] Emp. KRS 394, p. 311; see Chapter 2, n. 102. Boiling blood: Arist. *De anim.* 403A31 (of blood around the heart); boiling *psuchē*: Pl. *Crat.* 419E; cf. Chapter 2, n. 52. Flux of blood in sleep: see Lloyd 1975:126 n. 59. Impact of this thought on tragic images of murder: cf. Chapter 8, n. 34.

[14] *PV* 370 (*cholos*), *OC* 434 (*thumos*), Pl. *Ti.* 70B (*menos* of *thumos*), cf. Onians 1954:46–48.

[15] *Hum.* 10 (Loeb 4:160), *DMS* 8–13 (Loeb 2:154–68), Hp. *Breaths* 8.35 (Loeb 2:238). Heraclitus: KRS 229, 230 (p. 203); C. Kahn 1979:244–52.

full, and great melting happens, [the child] will have a diseased head as he grows," and afterwards will suffer "excessive flux," which can move of its own accord. In another treatise, bowels are upset by phlegm running down from the head. The idea of inner flux informed eighteenth-century humoral pathology: passions caused movement in "humors," which made patients think of things that "excited" them.[16]

Organs that swell in disease are *plēmuron*, "waved," that is, "congested." External swelling is treated with squeezing, lancing, or draining, which forces excess liquid out. Skin swellings are relieved by "drippings out," *apostasies*. Doctors try bloodletting, or encourage water to bring up sputum, "since it causes a kind of flood." Any flood, dripping, or swelling should force unwanted liquid out.[17]

All this is visible swelling. Inner organs, which cannot be seen, are treated in the same way. If the doctor suspects an inner organ may be *plēmuron*, he prescribes a purge or bloodletting. Inner "waves" must flow out. If the extra liquid does not drain away, it must be made to go.[18]

Popular assumptions behind these medical principles and treatment underlie the poets' language of feeling. This is the background in which we should set tragic language like that of Electra, alternately hoping and despairing that the lock of hair she finds could belong to her lost brother: "A wave of *cholē* stands near against my heart."[19] Unstable, liquid feeling waves and rages in her. Unseen emotion, swelling the innards, is a sign of danger. Treat it like any swelling:

"Words are the doctors of a diseased pride."
"Yes, if one soothes the heart at the proper time
and does not press with force the swelling *thumos*."[20]

[16] Winds cause flux: Hp. *Breaths* 10 (Loeb 2:240–42). Dreaming of flood means disease: Hp. *Dreams* 90.50 (Loeb 4:440). Flux to brain causes epilepsy: *DMS* 8–10 (Loeb 2:154–58), *AWP* 3 (Loeb 1:74). Heat or cold moves (*kineein*) bile and phlegm, see Lonie 1965:127–29. Eighteenth-century images: Foucault 1971:86.

[17] *Hum.* 20 (Loeb 4:92–94), *Reg. Acut. Dis.* 62 (Loeb 2:116) *plēmurida gar tina empoiei*, cf. *DMS* 13 (Loeb 2:166); Majno 1975:154–58. Cf. Chapter 3, nn. 17–19.

[18] See Majno 1975:184 (cf. 336 on Alexandrian development of this theme).

[19] *Emoi prostē kardias kludōnion / cholēs*, *Cho.* 183–84. *Prosistēmi* with the dative can mean "offend against" (e.g., the stomach, of food: Plato Comicus 102.2, *PCG* vii 475), but in intransitive tenses the active usually means "stand near, stand by." With the accusative, it can mean "attack," but we have the genitive here. *Kardias* has been explained three ways. Each implies a different picture of what liquid does to the heart: (a) "Place from which" (Verrall)— grammatically unlikely, since there is no *ek*, and *pro* in the verb suggests the opposite; (b) "movement toward" (Klausen)—grammatically unparalleled (S. *El.* 900 is not a true parallel; the genitive there is governed by *aisson*), but more likely on grounds of sense, cf. below, n. 23; (c) local, "at, by the heart"—also grammatically unusual (though cf. perhaps *Cho.* 390), but giving the best sense. It suggests a relation of liquid to heart similar to *Ag.* 180 (though there we have *pro kardias*). Either "stands against" or "comes toward" would do.

[20] *PV* 378–80. Imitating this passage, Cicero (*TD* 3.31.76) and Milton (*Samson Agonistes*

Boastful words are "swollen with wandering of mind," with madness. When the frantic chorus men ask Clytemnestra what is happening, they say, "Be healer of [my] worrying thought." Their thought is swollen. She must cure it. Plato hears the word *thumoeidēs*, "spirited," "angry," as *thumos* joined to *eidos*, "form." Aeschylus uses *thumuidēs*, from *oidanein*, "to swell."[21]

Poets represent emotion as Hippocratics represent the causes and symptoms of disease: internal liquid "falling," "dripping," flooding in and to the innards. Aristotle says men pale in fear because blood runs to the heart, away from other parts. This massed swollen liquid has internal "weight." "Why does a heavy *cholos* of *phrenes* fall forward to you?" the chorus sings in rhetorical address to Medea, who has left the stage for her murder: meaning, why has this terrible anger overpowered her? An "evil chill falls round my heart," sings the chorus of the *Seven against Thebes* at an equivalent place, when Eteocles goes off to fight his brother and the Thebans see the curse on the royal house at work. A "saffron-dyed drop runs to the heart" of the *Agamemnon*'s chorus members when they begin to understand Cassandra's truths.[22]

Words compounded with "falling" and "dripping" are common both to Hippocratic images of flux and to tragedy's account of passion. In Homer, *cholos* "seizes" but also "falls" and "sinks" into the innards.[23] In tragedy, feeling drips within us like disease:

> Instead of sleep, a reminding bitterness—
> suffering—drips before the heart.

We should connect such inner flowing with the *poroi*, the "channels" important to fifth-century accounts of perception and disease. Empedocles spoke of a *poros noēsai*, "channel for understanding." Perception, thought, emotion, and disease-causing flux move through passageways in the interior. Zeus's mind contains *poroi* hard to calculate.[24]

---

184) add the notion of a wound or tumor. But Aeschylus suggests an internal swelling. *Ischnainein* is "to reduce" swelling (as beer, at A. fr. 124, is "reduced" or "thinned" by age).

[21] *Sept.* 660–61 (on one interpretation); *paiōn genou tēsde merimnēs, Ag.* 99.

[22] *Med.* 1265, *Sept.* 834, *Ag.* 1121 (see Chapter 2, n. 59; Stinton 1990:112). Weight of liquid in mind: cf. *Aj.* 41 (*cholōi baruntheis*), *Phil.* 368. Haemon's indignant mind is heavy when hurt, *Ant.* 767. Cf. Ajax's *barunomenon noēma, Iliu Persis* 5.8 (H. *OCT* 5:139).

[23] Cf. Hp. *Breaths* 10 (Loeb 2:242): "breaths" cause internal *reumata*, the throat goes rough and sore whenever phlegm *an prospesēi*, with *reuma prospipton. Empiptō* is used of disease and its symptoms (*Trach.* 1253, *sparagmos*; Th. 2.49, *lunx kenē*, empty retching), and of passion (*deos empese thumōi, Il.* 17.625): see Chapter 3, n. 20. It is a technical medical term for the start of illness (and passion), see Miller 1944:165; Long 1968:134 n. 73. Some commentators on the tragic passages compare fate or *daimōn* "falling" from above, on the head. This, too, is a common tragic image (see below, pp. 129–30). The resonances of *piptein* compounds differ in every context, but I suspect both ideas always play some part.

[24] See *Ag.* 179–80, cf. *Cho.* 842, *achthos deimatostages* (where West prefers the pedestrian

I have concentrated so far on what comes into or toward the heart. But the inner flow of emotion or disease is two-way. Inward flux and outward waves fill innards, but the mind also "overflows" with passion, and then liquid is ex-pressed. Eyes express feeling as rays of light (Chapter 3). Tears, too, can seem like overflow from a wave of passion:

> For me a wave of *cholē* stands near against my heart. . . .
> Thirsty drops fall from my eyes,
> irrepressible drops of a stormy wave.

Here the juxtaposed words *kludōnion* (wave), *stagones* (drops), and then *plēmuris* (a second word for "wave" here) suggest tears flowing from a wave rising in the heart and overflowing through the eyes. Grief, desire, and anger flow outward to their object. Eros "drips *pothos* [longing]" from his eyes. Odysseus, pitying Penelope, hides his tears "with guile." His eyes stand dry "as if they were horn or iron," the opposite of what eyes are expected to be in grief or pity.[25] The Erinyes brim with rage and hatred. Their eyes ooze blood or foul rheum. The lava flow from Etna is overspill from the boiling *cholos* of the Titan buried beneath.[26]

Grief makes flesh, cheeks, innards, life itself, "melt." Penelope has "melted away her *thumos*, lamenting her husband." When she heard tales about him, "she let tears flow and her flesh melted, as the snow melts away on the mountains." The image of overflowing tears merges with images of body and soul flowing, "melting" away in longing and grief, as a body "melts away [*tēketai*]" in disease. Emotion, like disease, is liquefaction.[27]

I suggested (Chapter 3) that we inherited from the Greeks a discourse of darkness about mind, so much a part of our own imagination that it is hard not to call it "natural"—an ancient pitfall for classicists. It goes against our instincts to identify this discourse as a living part of a mentality encumbered with the alien quirks of fifth-century Greek thought. The same is true of inner flow. From flux to storm, inner flow has directed the imagery of feeling in modern European languages for so long that we do not want to relate it to the rebarbative physiology of its original Greek use. We have abandoned most of the physiological perceptions of which these images

---

conjecture *haimatostages*). Cf. above, pp. 25–26. Zeus's *poroi*: see A. *Supp.* 90; Chapter 6, n. 74. Empedocles' *poros noēsai*: see Chapter 2, n. 99.

[25] *Cho.* 183–86; *Hipp.* 525–26 (*kat' ommatōn stazeis pothon*), see Barrett *ad loc.*; Lebeck 1973:278–80 (liquid *himeros* flowing through eyes in Pl. *Phdr.*). Odysseus: *Od.* 19.211. Cf. Chapter 3, nn. 31–32.

[26] *Cho.* 1058; *Eum.* 54 (see below, p. 176). Typhos: see *PV* 372–73.

[27] *Od.* 19.263–64, 204–5; 5.396; *Heraclid.* 645 ("wasting away the *psuchē*"), Pl. *Rep.* 609C (the *sōma*), *Med.* 141 (*biotan*). The image appealed to Hellenistic poets, e.g., *AP* 5.277 (*kradiēn*).

were part, yet we have kept on their image-system, calcified in our newer languages.

This flux imagery—a verbal system, still in use—began in a past world of quite different experience and perception. From our belated vantage point, we cannot know how it actually felt to have those perceptions and to rest on those assumptions. All we can do is to collect material that suggests fifth-century imaginative connections and assumptions. A further step is to study it as an origin of verbal systems we do still share.

We share with the Greeks a secondary effect, this network of imagery for disease and emotion, but not the primary physiological assumptions that patterned it. We might compare this imagery to early mediaeval commerce, whose driving force was a contemporary passion for spices. This passion created a network of commercial relationships that operated also in later Europe. The secondary effects "were of more importance than the primary cause." The mediaeval appetite for spices passed away. But "the activities and organization it produced . . . are the foundation of modern commerce and industry." A set of relationships patterned by a specific earlier culture, fifth-century physiology in our case, mediaeval lust for spice in the other, laid foundations for connections and systems carried on by those who no longer share its primary impulse or assumptions. Here is the "dissociation" I spoke of, between how we speak about what we feel, and what we believe happens inside us.[28]

Inevitably, writers in later European languages have found it "natural" to use Greek wave and storm imagery of feeling and thinking, and still do. They are affected, sometimes directly, by Greek poetry or philosophy and its strong shaping pressure on European thought. They are also influenced, partly invisibly, by Greek metaphors that seep through in translation, and via Latin and mediaeval languages, into modern discourse. Their reading and their language endorse the imagery, though their physiological ideas, on the whole, do not. Cataracts and external hurricanoes designate the storm *in* Lear. The opening of that famous central scene crystallizes the parallel between inner and outer tempest. "Who's there, besides foul weather?" is answered: "One minded like the weather, most unquietly." Madness, rage, profound inner turmoil, such as religious conversion or grief: all are "storms" and floods in the mind. In Plutarch's day (first to second century A.D.), anger is familiarly portrayed as a stormy sea. Conversion is spontaneously expressed in the nineteenth century through fluent liquid language, as William James documents: "All my feelings seemed to rise and flow out." Virginia Woolf's Mrs. Ramsay experiences her own pity—for a girl whose father is dying in *cholos*-like images: "Bitter and

[28] Discourse of darkness: see Chapter 3, n. 84. Mediaeval commerce: see Southern 1967:42. Our own dissociation: see Chapter 2, nn. 83–85.

black, halfway down, in the darkness, in the shaft which ran from the sunlight to the depths, perhaps a tear formed; a tear fell; the waters swayed this way and that, received it, and were at rest. Never did anybody look so sad." Freud pictured the id as a vessel of liquid, "a cauldron full of seething excitations."[29]

We meet a great deal of storm and wave imagery of feeling in Greek poets. Distancing ourselves from our reading experience of later literatures, and concentrating on Greek physiological resonances of these images, is one way to respond. But some readers of Greek poetry may prefer to feel that they do entirely share a world of experience with fifth-century Athenians. The sense of community of feeling between reader and poet is precious. I do not want to take it away or reduce the poets' imagery to phlegm flowing through *poroi*. I want to enlarge understanding of tragedy, not restrict it. Though some of these ideas are absurd to us, they do illuminate a mentality in which mind and body, metaphorical and literal meaning, divine and human impulse, are inseparable.

I should like to hold fifth-century physiology of flux in play even behind the prior epic images of inner "sea." In Homer, a "black shiver" runs over a sea whipped by wind. When a man "greatly moved" dared to face Achilles, "his heart dark-purpled many things as he waited." The sea darkens and swells even before the wind blows, like Nestor's mind when he sees the Greeks routed. He hesitates, not knowing what to do:

> As when the sea dark-purples greatly with a silent wave,
> anticipating swift paths of howling winds
> but not rolling forward
> to one side or the other till some gale comes down
> from Zeus. So the old man agonized,
> divided in his *thumos*.[30]

The dark, swelling sea as an image of mental agony belongs with specific ideas of innards. The mind is already thought of in terms of breath, wind, liquid, darkness: images that will pattern Hippocratic theory later on.

For the tragic poets, the innards' darkening in passion is already linked by Homeric imagery to the darkening of the sea-swell whipped by wind. The Homeric phrase *kradiē porphure*, "his heart purpled," blends *porphureos*, "heaving, surging" (of sea), or "gushing" (of blood), with the "purple" of dyed clothes. There is an implicit connection between surging liquid and a red flush. Applied to the heart, this verb must mean both "surge, swell [with liquid]" and "darken, purple."[31]

---

[29] *King Lear* 3.1–6; Plu. *De cohibenda ira* 456C–E; W. James 1952:254–55; V. Woolf, *To the Lighthouse*, 1.5. Freud [1932] 1933:73.

[30] *Il.* 14.16–20, cf. *Od.* 4.402.

[31] See *Il.* 21.551, *Od.* 4.427, etc. The two ideas are often combined (e.g., Theoc. 5.125).

The connection of purpling, darkening, swelling liquid with seas in the outer world, with *splanchna* within, underlies tragic images of madness (or of *atē*, seen sometimes as "disaster," sometimes as madness or its cause) as "waves" beating against a shore. Io's madness is a blast carrying her sideways. Her mad stormy words are waves beating aslant against a shore, a torrent beating against sea waves.[32] Ideas of a sea of troubles, of misfortune's "waves," suggest a flood rushing in from outside but are intensified by the idea of an inner storm that swamps the *phrēn*.[33]

These connections underlie extended tragic imagery, such as this ode from Sophocles, which flings its range out to elemental disaster, but ends with the madness of mind:

> As when the undersea's darkness sweeps up and on
> with the bitter-blowing winds from Thrace,
> and rolls black sand up from the depths,
> and the shores are struck against, blown against hard;
> they groan and howl. . . . I see the sufferings
> of the Labdacid house fall on past sufferings.
> The race doesn't change. Some god crushes it to splinters:
> it finds no resolution. For now . . . another
> blood-filled blow strikes from the underworld gods:
> thoughtlessness of reason, Erinys of *phrenes*.

The immediate point here is the misfortune of Antigone's family, the Labdacids. But the fullest attention is given to the inner conditions in that family: their *phrenes*. The passage has always been hard to interpret. It seems consciously Homeric, perhaps also Aeschylean. Scholars have wondered what precisely the wind, sea, and dark sand were intended to convey. (Is Aristophanes' phrase "how you do disturb my sand" a mocking little echo?) The context is the central paradox of the family's "innocent guilt."

Scholiasts long ago connected them, and saw allusions to the darkening sea in short phrases describing passion (e.g., A. *Supp.* 785, *kelainochrōs de palletai mou kardia*), explaining, "The sea . . . blackens when it is disturbed." Jebb *ad Ant.* 20 suggests that in *kalchainō*, the idea of dark color "precedes" that of turbulence, while in *porphurō*, turbulence "precedes" color. "Precedes" is a belated heuristic device (cf. Chapter 2, nn. 86–92). What matters is the general connection (which Jebb illuminates) between turbulence and deepening color, and the specific connection between darkening turbulence of sea and of mind. Both verbs, in their range of usage, make these connections clear.

[32] *PV* 883–86 (for the violence of these images, cf. *Od.* 5.401–5, *Il.* 17.263–64). Cf. *Aj.* 206–7 (a storm of madness and misfortune), *Phil.* 1194 (a mind distraught with "stormy pain"). Waves of *atē*: Dawe 1968:95 n. 10. Too much drink is a storm, moderate drink is a calm safe passage: Slater 1976.

[33] Waves of disaster "swamp the *phrēn*" of Creusa's servant, *Ion* 927. Waves of misfortune and troubles: see *Pers.* 599–600; *Sept.* 758–61; *OT* 1527; and the *trikumia*, *PV* 1015; Pl. *Euthydemus* 293A. The "terrible wave" that "overwhelms me" comes from gods, *Tro.* 696. "Sea of troubles": *Hipp.* 822, *HF* 1087.

This comes from inside. The "undersea" is coming up, Erinys is in the *phrenes*. But it also comes from outside. Bitter winds assault the sea, gods "strike" the family. The Greek assumption that the stuff of the outside world is the stuff of the inner enables the image to speak of sea and mind at once.[34] Remembering "flux" imagery of passion does not reduce our understanding of Sophocles' words, but connects them to profound principles of Greek thought.

An untroubled mind is "calm" in language that belongs to the sea. "Peaceful thought" is "windless *galēnē* [sea-calm]." Plato, talking of pleasure and pain as "movement," freedom from them as peace (*hēsuchia*), pointed the way to the psychic *galēnē*, inner tranquillity, a central concept in Hellenistic philosophers who value the stillness of a soul "undisturbed" by passion. Passion muddies, ruffles. An untroubled mind is clear fluid at rest.[35]

BREATHS OF PASSION

Do winds cause flux? Does wind whip up the sea? Does breath of passion muddy and swell inner waves of emotion?[36] In a sense, all these are the same question for the fifth century. Tragic imagery of feeling as sea whipped up by gales, of inner calm as windless sea, is underpinned by contemporary ideas that liquid inside the body enters channels that also hold breath.

We start with medical writers and philosophers: with the Hippocratic assumption that breath or air is present in inner channels that hold liquid. Veins "receive" phlegm and air as well as blood. Some "structures" (*schēmata*) in the body are hollow, some are "close-textured, some loose-textured and fleshy, some spongy and porous," some "always full of fluid from

---

[34] In this rendering of *Ant.* 586–603, I ignore most textual difficulties and read *kopis*, not *konis*, 602. Cf. Ar. *V.* 696; Steiner 1984:255–56; Chapter 8, n. 61. Goheen (1951:61) speaks of a "fusion of thought," an interweaving of mindstorm and stormy misfortune. But "fusion" implies the two are originally separate (cf. Chapter 2, n. 93), whereas I am arguing that fifth-century imagination sees mind turbulence as part of the same thing as sea turbulence, since inner and outer are the same fabric (Chapter 2, n. 120) and gods send both.

[35] See *Ag.* 740; Pl. *Rep.* 583E–584A, and *Legg.* 791A, where Plato links *hēsuchia* and *galēnē* (the result of calming any inner turbulence) in the mind; *ataraxia* comes when *ho tēs psuchēs cheimōn* is put to rest, Epic. *Ep. Men.* 128 (see Long 1978:84, 87 nn. 15, 42; Burnyeat 1980b). In the earliest painting of Pentheus's *sparagmos*, one of the maenads is labelled Galene. Euphemism? Or embodiment of post-maenadic calm? See Henrichs 1978:132 n. 34. In later times, Galenos and Galene were proper names (cf. "Irene"). On *galēnos*, see Wilamowitz *ad HF* 698. With the mind's calm water, cf. the clear *phrēn* at *Hipp.* 1120 (with Barrett *ad loc.*): a *katharan phrena* unmuddied by religious doubt. Cf. *Alc.* 1067 (*tholoi kardian*: she upsets, disturbs my heart) and the use of *suncheō* to mean "I confuse, trouble" with an inner organ as object (e.g., *Il.* 9.612, *thumos*; 24.358, *noos*). It literally means "I pour together."

[36] See above, nn. 16, 31–35; Chapter 2, n. 65.

outside." The porous ones, like the spleen and lungs, "enlarge when fluid is added." When they "receive or drink up the fluid . . . the porous hollows are filled." According to this writer, pain happens when liquid and breath enter the same inner parts. Empedocles' image of respiration illustrates the idea that the same channels can hold liquid or breath. "When the fluid blood rushes away, the bubbling air rushes in. . . . When the blood leaps up, the air is breathed out again." Then follows the image of a girl playing with a brass *clepsudra* (a perforated pipette with a narrow neck):

> When she puts the pipe's mouth
> against her well-shaped hand
> and dips it in the flickering water's mass,
> no moisture enters. The air's bulk inside,
> falling upon the many close perforations,
> holds it back till she uncovers the full flow.
> Then the air goes; an equal mass of water enters in.[37]

Fifth-century intellectual interest in the internal passage of breath comes out in Aristophanes' mockery: "The gnat's *enteron* [gut] is narrow. Through it the *pnoē* [breath] goes violently—straight to the rump!" Later, Aristotle speaks of *pneuma*, "breath," that is "innate" in generative froth, in the *poroi* of smell and hearing. This, too, seems to be breath within inward liquid.[38]

From earliest lyric, Greek poetry assumes that wine goes into the lungs. Plutarch thinks that Euripides (who speaks, in a fragment, of wine crossing the lungs' channels) "saw that the lung has cavities and is pierced with *poroi* through which it sends moisture."[39] Philosophic, scientific, and poetic language assumes breath can be in or move in the same inner places as liquid. This is vital: it helps us understand how some words (*thumos* for example) suggest now liquid, now breath.[40] It also puts into wider perspective the poets' many images of emotion as liquid swelling, which interact with other images of emotion as rising wind or breath. The two-way, inward and outward movement is an important ingredient of Greek fantasy about innards and their relation with the world. We see it at work in explanations of vision (Chapter 3) and in the language of breathing. In-fluence, ex-pression: breath in the "mind" is instantly ambiguous. It goes out and in: a

---

[37] *Anc. Med.* 22 (Loeb 1:56–60), cf. *DMS* 10–12 (Loeb 2:160–64), Hp. *Breaths* 8.25–50 (Loeb 2:238–40). Emp. fr. 100, KRS 471, pp. 359–60.

[38] Ar. *Nub.* 161–62; Arist. *De gen. an.* 762A20, 744A2 (though *pneuma* here may not mean ordinary "breath" but a divine substance, constituent of the heavenly bodies, Nussbaum 1978:159–63).

[39] Alcaeus fr. 13.1, E. fr. 983N, Plu. *Mor.* 698–700 (who cites and discusses these and other poets, hoping to save the physiology of Pl. *Ti.*, e.g., 70C, 91A).

[40] See above, pp. 26 and 29–30.

simple physiological basis for all kinds of poetically and theologically rich ambiguity. Often it is impossible for a listener to know which way the breath of emotion is flowing, and therefore where its source is. When Homeric warriors "breathe *menos*," for example (as they often do), do they breathe it in or out?[41] Sometimes several warriors together "breathe *menea*" (plural of *menos*). Is each warrior breathing one *menos*, his own? Or are they all panting a series of *menea* (in which case, are some in and some out)? Angry poised fighters, "filled with *menos*": do they breathe it out, expressing what is in them, as the Chimaera "breathes out a terrible *menos* of fire"? Or do they breathe it in, as if it were the war-god himself, filling them with necessary fury from outside?[42] The Homeric image is gladly unclear.

Tragic poets work from that unclarity. These tiny points that exercise philologists might seem trivial, but they speak to an entire way of seeing: to the Homeric representation of human beings in relation with their own feelings and the outside world, a representation that tragedy makes its own. When Aeschylus speaks of a man "breathing Ares," we could take it as "breathing out a fighting rage," and imagine that the warrior's breath breathed *out* in battle "is" the war-god. Later in the same play, Cassandra sees the house breathing *phonon*, "bloodshed" (in some manuscripts *phobon*, "fear"), which is "blood-dripping." Aeschylus may be thinking with the Odyssean passage where Theoclymenus has a vision of walls and rafters sweating blood. Both diviners see blood on the walls, an omen of approaching slaughter in the house. Cassandra suggests that the walls breathe blood, a bubbled-out expression of the house's self-contained rage. Later in the trilogy, the Erinyes "breathe *menos* and every kind of fury."[43] All this looks like fury breathed *out*.

But in another play, "breaths of Ares" appear as if they came from the god *into* people, blasting the city, urging besiegers on. Someone is "*entheos* [possessed] with [or by] Ares." Given general Greek resonances of possession as an incoming divine breath, this suggests that Ares breathes *into* the warrior.[44]

---

[41] E.g., *Il.* 2.536; see Chapter 2, n. 56.

[42] Cf. *Il.* 22.312, "He was filled with *menos* in his *thumos*"; cf. Ar. *V.* 424, "filled with rage and *menos*." Chimaera: *Il.* 6.182.

[43] *Arē pneontōn meizon ē dikaiōs*, *Ag.* 375–76. Fraenkel objects, both (as others do) on grounds of sense, and for grammatical reasons. He reads *arē* and obelizes (as do West and Page), but *pneontōn* here does not seem particularly odd: poets do sometimes characterize people by the way they "breathe," e.g., Pi. *P.* 11.30, *Andr.* 189 (cf. Erinys "breathing fire" from her clothes, *IT* 288). *Haimatostagē*: *Ag.* 1309; above, n. 24; cf. *Od.* 20.534; and Clytemnestra's dream where something "breathes *koton* from sleep," *Cho.* 33. Erinyes: *Eum.* 840 (cf. *PV* 720 *potamos ekphusai menos*, where *ek* makes the direction unambiguous).

[44] *Sept.* 63, 115, which prepare for 497, *entheos d'Arei bakchai pros alkēn. Entheos, epipnoos, epipnoia, bacchaō*, see Padel 1983:13.

The crucial ambiguity of "breathing" allows a simultaneously external and internal causality. Why should a poet decide either that raging feelings start as outside in-fluence, or that they belong within and are ex-pressed out? Why should he, or indeed a real-life warrior, know? The physiology of breathing is there to think with. It enables a poet to write about feeling in two ways at once. When a man is fighting, the breath that is war is in him. It comes from Ares into him, and it is breathed out by his innards. It is at once his and not-his, inward and outward.

When Sophocles' Electra hurls a furious speech at her mother, the chorus says, "I see her breathing *menos*." The ambiguous direction of breath reflects the tragically reciprocated fury between mother and daughter. Does the chorus see Electra breathing *menos* in from her hated mother's presence? Or breathing it out on the hated object? Or both? Another oppressed chorus joins Aeschylus's Electra in a song of *thumos* against Clytemnestra. Their *thumos* is breath rising in front of the heart, a gale rising before a boat's prow, giving a pointillistic background of inner emotion long kept "below": kept politically below (like the chorus) and simultaneously battened under in the mind. What was "below" now rises "in front":

> In front of the prow of the heart
> a bitter *thumos* blows,
> an inraging hatred.[45]

Yet another chorus sees Antigone's passion as a wind:

> From the same winds still
> these blasts of soul hold her.

This is the same chorus that tells of "bitter-blowing winds from Thrace" pounding Antigone's family, leading to "Erinys of *phrenes*." The winds enact fate, and they act upon Antigone. They are also of and from her own soul.[46]

In another play, Ajax's recovery of sanity is a wind dying down:

> As the sharp south wind, after rushing on
> without bright lightning, dies,
> now Ajax, sane, has new suffering.

[45] S. *El.* 610; *Cho.* 390–92, where I follow Murray's text, not Page's, taking *kardias* dependent on *prōiras*, and *enkoton stugos* in apposition with *thumos*, as in Lloyd-Jones's translation: "Before my heart's prow blows a cutting wind of rage, my mind's rancorous hatred." Bitterness: Chapter 2, n. 45. Heart's "prow": cf. the suggestion adopted by West at A. *Supp.* 989, *ek prumnēs phrenos*, which Page rejects (inconsistently, since he invents an *ek* here, breaking 390 at *paroith'*). His conjecture makes *thumos* blow unambiguously *out* of the heart. This is too explicit. In Homer, *thumon apopneiōn* (*Il.* 4.524, 13.654) is "gasping out *life*."

[46] *Ant.* 929–30, cf. n. 34 above.

This image presents his angry madness as an external force, not a part of him. It helps to constellate round Ajax a sense that he and his emotions are irresistible, elemental, not to be judged by human measure. This sense of his madness fits Hippocratic explanations: "Apoplexy is caused by breaths. . . . If breaths rush through the whole body, the whole patient becomes *apoplēktos* ["struck out," delirious, mad]. . . . If the breaths go away, the disease ceases. If they stay, it stays." Like this Hippocratic master, tragedy generally presents madness as temporary, and often due to external windlike force.[47]

In such passages, the breath or wind, whether the poet imagines it coming from inside or from outside, is somehow responsible for the central tragic act. In the Aeschylean lines of *thumos* "blowing," the windlike choric anger is the emotional backdrop for the play's act of vengeance. The choral comment on Sophocles' Antigone gives an elemental register to her rebellion: winds drive her soul. A blast of madness thrusts Ajax to the act that starts his play. In each case, the ambiguity of breath and wind—inside or outside?—leaves the ultimate cause of the emotion, and so of the action, dark.

"Gusts" of passion are common in single images—a raging *pneuma* of madness carries off Io, "blasts of hostile winds" are breathed by an impious besieger of Thebes[48]—though they also play their part in the overall dynamics of each play. The most extensive example is the breath Agamemnon takes when he decides to sacrifice his daughter.

Aeschylus embeds this breath in a context of paralyzing wind and impious breath. This lyric structure of astonishing verbal violence prepares his audience for the oncoming trilogy. Agamemnon decides to kill his daughter, while

> breathing a wicked [breath? wind?] of *phrēn*,
> turning, unholy, impious. From that moment on,
> he learned how to think to dare everything.

This grammar is ambiguous. The adjectives "turning" and "wicked" qualify the object of "breathing," but what he breathed is not spelled out. Agamemnon breathed (something that was) turning. And wicked. We have to understand a noun like "wind" or "breath." Taken by themselves, these lines might imply that Agamemnon breathed in a wicked wind from outside. It "turned" his mind. In Homer, Agamemnon "turns the *phrenes*" of

---

[47] *Aj*. 257–59. Commentators dither in their efforts to explain "without lightning." Whatever its significance, it plays a part in the loss of light that hangs round Ajax through the play. Tragic madness is dark and temporary, see Padel 1981:109. Wind dying: Hp. *Breaths* 13 (Loeb 2:248).

[48] *PV* 883–84, *Ant*. 137.

Menelaus; even Zeus's *phrēn* can be "turned."[49] Being "turned" is traditionally something that happens to the *phrēn*. Agamemnon's has been turned away from its proper function of thinking properly, rightly. Which should our imagination supply: "wind" or "breath"? "Wind" would suggest that the cause of impiety lay outside. "Breath" might imply that the impiety was his own. Further, is the "turning" transitive, that is, does it have an object? Or intransitive, with no object? Transitive (as if from that Homeric *trepen phrenas*, "he turned someone's *phrenes*"), might suggest something from outside, "turning" Agamemnon's mind to crime. Intransitive might suggest a series of "turning," that is, "alternating," "changing" breaths.

Aeschylus simply says that what is breathed is "of the *phrēn*." Where it comes from is crucial to the play's theology. On it depends Agamemnon's guilt for his daughter's death, and the play's vision of the ensuing family murders. Does what is breathed come from the *phrēn* itself? Does "of the *phrēn*" mean "made there"? Or does it mean that evil entered the *phrēn* from outside, that *phrēn* was simply the place where evil was breathed? We do not hear the direction of that breath before or after the "turning." It may be in or out, just as "turning" may be transitive or intransitive.

So the lines presenting Agamemnon's choice also present choice to their listeners. What should they decide to have heard? That an evil wind came into Agamemnon, influencing him to make an impious choice? Or that the decisively impious impulse came from within his *phrēn*? The evidence has come before them, but they cannot know how to choose. Through Aeschylus's phrasing and timing, the ambiguity of breathing becomes an ambiguity of interpreting and gathers a vital ethical force. Agamemnon's will and breath are involved as deeply as, and together with, breaths or winds of the outside world. Agamemnon brings himself to implement a decision whose source is partly outside him.[50] Breath within responded, somewhere, to breath from outside.

Euripides suggests a similar idea in smaller-scale phrases. When his chorus praises Electra for a pious change in attitude, it says, "Your thought

[49] *Ag.* 219–21; cf. *Il.* 6.61, 10.45. Fraenkel (*ad loc.*) compares *Cho.* 390, *Ant.* 929, and *Phoen.* 454. He remarks that stormy blasts represent the irrational force of emotion coming from outside, and says the wind image is more explicit at *Sept.* 705–8, *daimōn / lēmatos an tropaiai chroniai metal- / laktos isōs an elthoi thelemōteröi / pneumati*, which casts responsibility for shifting moods onto *daimōn* and its breath. But the ambiguity of *tropaian* (*Ag.* 219) is far greater than that of *tropaiai* (*Sept.* 706), and the theology is correspondingly more complex. The connected passage at 187, whose imagery (Fraenkel says) "belongs to the same sphere," shows Aeschylus consistently ambiguous about the source and direction of the wind. "The direction of the will that is resolved upon action" (Becker 1937:160) is intricately and confusingly dependent on the direction of the wind that shapes its resolve.

[50] Cf. Stinton 1990:112. *Tolmē* in *to pantotolmon*, *Ag.* 221, speaks to the practical outrage: that Agamemnon's decision was translated into action.

(*phronēma*) has veered back again (*palin metestathē*) to the breeze." Peleus thinks Menelaus should have ignored Helen's departure: "But not that way did you set your thought to the wind (*son phronēm' epourisas*)." Menelaus was helmsman of his thought, but there were real winds outside him.[51] Gale and breath images in this Athenian, sea-turned culture economically imply that responsibility belongs both outside, to *daimōn* or its weather, and to the human mind. We turn our thought to the wind.

For Agamemnon, context fortifies this interaction of wind and breath. These lines of his breathing, of his fatal decision, are the climax of a song that begins with external winds beaching the ships, "breathing against," "causing no sailing." The poet introduces Agamemnon as "breathing with sudden-hitting winds."[52] Our response here must be uncertain. Are these that he breathes the same, exterior, winds? Are they metaphorically external winds of fortune? Or are they beginning to be his own breath from within? Aeschylus mentions again the real winds, blasting the ships. But the chorus calls them "breaths":

> Breaths coming from Strymon
> creating cruel leisure, starvation,
> distracting the men,
> harming boats at their anchor,
> not sparing ships and cables,
> adding and doubling the time: they rubbed away
> in delay the bloom of the Greeks.[53]

These "breaths" appear in the song's fourth strophe (a verse whose structure and rhythm is precisely mirrored in the next stanza, the antistrophe). In the following strophe, at precisely the same point in the structure, comes Agamemnon's decisive breathing. So the point in the pattern where we hear compound adjectives describing winds and their effect on the boats corresponds to the point where compound adjectives describe that impious breath and its effect on Agamemnon, who as the fleet's commander is the person most pressured by those winds.[54]

[51] E. *El.* 1202, *Andr.* 610.

[52] *Ag.* 147, 187.

[53] *Ag.* 192–98, a famously ambiguous passage. Borthwick (1976) takes *anthos* as *aōtos* and *triböi katexainon* to mean "wore away the nap," reviving Housman's derivation of *alai* not from *alasthai* but from *alein*, "winds that wear men away." Borthwick admits that *alai* stays uncertain in meaning. It is normally thought to belong to words of anguish and physical or mental distraction, and I think this connection works better in the context.

[54] With the fourth strophe, *kakoscholoi, nēstides, dusormoi / brotōn alai*, cf. the fifth, *phrenos pneōn dussebē tropaian / anagnon anieron*. Dawe (1966) transposes the "hymn to Zeus" (to make Zeus, not Artemis, the ultimate cause of events, pp. 15–16). He claims the references to breathing are "natural" in the new context he gives them (p. 9). Removing them from

By the time he shows Agamemnon taking his "wicked" breath, Aeschylus has activated in his listeners' imaginations an intricate set of associations to winds and breaths. These winds are breathing, the poet implies, not only onto the ships, but maybe into Agamemnon, "turning" his mind into a wicked course. He does not say so explicitly. By saying the breath Agamemnon breathed was "of his *phrēn*," Aeschylus hands us in a single phrase the ambivalence of tragic causality. The chorus does not say Iphigeneia's death was only Agamemnon's fault. But it does not say it was not his fault, either. Ambivalence about the direction of breathed emotion becomes ambivalence over cause, both of the ensuing trilogy and of the Trojan War. The song is a tapestry of external and internal causes for human evil. Its center and climax is Agamemnon's breath. This will resonate in the spectators' imagination as they respond to Agamemnon's son, when he faces in the next play, as his father was reported to face, the decision to do what he "should not." To kill his kin.[55]

Despite their framework of ambiguity and paradox, tragedians reflect the medical writers' equilibrium. Tragic breathing is not symmetrically ambiguous between two possible directions, out and in. The breath-source of human violence seems to be more often outside, like diseases that come "from the *pneuma* that we breathe to live."[56] In the fifth century, the human interior is the recipient, more often than the origin, of violence. Gods drive mad violence into us by breathing. "Breaths coming from Strymon" are essential to tragic nosology of evil, as "breath" is central to the idea of daemonic possession.[57]

The idea of some distracting breath or wind in the mind had a long postclassical afterlife. In *The Anatomy of Melancholy*, for instance, that medical treatise which reaches out, like the Hippocratics, to philosophy, Burton assumes in 1621 that wind and air have a harmful effect on the mind: "The devil many times takes his opportunity of such storms, and when the humours by the air be stirred, he goes in with them, exagitates our spirits, and vexeth our souls; as the sea waves, so are the spirits and humours in our bodies tossed with tempestuous winds and storms."[58] Greek physiol-

---

pnoai apo Strumonos molousai, he destroys the interaction of internal with external breath and motivation and does not examine his own idea of "natural."

[55] Orestes' motivation is a mixture: *Cho.* 271–97 (divine compulsion), 299–301 (human reasons), 899 (anguish), 900–903 (must respect divine will), 910 (anyway, Fate is doing the murder), 923 (it is Clytemnestra's own fault), 927 (if he does not kill her, he cannot escape his father's "hounds"). But in spite of all this, it is still a deed he "should not" do. His last words before the murder are, "You killed whom you should not; now also suffer what you should not," 930.

[56] *Nat. hom.* 9 (Loeb 4:24).

[57] See Padel 1983:14.

[58] Burton, *Anatomy of Melancholy* 1.2.5.

ogy releases into European imagination complex ethical, medical, and dae-monological explanations of events within the mind.

For the Greek tragedians themselves, breath in the mind interacts with other images in which the mind contains wind or air. Emotion "flies" in the mind. In the *Bacchae*, Pentheus, like his mother, falls under Dionysus's maddening influence. He resisted Dionysus in spite of evidence that this was insanely risky. Before he succumbs, the stranger tells him,

> Now you are flying, and though you are sane
> you are not thinking sanely.

Later, when Agave under Dionysus's influence sees Pentheus's severed head as that of a lion, her father asks,

> Is the flying element (*to ptoēthen*)
> still in your soul?

Pentheus's resistance is unsafe, a kind of madness. His mad attitude, Agave's bacchic madness: both are a "flying" in the mind. Elsewhere, in an ambiguous, textually corrupt passage, Aeschylus seems to suggest that a hidden feeling, perhaps daemonic, is flying in the *phrēn*:

> Why should I hide
> a divine thing,
> a thing of my *phrēn*, which flies . . .?

In another context, he speaks of fear that "flies in front of the heart."[59]

"Flying things" in the mind shade into an iconography of emotion as flying daemon or winged figure. Greek easily endows personifications with wings (Chapters 6, 7), especially anything that enters, affects, or comes from the mind. Thought is windlike: in Homer, gods move "swift as thought," Phaeacian ships are "swift as a winged thing or as thought." In the *Antigone*, *phronēma*, "thought," is "windlike."[60] Prophecies, laments, curses, dreams, songs, and words are winged. Windlike, they fly and hover in the air. Plato plays on this, representing the mind as an aviary. To recap-

[59] *Ba.* 332, 1268; *Cho.* 388–89. Here (see above, n. 45, for the lines that follow) Murray's reading *theion* is metrically and grammatically suspect. Hermann proposed *hoion*, which Page adopts. Murray preserved but obelized *theion*, suggesting *phreni theion empas*, but his parallels do not carry much weight. *Theion* is overexplicit, probably a gloss. *Hoion* also looks like a gloss and is weak, though it heals the meter and helps one relate *ti keuthō* to *potatai*. My point is *potatai*. Cf. "fear flying," *Ag.* 976–77 (*potatai* again), with the tragic parody of Ar. *Nub.* 319, "My soul fluttered when I heard their voice." Cf. Ate above men's heads, winged per-sonifications: Chapter 6, n. 64; Chapter 8.

[60] Swift, windlike, winged thought: *Il.* 15.80–83, *h. Apoll.* 186 (see Allen and Sikes, *ad h. Herm.* 43), *Od.* 7.36, *Ant.* 354: an ode connected closely to the first stasimon of *Cho.* (see Stinton 1990:389); cf. *anemoenta koton, hostis ouch hupopteros phrontisin, Cho.* 591–92, 602–3.

ture some piece of knowledge, you put in your hand, but the birds, winged living units of knowledge, flutter chaotically within. You may catch the wrong one, "a ringdove instead of a pigeon."[61] The mind's contents and products are winged things, flying either in air outside or in spaces you yourself contain. The same things are "windlike": emotion is wind, breath, or what flies in it.

The mind itself "flies." When people are mad, very afraid, drunk, angry, youthfully reckless, or much in love, their soul, *thumos* or *nous*, "flies."[62] The soul returns at death to the air, the element of which it is made, and flies down "winged" to Hades.[63] Air, breath, wind are the soul's element. Of course it flies.

In much of this imagery, the external "in-spiring" is destructive, the "flying" unwelcome. But sometimes "breaths" nourish the mind. In some theories, air brings in energy, life, intelligence. Primitive people, according to one argument, "in contact with the air all round them, nourished by the ceaseless inflow of *pneuma*, sucked in moist air as infants suck in food." And in Aeschylus, Apollo breathes *charis*, "grace," into Cassandra.[64] Wind impregnates mares in the meadow. It also feeds plants. Nourishment and pregnancy caused by wind: these ideas merge with wind imagery, erotic imagery, food and drink imagery, in Greek understanding of daemonic possession.[65] Breath nourishes mind and soul. When Ajax takes leave of his little son (and only he knows this goodbye is forever), he tells him:

[61] With *epea pteroenta* (*Il.* 1.201, etc.), cf. *humnos* (Pi. *I.* 5.63), *ptēnoi muthoi* (*Or.* 1176), *oneiroi* (*IT* 571), *elpides* (E. fr. 271), *pteruges goōn* (S. *El.* 241–42). Prophecies *peripotatai* over Delphi: *OT* 482. Aviary: Pl. *Theaet.* 197D–199C.

[62] Madness: Thgn. 1053 (*ton . . . mainomenon petetai thumos te noos te*). Fear: *Ant.* 1306 (*aneptan* when Creon hears of his dying wife's curse), E. *Supp.* 89 (*phobos m'anapteroi*). Drink: *Cyc.* 497, happy is he who comes to the *kōmos*, *ekpetastheis* "on beloved streams" of wine. Eros: Anacreon, *PMG* 33 (24B, 52D), (*anapetomai pros Olumpon . . . dia ton Erōt'*). Joy: *Aj.* 693 (*aneptoman*), cf. "with hopes," *OT* 487. Rage, cf. E. *El.* 1255: Athene will restrain the Furies *eptoēmenas . . . drakousin*, "raging [sc. against Orestes] with snakes," or (Denniston, following Murray) "hot with flickering serpents" (Denniston says snakes "add to the fury"), or just "fluttering with snakes." Cf. *Il.* 3.108, where *phrenes* of armed men (i.e., of the young) *aiei . . . ēerethontai*: they wave in the air, turn with every wind, are reckless and unsteady compared to the minds of the old.

[63] See Chapter 3, n. 4; Chapter 4, n. 4. *Ptamenē Aidosde bebēkei*: *Il.* 22.362; cf. Chapter 2, n. 74.

[64] Dio Chrysostom 12.30, *Ag.* 1206, cf. A. fr. 178aR (sleep breathes *dia pleumonōn*), *DMS* 19 (Loeb 2:178) *tēnde phronēsin ho aer parerchetai*.

[65] Mares impregnated by Boreas: *Il.* 20.222 (cf. 16.150, foals born to Zephyrus by a harpy "as she grazed in the meadow"), cf. Arist. *HA* 572A13, V. *Georg.* 3.275 where mares are impregnated by wind. Plants nourished on wind: Pliny *NH* 18.34, *Zephurum dicit in plantas nutricium exercere*; Lucian *Bis accusatus* 1, *tous anemous phutourgountas*; cf. Cat. 62.39, 41: *ut flos in saeptis secretus nascitur hortis / . . . quem mulcent aurae, firmat sol, educat imber. Exanemousthai* is "to be blown up [i.e., made pregnant] by wind." Cf. the infertile *anemaion*, "wind-egg," Pl. *Theaet.* 161A, and erotic imagery of possession, Padel 1983:14.

> Feed on light breaths,
> nursing your young soul.

Tragedy, like medicine, knows that breath, wind, or flying things will and must come in.[66] All we can do—for ourselves, our children, human beings everywhere—is hope that these breaths will be gentle, light, nourishing.

But tragedy, like medicine, is needed because something within goes wrong. Both exist to explore the causalities and consequences of things going wrong inside. Incoming breaths of which they speak are more likely than not to do harm.

[66] See *Aj.* 558–59; Chapter 3, nn. 8, 13, 15.

Chapter 5

INNER WORLD, UNDERWORLD, AND GENDERED IMAGES OF "MIND"

"Mind," Earth, Womb, Hades

The black-faced Madonna, in the shower of wheat, among the animals, was no sorrowful Mother of God, but a subterranean deity, black with the shadows of the bowels of the earth.

—C. Levi, *Christ Stopped at Eboli*

MANY ASPECTS of this material (Chapters 3 and 4) suggest that Greek understanding of innards is profoundly patterned by Greek perceptions of, and constructions of, gender. Breath enters and fills *splanchna*. Wind makes mares pregnant, swells plants, and fills innards with emotion or disease. Innards are black like the underworld. Power-charged dark liquids flow within them. There seems to be a homologous relationship between underworld and innards at work in Greek mentality, fuelling fantasy about both. Hades' unseeable rivers are at one end of the spectrum in this fantasy, menstruation—and any other unmentionable inner "flow" controlling Greek male perceptions of bodies, especially women's bodies, in medicine, myth, and cult—at the other.[1] In between is the flux of feeling into, within, and out of *splanchna*.

Inward flux and darkness are characteristic of innards, of Hades, and of women's inwardness. Perceptions of both Hades and fluid female innards are background to the Greek images of feeling's flow. The dominant fifth-century imagery of innards, I suggest, is female. The mind is centrally like—but not only like—the womb.

Philology suggests three connections between mind, underworld, and womb. One meaning of *splanchna* is "reproductive organs," occasionally men's, more often women's. By itself, *splanchna* can mean "womb."[2] Hades can also be spelled "Haides" or "Aides," and the Greeks related it to *a-idein* ("to not-see"), *a-idēs* ("unseen"). By 500 B.C., Heraclitus is making significant play with the chime between *aidēs* and *Aidōs*, as well as *aidoia*, the

[1] See King 1983.

[2] *Splanchnon* of womb: *Sept.* 1031; Pi. *O.* 6.43, cf. Pi. *N.* 1.35; *IG* 14.1977. Male "loins": *Ant.* 1066.

standard word for "genitals."[3] Like *splanchna*, *aidoia* can mean either male
or female genitals. The word is actually from *aideomai*, "I feel shame [*aidōs*]." Female *aidoia* more closely resemble Hades as being unseen, *aidēs*. A
related adjective, *aidēlos*, can be active—"making unseen, destructive"
(used in the *Iliad* of warring gods and fire)—or passive: "unseen" (used by
Sophocles of Hades). In male Greek imagination, a woman's interior is
aidēlos in both meanings: it is both unseen and potentially destructive. It
makes what enters it "unseen." Fifth-century Athenian prostitutes often
had names like "Lioness," "Panther."[4] Female *aidoia*, therefore, might be
called *aidēla* in both senses.

The words *keuthos* and *muchos* are used of the inmost quarters, the wom-
en's quarters of the house. *Muchos* can be used of a prophet's "cave" or a
body's "cavity." But these words can also be used for Hades.[5] The "woman's part" of the house, like her own *aidoia*, is unseen, a "recess" (core sense
of *muchos*). So is Hades: it is the potent recess of that dark mother, Earth.
In Greek culture, as others, women are identified with the interior. The
culture generally confined and guarded its women. The house was a woman's place. Middle-class women spent most of their time indoors. This was
particularly true of fifth-century Athens. "House" is also, from early times,
an apt word for Hades. In Homer, Hades appears mainly in the phrase "the
[house of] Hades."[6] Hades, which is a *muchos* ("recess," or "women's quarters"), suggests not only parts of the house that hold women, but also recesses contained within them.

"Dark Earth" "covers" the dead and nurtures plants. She, too, is
"Mother." Funerary speeches and epitaphs speak of the dead "returning"
to earth, to the dark from which they came, repaying their "debt" to Earth.
A warrior "pays Earth his nurture-charge by dying." Plato parodies common Athenian rhetorical images of earth as mother in his *Menexenus*, and
in general fifth-century imagery of women's bodies, field and "furrow" play
an important role. The "dark from which you came" is the dark of the
earth, and of the womb. Polyneices was unjustly minded from birth, "flee-
ing darkness from his mother," that is, when he left his mother's womb.[7]

---

[3] *Aides*, *a-idein*: see Lloyd-Jones 1965:242 (esp. nn. 2–4), Jucquois and Devlamminck
1977:20; cf. Burkert 1985:426 n. 13; Heraclitus fr. 15DK; C. Kahn 1979:265.

[4] *Il.* 5.897, 880, 2.455; *Aj.* 608. Prostitutes: see Taillardat 1965:107. Potentially destructive female interior: see Padel 1983:3–8.

[5] *Muchos* as "women's quarters" (*Cho.* 447, *Trach.* 686): Gould 1980:48 n. 73. Used of
Hades: *PV* 433; cf. Chapter 3, n. 85. Cf. *keuthos nekuōn*, *Ant.* 818: *keuthos* is also used with
oikōn, *Alc.* 872. Cf. Hades as *keuthmōn*: *Tartarou*, *nekrōn*, *gaiēs*, *PV* 222, *Hec.* 1, *Theog.* 158.

[6] Women identified with interior and house: see Gould 1980:47–48 (with nn. 72, 74);
Padel 1983:8, 14–15; see also Bachelard 1969:44. For arguments, evidence, and qualifica-
tions over the degree to which Athenians enclosed women: see Schaps 1979:198; Just
1989:111–25. "House of Hades," e.g., *Il.* 3.322, 22.52: see Sourvinou-Inwood 1981; cf.
house of Night, above, Chapter 3, n. 78.

[7] *Sept.* 477–79, see Lattimore 1962:101. Return "to darkness whence they came": E. *Supp.*

It is a cliché in feminist thought today, but it is an important factor in Greek language of mind nonetheless, that (in the male perceptions that shape Greek literature) the place from which one came, to which one must return, is desirable but also a source of fear. It is a covering, a repository of the dead. Earth, womb of world violence, is fertile with fearful as well as beneficial forces. Night, too, gives daemonic vitalities a dark mothering. Hesiod's Night is an archetypal lonely fertile blackness. "She did not lie with anyone," but bears (among others) Fate, Death, Sleep, Dreams, Deception, and Conflict who becomes mother to Ate, that disastrous self-damaging of mind. Hesiod's Earth is mother to (among others) Erinyes, Cyclopes, and Giants. She makes within herself "the element of grey flint," which forms a sickle "with jagged teeth." This tool will castrate Heaven (that is, male Ouranos), whom Earth herself bore, who then had sex with her, and whom she decides to emasculate. "Dark Earth" is from early times the "mother of all creatures." The archetypal dangerous mother.[8]

Earth and Night both have central roles in early prophetic cults. Dark innards supposedly have prophetic powers like those of Earth and Night. Women supposedly practiced magico-medical root-cutting at night (see Chapter 3), like Medea in Sophocles and in a famous Hellenistic poem, whose language is layered with images of hollow darkness and primevally destructive sexuality:

> Medea took from a hollow box the drug
> men call Promethean. . . . It sprang up first
> when the eagle dropped bloody *ichōr* to earth
> from tortured Prometheus. . . . In the ground
> its root was like new-cut flesh.
> Medea collected its juice, dark as mountain beech. . . .
> Seven times she called on Brimo from the underworld,
> queen of the dead, who travels at night, black-clothed. . . .
> Dark earth groaned and shook below as the root was cut.
> Prometheus cried in agony. Medea took this drug,
> tucking it in the scented strap under her breasts.[9]

Women are credited with power over and secret knowledge of what is within and dark. Background ideas—Earth prophecy, the goddess

---

532–34; Lattimore 1962:31–34, 49 (n. 199); Burkert 1972:4 (with n. 55). Pl. *Menex.* 238A (ending outrageously, *ou gar gē gunaika memimetai kuēsei kai gennēsei, alla gunē gēn*). Dark womb: *Sept.* 664. DuBois (1988:39–85) collects images of women's bodies as earth or furrow.

[8] Night as mother: *Theog.* 211–30, see West *ad loc.*, *Eum.* 321–22, and Orphic theogonies (see West 1983:70–71, 116). Earth as mother to Erinyes, Cyclopes, Ouranos: *Theog.* 185, 137, 127; producing flint for the sickle: 161 (cf. 180). Mother of all: e.g., Alcman fr. 58.3D (*PMG* 89, p. 62), *Cho.* 585; cf. Vernant and Vidal-Naquet 1981:141–42.

[9] Ap. Rh. 3.838–67. Oracles of Night and Earth, root-cutting: see above, pp. 69–71.

Night—interact with fantasy about women's unknowable and alien *splanchna*, which produce potent knowing forces from an unseen place.

Greek notions of femaleness interact with the basic Greek principle that the outer world, the *kosmos*, is made of the same fabric and structure as the inner.[10] In male perceptions, women's inwardness merges the underworld, unseen recess of the world outside human beings, with the inner world, unseen recess within. Greek ideas of femaleness link the flux, darkness, magico-prophetic powers, and (we shall see) fertility of the innards with those of the underworld, earth, and night.

INNER IMPURITIES AND EMISSIONS: "GOOD" TURNED "BAD"

> But to the girdle do the gods inherit, beneath is all the Fiend's; there's hell, there's darkness, there is the sulpherous pit.
> —*King Lear* 4.6

Associations with the human interior, paradigmatically but not only the female interior, resonate in Greek attitudes toward cults associated with the underworld. What comes out of women is impure. Womb's blood pollutes men. Words for intestines and bowels, *entera*, *koilia*, can also be used for "womb." *Koilia* can also mean "excrement." The womb is easily aligned with excremental language. It emits what is dirty and polluting.[11] The dark human interior contains and sends forth polluting waste substances, but also necessary and welcome new life. This precisely resembles dark earth and underworld. Earth brings forth new growth. But her "womb," like Night's dark "house," also "breeds" nightmare. Terrifying, impure things: Erinyes, Madness, Conflict, Giants.

A vague and many-faceted impurity characterizes chthonic gods. Hecate's persona, for example, resonates with dirt, human waste, waste food, pollution. Each month (emblematic, maybe, of women's monthly "waste")

[10] See Reinhardt 1926:27–33 (stressing the debt here of later writers like Galen or Poseidonius to Empedocles and the atomists); Kranz 1938; Lloyd 1966:233–40, 265–70 ("vitalist" cosmological theories and their influence, cf. Chapter 2, n. 120), 252–54 (analogies between body and universe, Chapter 3, n. 4). On "light and dark" in the cosmos and human beings: Bultmann 1948:11–23, 29–35; Classen 1965:105–6, 114–15.

[11] See Padel 1983:5–7. *Entera* distinguished from *splanchna*: e.g., Hdt. 2.40; used for "guts": e.g., *Il.* 13.507, Ar. *Eq.* 1184; "womb": Archil. 142(B); "belly": Lucian *Lexiphanes* 6. *Koilia* (from *koilos*, "hollow") can mean any bodily cavity, especially "thorax-plus-abdomen" or "intestines." In Hippocratic works, singular and plural can both mean "excrement," e.g., *AWP* 9, 10 (Loeb 1:94, 98). Attitudes toward defecation: see Parker 1983:293; Owens 1983; *RE* s.v. excrementum. For men at least, it was probably standard practice to defecate in the streets. Laws controlled it in the agora, and perhaps on routes of religious processions. Egyptians saw feces before defecation as an inner mass of decaying, disease-causing material: Majno 1975:129. As a bodily activity, defecation would defile a Greek shrine anyway, but it is particularly polluting, see Ar. *V.* 394, *Ran.* 366; Parker 1983:162.

food is left for her at the crossroads, apotropaically, to keep her away. Central to Greek ideas of emissions from the human interior and from earth is the change in nondirty things like blood or food when they leave the body or table and come in contact with earth. What was nourishing, "good," part of the living body, is defiled and defiling once it falls on ground, is left at crossroads, has been through the body and emerges as dirt.[12] A person who wants to harm another uses Hecate's pollutedness, summoning her to pollute that other person as they curse. Within the threat of Aeschylus's Erinyes to pollute the land and people of Athens is the polluting charge of spilled blood.[13] "Dark" divinities of earth and night are polluted and polluting. They are the earth's emission, waste on the ground.

The opening of *Eumenides*, a play that challenges how the Athenian spectators will "see" Erinyes, thrusts them into this territory of pollutedness. The priestess prepares the audience to see Erinyes as disgusting, worse than food-snatching Harpies:

> An unthinkable herd of women . . . no,
> no women, Gorgons. Yet, not Gorgons either. . . .
> Once I saw female creatures pictured
> carrying off the feast of Phineus:
> but these are wingless, black,
> foul in every detail. They snort
> with revolting breath—keep out of range!—
> and ooze repellant liquid from their eyes.
> Their clothes should be nowhere near
> gods' statues or human homes.

This is the audience's introduction to them. Apollo further says that they belong to killing-grounds, to places where human bodies are mutilated: places of execution, gouged eyes, slit throats, where men are impaled through the spine. "Do you hear," he asks,

> what sort of feast you love
> which gods hate? Every aspect
> of your figures proves it:
> such creatures ought to live
> with a blood-licking lion,
> not rub your pollution off
> on this oracle.[14]

---

[12] Defilement of fallen food: *Od.* 22.20–21; Vernant 1980:119–22; Parker 1983:307, 393, 107, 30 n. 65, and 295 n. 66, on the Pythagorean rule not to pick up fallen scraps. They "belong to *heröes.*"

[13] See Parker 1983:223–24 with nn. 84–86; *Eum.* 782–85; and pp. 174 and 181–84 below.

[14] *Eum.* 46–56, 190–95.

But earth is also mother of growth. *Koilia* bring forth new human beings as well as waste and defiling liquid. This play pivots on the Erinyes' doubleness, repulsive destructiveness inseparable from fructifying force. By the play's end, the audience sees them in their fertile role. Inhabiting "primal hiding-places of earth," the Erinyes will turn their presence into a force for prosperity. They have power to give blessings "from earth, from sea's wetness, from the sky," to foster good growth in earth, animals, and people.[15] That is why Athene wants them here. She cares like a gardener, "like a grower of plants," about Athens's growth. The Erinyes have power to wither, to make land and human beings barren. Their anger can be poured out as drops that "wither human seed." They bloodily grind human *splanchna*. But they also have power "to save human seed," to quicken growth in earth and in human bodies, to protect the community. "From these terrifying faces great benefit" will come to those who inhabit land that honors them, land under which they will live.[16]

Like Erinyes, polluting Hecate has power to bless and increase human work. In Hesiod, she benefits kings, warriors, horsemen, athletes, sailors, fishermen. She has power and privilege "in earth, sky, and sea." With Hermes, she increases farmers' stock. She also takes it away. She diminishes as "easily" as she gives. She has *dunamis*, "power," to increase and decrease, bring wealth and remove it. Like other divinities, chthonic gods have power to help in that sphere in which they harm, and vice versa.[17]

The culture's associations to excretions of the human body and human mind are entangled with Greek attitudes toward the contents and emissaries of Hades. Thoughts, feelings, and words, like foul-oozing Erinyes or black-winged Madness, are pictured as daemonic flying figures and, like human emissions, as wind or liquid.[18] Feelings and words can have transformative, potentially polluting force. Curses—connected with Hecate, with chthonic impurity—have damaging potency like Hades' emissaries. But words also have the force of new life, like the living, rather than the waste, products of the womb. Words have a chthonic doubleness. This is at its most intense in tragedy, that structure of staged words empowered to change, enlighten, damage. Thoughts, feelings, and words, within and emergent from one person's interior, wreak fruitful *and* destructive change among other people.

The scatology of comedy, which followed and parodied tragedy, translates tragedy's concern with the interior and what comes out of it into concrete bodily terms about which extant tragedy is mostly silent. The ex-

---

[15] *Eum.* 1036, 1030–31, 906–10.

[16] *Eum.* 911–12, 333, 787, 803, 859, 909, 991.

[17] *Theog.* 430–43, 427, 442–47, 487, 443, 420. Gods' power to help in areas where they harm, and vice versa: see Chapter 8, n. 11.

[18] See Chapter 4, nn. 60–61.

ception is the nurse's speech in the central scene of the *Oresteia*. The nurse emerges in despair. She has heard of Orestes' death, and she remembers his babyhood:

> You must nourish a baby like an animal.
> It cannot think. That's the way of its *phrēn*.
> A baby still in nappies cannot say
> if it's hungry, thirsty, or needs a pee.
> Infants' young innards [*nēdus*, "bowels," also used for "womb"]
> are independent. I guessed ahead of time
> but often I was wrong. Then, nurse and washerwoman,
> I had to wash the nappies.

Words and excreta are parallel. The nurse washed away waste. She who fed Orestes now thinks of him dead and believes her trouble went, precisely, to waste. Her role now in the plot, though she does not know it, is to strip Orestes' enemy, Aegisthus, of protection and prepare him to be killed. She has been sent to carry a message to him. The chorus changes this message: she must tell Aegisthus to come *without* his bodyguard. So she who combined both roles, nurturer and washer-away of waste, continues them unwittingly in her changed message. She nurtures Orestes' plan, and prepares to get rid of Aegisthus, the pollutor and waste product of the house.[19]

She does this by carrying and changing words, cleaning up, as it were, the message emitted by the house. A child can neither speak nor regulate what comes from it. Children learn speech as they learn to control what comes out of their bodies. One emission resonates with associations to the other. Comedy's many jokes about what comes uncontrollably out of people at moments of terror articulate the body-resonances within tragedy's occupation with uncontrollable emotion, with words that come out of people at moments of passion: coming out helplessly—"independent," in the nurse's word—sometimes for good, but often for harm.[20]

Much psychoanalytic theory has a bearing on this symbolism, of course. Freud connects Prometheus's creative theft of fire with urination; Bion pictures thinking as excreting, as evacuation.[21] I suspect that Greek associations of thinking and feeling to what comes into and out of innards consciously or unconsciously influenced these theories, through Freud's susceptibility to Greek language as well as Greek ideas. A thought central to psychoanalysis is that we (the universal "we" of psychoanalysis) have an innate tendency to understand things that are not-self by comparing them to basic organs and processes that are self, and so to assimilate the outer

---

[19] See *Ag.* 1669, *Cho.* 944, 990, 753–60.
[20] See Henderson 1975:187–94.
[21] Freud [1931] 1932; Bion 1962:31, 57, 84; Wollheim 1974:42–43.

world into the familiar world of one's own body.[22] Children think of new powers they acquire, like language, like consciousness of their own thought-processes, partly in terms of control they simultaneously acquire over what comes into and out of their bodies. The "independent" power of bodily and verbal emissions is one factor at work among many in this vital scene when the Trophos ("Nurturer"), remembering Orestes' dirty nappies, mourns a fictive death, constructed by words that have come from Orestes himself.

The Mainly Female "Mind"

What sex is a heart (the word is feminine in Greek)?
—M. Detienne, *Dionysus at Large*

In all this, the model of "mind" is something basically enterable, a container, like female innards in contemporary perceptions. Innards are susceptible to the external. The outside world divinely and materially inscribes, invades, and interferes with them. One concrete image for the relation between a possessing god and the mind is erotic penetration of female by male.[23]

Innards also act, speak, know (Chapter 3), and are somehow potent themselves. Their relation with the outside world is twofold. Impinged on from without, they also express themselves outwards. Sometimes this is a breeding, sometimes an overspill: something has come in from outside and caused swelling, growth. But sometimes the powers seem to come from within.

The vessel image of the mind predominates in fifth-century tragedy, just as fifth- and fourth-century science, in balancing external and internal causality, allows the external more weight. Tragic innards are penetrable. They flow with liquid. Their movement is reactive, rarely unambiguously autonomous. In passion or in madness they move, they wander out of place, as the womb was thought to do in "hysteria." In relation to the daemonic world, they are invaded, hurt.[24] All this seems to fit a female model of mind.

So, on the face of it, would "mind's" creativity. But Greek thought was divided about the creativity of female innards themselves, and this confuses our understanding of Greek attitudes to the creativity of a mind conveyed mainly through female images.

Many Greeks denied that the womb had power to engender. In the *Oresteia*, at the climax of the argument about Orestes' relation to his par-

---

[22] See Milner 1952:187–91; cf. Chapter 3, nn. 5–6.
[23] See Padel 1983:11–15.
[24] Cf. Padel 1983:14. Womb in hysteria: B. Simon 1978:251–60.

ents, the male god Apollo, arguing against female chthonic deities, protecting the male child against his mother's avengers, claims that the male is the one who engenders (*tiktei*). The male is "he who leaps," *ho thrōiskōn*. Aeschylus is the only author to use the verb *thrōiskō* transitively.[25] Normally it means "I leap, spring up," like the related verb *thornumai*. There may be resonances here of *thoros*, "semen," and a scholiast explains *ho thrōiskōn* by *ho spermainōn*, "the sower of seed." But there must be in the word some of its normal "leaping" force. The active, up-rushing male act: this is what Apollo claims engenders. The female is all passive reception.

In this speech and argument, Aeschylus is pressing idiosyncratically on the language, creating ambiguities and ironies important for his whole trilogy. *Tiktein*, "to engender," is traditionally used of both male and female, people and animals, but with some differences between Homer and tragedy here. The different tenses seem to make mysterious differences. Homer, using *tiktein* of people, tends to use the imperfect (denoting continuous or repeated activity) mainly of the father's activity, occasionally of the mother's. Tragedy uses present and imperfect far more often of the mother. In Homer and elsewhere, the aorist (denoting a single, instantaneous act) is particularly the mother's (but is sometimes the father's). Used of animals, the verb mainly refers to the female's activity. It is also often used of the earth. *Tiktein*'s range of usage implies a jostling of inconsistent assumptions about procreation, which evade the question of the female's creative contribution, and are summed up in the English lexicon's explanation: "of the father, *beget*; of the mother, *bring forth*."

Distinctions between *tiktein*, "to engender-or-produce," and *trephein*, "to nurture," have increasingly ironic force in the *Oresteia*. The *Trophos*, "nurse," "nurturer" (from *trephein*), unwittingly nurtures the son's plan to kill his mother, who apparently rejoices at his death, yet claims she "nourished" him.[26] According to Apollo, the mother merely receives and nourishes the seed:

> She who is called mother of the child is not its parent (*tokeus*)
> but nurse of the new-implanted flood (*trophos kumatos neosporou*).

That word *kuma*, "flood": what is it doing in Apollo's argument? It means a swollen thing, usually liquid: a "wave." Aeschylus "extends" its use elsewhere to lumpy molding on a ceiling. Is it "extended" here to *mean* "fetus"?[27] Or does it carry its normal liquid sense?

[25] *Eum.* 660, cf. A. fr. 15.

[26] See the irony of *Cho.* 698–99. Clytemnestra's claim to have nurtured him, 908.

[27] *Eum.* 659, and *Cho.* 128 (the two places it has been taken to mean fetus); cf. fr. 78. Later, *kuēma* can mean fetus (e.g., Arist. *De gen. an.* 731A4). In two later passages, *kuma* might mean fetus (one, E. fr. 106 *gemousen kumatos theosporou*, is anyway an echo of this passage, the other is *AP.* 6.200), but neither illuminates Aeschylus.

In the *Choephoroe*, Electra appealed to Hermes Chthonios and "daemons under earth" for help against her (and Orestes') mother. That earlier passage resonates now in Apollo's argument against mothers, used *against* "daemons under earth." Electra had called on Earth, "who brings all things to birth (*tiktetai*), and having nourished them (*threpsasa*) receives in turn their *kuma*": a generative *kuma*, a "flood" of sperm that makes her swell (rather than a "fetus," that seed's result). *Kuma* there was "liquid seed," as I think it is in Apollo's speech. *Kuō* is used of females to mean both "I conceive" and "I am pregnant with." But elsewhere Aeschylus also uses it causally of male rain on earth in the marriage of sky and earth.[28]

Electra pictured earth receiving rainlike seed of "all things." Apollo pictures the mother receiving a flood that sows, making her, or the seed, swell. (Euripides will elaborate the scenario in a later play in the same family context: mother is field receiving "the seed."[29])

Mother, then, is nurse. *Tiktein* and *trephein* ironically collide. Apollo continues:

> He who leaps engenders;
> she, like a stranger for a stranger,
> preserves the seedling—
> those god does not harm.

Within the trilogy's dynamics, the argument and language here have a complex role. The pivotal point is approaching: the judgment on Orestes. From this will flow the conversion of Erinyes from withering and repulsive to frightening but fruitful powers. Two ways of seeing Erinyes interact with two ways of seeing parenthood, the source of growth. This is all retested by Euripides, whose Orestes flings this argument (in Euripidean irony) at Clytemnestra's *father*. Clytemnestra was his "own child." So father is paradoxically identified with the mother Clytemnestra, on the self-refuting argument that paternity is the real parenthood:

> My father begot me [*ephuteusen*, "implanted"];
> your own child brought me forth (*etikte*),
> a field receiving seed from someone else.
> Without a father there would be no child.
> So I thought: better to defend the founder (*archēgetēs*)
> of my existence in the family (*genous*),
> than the one who supplied my nurture.[30]

---

[28] A. fr. 44.4, *Cho.* 124–28. *Neosporos* (*hapax legomenon*) could be active or passive.
[29] *Or.* 552, cf. duBois 1988:57–61.
[30] *Eum.* 658–61, *Or.* 552–56.

The argument about creativity, and its language, have complicated resonances (self-consciously brittle in Euripides), not merely in each play, but
in the general conflict between male and female in tragedy. It has its place
in the wider context of contemporary theories about what makes things
happen in and to human beings. Some writers stress the external cause, the
flow into the human being. Others, fewer, talk of internal causes, a flow
outward from person to world. Interactive explanations were available, to
say that what is within works together with what comes from outside. Vision and disease could be explained as an interdependence of *esionta*, "coming-in things," and innate powers. But in contemporary explanatory patterns, the internal source is rarer than the external. The mother's role in
creating the child is stressed less than the intrusive "coming-in" role of the
father. Apollo stresses external causality. Mother, womb, and field receive,
hold, nourish seed. What comes out is the result of the input. New life is
not engendered within, but owes its existence to the external intruder, father, seed.

One can see why this causality should be applied to human conception
so nakedly in tragedy, jarring though it is to modern minds. It meshes with
external explanations of other things that happen to people: in tragedy as
in medicine, external dominates internal causality.

Outside tragedy, however, others were more willing to allow women
some part in creation. Hesiod released a model for women's sole creativity
when he pictured Earth and Night bearing children without intercourse.
Gaia bore (*egeinato*) Ouranos and Sea "without *philotēs*," love, sex. "Afterwards she bedded with Ouranos and bore" others. Night, "not couching
with anyone," bore Fate, Death, Sleep, Dreams, Blame, Woe.[31] No fifth-
century theorist suggests the mother can do it all, but some, using an interactive explanation, argue that the mother's "seed" does contribute to
genesis. Democritus thinks fetal gender is determined by whichever seed,
mother's or father's, predominates: each parent supplies the full range of
parts for the child. Empedocles, with a rather similar theory, thinks each
parent provides half. These types of theory clearly went the rounds alongside the view, supported by Anaxagoras and voiced by Aeschylus's Apollo,
that the father did it all.[32] Ambivalence about creativity, summed up in the
range of *tiktein*, becomes articulate in competing theories about procreation in this age of theory-making.

These assumptions and theories about the *womb*'s creativeness interact
with ambivalence about creativity of the mind. This was inevitable, given
the pervasive idea, crystallized in one Hippocratic treatise, of an "exact par-

[31] *Theog.* 126–32, 211–25.
[32] Discussed in Arist. *De gen. an.* 764A6, 722B; see Plot. 3.6.18–48; Lloyd 1966:17 n. 5.

allelism between things produced from the earth and things produced from human beings."[33] Some writers about thinking and the origin of thought opt for the mind that only produces when something has been put in from outside. Others feel the mind might be innately creative by itself, or that its products are the result of interaction with outside input. In Plato's *Theaetetus*, Socrates implies that some souls simply are pregnant. They "discover within themselves" beauties of wisdom when he uses his midwifery art. On others he has to use the matchmaker's art instead, sending them off to experts like Prodicus to get impregnated.[34]

Most writers, including tragic poets, do not choose between competing explanations—external, internal, or interactive—of mind's creativity. They simply imply the mind somehow has the capacity to engender. "My soul . . . was not looking out for the safest course, but was continually pregnant with the following thought," says a character in Xenophon. Thoughts and words come out of the mind. "I shall speak the word from my *phrēn*," the chorus tells Electra.[35] It is not in the chorus-members' brief to say where they think the word came from in the first place.

Sometimes poets imply that the mind's products—words, deeds—have an external source. One female chorus, singing around Clytemnestra's murder, singing about women's crimes, asks self-subvertingly, "Who could tell of man's [*sic*] over-daring thought [*phronēma*]?" *Phronēma* (related to *phrenes*) is a "daring": often an "over-daring," leading to crime. The chorus illustrates this by the *pronoia* ("forethought," "plot") of Althaea, who killed her son.[36] Even as the singers list women's crimes, they offer an external explanation for female wickedness: Eros "over-conquers," is *thēlukratēs*, "stronger than [or 'in control of'] the female." In tragedy, what *phrenes* produce, especially in women (given tragedy's readiness to articulate its culture's distrust of women), is often disastrous and destructive. But this destructiveness may be due to an "overmastering" force that entered those *phrenes* from outside. The more so because women are supposedly more penetrable by the outside world, more open to violent passion.[37]

The female model of mind, passive *and* engendering, contains vital am-

---

[33] See *On the Nature of the Child*, 528.22ff. (Littré).

[34] *Theaet*. 148E–51B, see Burnyeat 1977:8–9.

[35] Xen. *Cyr*. 5.4.35, *Cho*. 107, *ton ek phrenos logon*.

[36] *Cho*. 594–95, 606. *Phronēma* and *tolmē* can both have a bad as well as a good sense. Over-boldness, recklessness, is a common tragic implication of *tolmē*, e.g., *OT* 125, *Ion* 1264. It is coupled with *anaideia* at Antipho 3.3.5. *Phronēma* can mean arrogance, presumptuousness, e.g., *PV* 953, *Heraclid*. 926. *Pronoia* is often used in a bad sense (esp. by orators, e.g., Aeschin. 3.212), of crimes done "with [malice] aforethought."

[37] *Cho*. 597–601. Tragedy's distrust of women: see, e.g., *Hec*. 884–85 (with 1269). Women distrusted as more open than men to violent passion: Padel 1983:4–17; Just 1989:196–216. Tragic anxieties and ambiguities over women's roles expressed in Greek myths: Gould 1980:52–58.

biguities. It is obscurely divided, rather like female *aidoia* themselves, which are perceived as obscurely folded, like writing tablets.[38] The center of tragic attention is the human mind in its suffering. According to perceptions of the female in Greek culture, "mind" suffers like a female. In imagery that runs through all Greek tragedies, the mind—like a woman in society, like female sexuality in relation to male—is acted upon, invaded, a victim of the outside world (especially of divinity), yet ambiguously generative.

Looking back on the concreteness with which Homer, the Hippocratics, and tragedy portray innards (Chapter 2), we might say there are two main models of "mind." In one, innards are a vessel acted upon and entered by the outside world. In the other, they are an agent with knowledge, imperious speech, innate autonomy. The Greek way of dealing with a problem most cultures face, how to understand the mind as both active and passive, subject and object, is to picture it concretely in two ways simultaneously: moving organ and recipient vessel. According to contemporary Greek perceptions, these work out as male and female respectively. The "female" image is more pervasive, as medical insistence on "coming-in things" is the dominant explanatory pattern for disease. Sophocles uses *splanchna* only once for men's reproductive organs, but the word is common for women's.

Swelling images of impassioned *splanchna* might seem apt for male sexual organs, but in fact are assimilated to the female interior. To put it another way, the sexualization of the innards is stronger in the passive than in the active model. Mind or soul can be imaged as vessel, as a female organ, more concretely than mind as agent, as male organ.

Outside tragedy, an active image of mind is implied in some verbs of mental or perceptual activity, verbs like "grasp," "arrive at." These proliferate in classical prose, particularly in and after Plato.[39] This image is sometimes overtly male. Plato argues that reason may "marry," "have intercourse with" the Forms, to "beget"—a male begetting—understanding and truth.[40] In this way, an active, implicitly male model of mind eventually dominates philosophical discourse. But this is not the case in tragedy, where the active imagery is less obvious or immediate than the passive, and the concrete imagery of vessel-like innards, flowing, darkening, entered,

---

[38] See duBois 1988:130.

[39] E.g., *ephikneisthai*, "arrive at" (in visual context), Pl. *Theaet.* 184D8; *ephaptesthai* (in a thinking context), ibid. 190D9; *haptesthai*, *Phd.* 99E (for the activity of the senses). Hellenistic philosophers favor *katalambanein* for "grasping" a perceived object, or cognitive "grasp," most famously Zeno of Citium, who compares perception to the act of physical "grasping" with one's hand, Cic. *Acad.* 1.41, 2.145. Arist. *Metaph.* 1051B24, 1072B21 speaks of intellect "touching" (*thinganōn*) its object.

[40] *Migeis tōi onti . . . gennēsas noun kai alētheian*, and *gennain dianoēmata te kai doxas* (*Rep.* 490B, 496A).

overshadows active verbs of learning and understanding. I have brought forward so far only the biological aspect of innard imagery. Its daemonology will tell us again, in a different register, that tragic innards are invaded by emotion (Chapters 6, 7).

Tragic language suggests self or mind primarily, but not only, through images of inwardness that have female resonances: house, womb, earth. Modern interpretive controversies about innard-words as "faculties indeterminately corporeal," as "organs" (Chapter 2), seem to me to stem partly from Greek doubleness in speaking, if not thinking, about innards. This doubleness begins in Homer and continues in different guises through different Greek communities. *Thumos* is presented as a sudden energy, speaking, commanding, rising. This might, if we are going to be concretely sexual about it, suggest male sexual activity. But tragedy, like the intensely controlled male society to which tragedy speaks, tends instead to image innards as reactive, entered, hurting and flowing within. Like women, as men imagine them. If these innards have innate power, it is mysterious. Poets often present it in language so ambiguous that it causes (among other things) textual controversy.

Tragedy's presentation of innards as predominantly "female" may reflect dominant interests of the tragic genre, as distinct from epic. But to say only this is to sidestep an issue, for tragedy, unlike epic, is a product of a particular society, and the shape and interests of the genre to some degree reflect a bias in its society. Homeric epic is centrally interested in actions and decisions. It portrays and elicits feeling mainly through these. But much of tragedy, especially the long lyric songs, is taken up with expressing feelings about an act. Fifth-century Athenian mentality, I think, underpins later European concentration on a female model of mind, by using ideas of female interiority as a structure good to think with about the inner equipment, the mental and emotional experience, of everyone, and most importantly, for most societies so far, of men.

Post-Homeric Greek thought, which delights in opposites,[41] images male feeling and knowing through female innards. The male philosopher comes to know from a dark female source. The speaker of Parmenides' *Proem* learns to know from a goddess in the house of Night. Plato's Socrates claims he learned from a woman a lesson about Eros that encapsulates the whole of metaphysics.[42] The light of male knowledge is found through a journey to or through a female dark.

The Homeric paradigm is Odysseus, who learns "his way and his homecoming" by facing inhabitants of Hades. When "all ways are shadowed,"

[41] Lloyd 1966:15–26.
[42] Parm., see Chapter 3, n. 79; Pl. *Symp*. 201D–12A. The motif is parodied at *Menex*. 235E–36A, where Pericles and Socrates learn *rhētorikē* from Aspasia.

he reaches a place "covered in mist," where "night is stretched over mortals."[43] The ghost of Teiresias asks him why he has "left the sun's light, to see the dead and the joyless place?" It promises to "speak true things." Odysseus learns about his home, about the nature of death, from his dead mother.[44] Like Teiresias, she underlines the strangeness of his presence there. "How did you come alive under the misty dark? It is hard for the living to see these things." True answers to your most urgent questions come when you leave light, and look at what is hard to see. They come from dark, joyless places, from the ghost of a blind seer or, most telling of all, from your mother's ghost, who tells you to "hurry back to the light, and know" all that you have learned in the dark, "that you may tell it later to your wife."[45] The first Greek intellectual hero learns about his own life and home, about his own death and death itself, from darkness, from tenants of Hades, especially his mother. He must bring this knowledge to his wife. The male Greek journey of knowing is bound to darkness, womanhood, coming from and returning to women.

Darkness is characteristic of the mind disturbed, endangered, maddened. But it is also characteristic of women's bodies and lives.[46] Darkness characterizes a mode of consciousness and living that is alternative to the norm. A sane man is *sō-phrōn*, "having a safe (*sōs*) *phrēn*": self-controlled, secure. But overwhelming passion can make his *phrēn* dark, mad, dangerous, at risk. In other words, it makes his mind be as women are.

In the outer world, the macrocosm, darkness belongs to the underworld and to forces like Erinyes or "Madness." In the inward human microcosm, it belongs to innards affected by such forces.

It is consciously important to Greek thought that what is destructive may also illuminate (Chapter 3). Sirens are fatal, but their knowledge is true. Women, and womanlike inner experience that alters safe male modes of consciousness, are illuminatingly dangerous. An apt medium for male tragedians, exploring human passion safely, on behalf of sane male citizens.

---

[43] *Od.* 10.537–40, 11.12, 15, 17, 93–96.
[44] *Od.* 11.181–203, 218–22, 155–56.
[45] Cf. *atrekeōs katalexon*, *Od.* 11.170; *dizēai*, 11.100, 223–24.
[46] Padel 1983:6–10.

Chapter 6

THE ZOOLOGY AND DAEMONOLOGY
OF EMOTION

TWO FIFTH-CENTURY THOUGHTS crucial for our understanding of tragedy are that human beings are made of the same stuff as the universe, and that we infer the inner, which we cannot see, from the outer, which we can.[1] I introduced these thoughts in scientific contexts, but they belong with a comprehension of the world that is also, at every point, daemonic. Daemons, like liquid and air, are part of the fabric of the world. Tragic audiences expected daemons both inside, in their innards, and outside, in the environment. From the visible surfaces of world or person, they inferred the unseen presences of daemon.

Daemon, the Anglicization of *daimōn*, covers forces that we, as Western observers, might call gods, but also what we think of instinctively as "demons": good, beautiful, articulate, but also repellant and bestial. In Athenian homes and cities, daemons were a force as live and considerable as electricity in ours. Later (Chapter 7), I explore their resonances and roles in the outer world. Here I chart their involvement in the inner. So far, I have treated passion as the inner moves of liquid and air. But tragedy also represents this inner movement as the moves of daemon within.

DAEMONIC WEATHER, WIND, FIRE

Let us start with another look at wind. I related storm imagery of passion to contemporary biology (Chapter 4), but there are gods, too, in storm. As in many cultures, lightning, flood, wind, fire, and storm are daemonic assault: a prime symbolic source for understanding and representing mental experience. We think of them as forces of "nature," but to the Greeks, "nature" was also (as we would put it) supernatural, a medium of daemonic expression, whether tender or aggressive. The elements are the gods' arsenal. The gods both use and are inherent in the weather.

The thunderbolt is Zeus's weapon, which Athene borrows. "Alone of the gods," she says, "I know the keys of his house in which his thunderbolt is sealed." With Poseidon, she plans to shatter the Greeks' ships going home from Troy and punish them for desecrating Trojan altars:

---

[1] See Chapter 3, nn. 4, 25, 59–60; Padel 1990:336.

ATHENE: Zeus will send rain, limitless hail,
              black blasts of air. He says he'll give me
              his thunder-flame to hit the Greek ships,
              burn them up with fire. You prepare the Aegean strait
              to roar with tidal waves, wild eddies of the sea. . . .
POSEIDON: I'll disturb the sea. . . . You go to Olympus,
              take the thunderbolts from your father's house.

The thunderbolt's lesson is coercive piety: the Greeks should learn to "reverence Athene's temples and the other gods." It strikes the sacriligious. It is also part of the storm.[2] The word *belos* means a thrown weapon. It is used for Zeus's "bolt," and also for "shafts" of snow, rain, sunlight, starlight. Living on earth we face continual "bolts" from above. *Belos*-verbs are hitting, throwing, shooting. "Sun's shining ray, a clear *shaft*, hit the ground." The moon's circle "threw *javelins* from above." The arrow of fire or stars is weaker than that which "Eros sends from his hands."[3] The elements bombard humanity.

The fifth century tended to date the beginning of civilization to some primal sheltering from the elements. The nonhuman Cyclops, boasting that he does not fear gods, grounds his confidence crudely in his power to shelter from weather:

> I don't shiver at Zeus's thunderbolt
> nor acknowledge Zeus a stronger god than me.
> I don't care for him! Listen—when he pours down
> rain from above, I've shelter in this rocky cave. . . .
> When he pours snow from the north, I wrap my body
> in wild-beast furs and light my fire.

For the fifth century, this was comically fallacious.[4] Zeus sent rain, but expressed his power in other ways, too. The weather was one manifestation of divinity, not, as primitive people imagined, the only one. But the idea that this was how earlier civilization saw things suggests that weather was still, in fifth-century eyes, a strong model for divine attack.

Winds are used by gods, but they are also rapacious, violent gods themselves. Boreas (North Wind), Zephyrus (West Wind): the one's *pnoiē* (breath) revives Sarpedon, the other's is unimaginably swift. In Homer, the winds feasting together, rowdily male, "in the house of fierce-blowing Zephyrus," jump up and catcall to Iris, the female messenger, "each telling

---

[2] *Eum.* 827–28, *Tro.* 78–93, 85–86. Zeus also hits Capaneus, Asclepius, Semele, Typhon: E. *Supp.* 640, 860; Pi. *P.* 3.57; *Alc.* 4, 128; *Ba.* 90; *PV* 360, 371 (cf. his threat to Inachus, 668). For a general anthropological perspective here, see Firth 1973:161.

[3] E. *Supp.* 650, *Ion* 1155 (*ēkontiz' anō*), *Hipp.* 531. Gods' weapons: see below, pp. 152–56.

[4] *Cyc.* 320–31; see Burton 1980:99.

her to sit beside himself." They rape mares in the meadow. Boreas raped the princess Oreithuia: Aeschylus brought him on stage in the lost *Oreithuia*. Jealous Zephyrus accidentally kills Hyacinthus, the boy he desires. Apollo (who desired him too and was teaching him quoits) complains that when he threw his quoit, "Zephyrus blew down and dashed it on Hyacinthus's head." Winds are authors of rape and death. Homeric storm-winds are "Snatchers," Harpuiai.[5] They are available agents of violence for other gods. Zeus sends rain and "black blasts of *aithēr*" on the Greek ships. Poseidon, furious at Odysseus,

> roused all blasts of every kind of wind. . . .
> The East and South winds rushed together,
> fierce-blowing West wind, and North wind,
> born in *aithēr*, rolling a massive wave.
> Odysseus's knees gave way.[6]

When winds shake *phrenes*, therefore, there are daemonic as well as breathy resonances. Hatred and fury are gusts in the mind. Antigone's soul suffers "blasts of the same winds" as before, when she persists in challenging Creon. Eteocles, when he sees his hated brother, gives out "a terrible glare and breaths of *thumos*," as if he had seen the Gorgon.[7] Sexual desire is a storm:

> Eros tossed my *phrenes*
> as a whirlwind falls on oaks in the mountains.

Helen's father let her choose among her suitors "wherever Aphrodite's *pnoai* [breaths, winds] might take her." Madness may be god's "breath." Ares' *pnoai* stir a *kuma* (wave) round Thebes. Bacchants are "mad with Dionysus's *pnoai*."[8]

Fire also is daemonic. The core image for fires of passion is disease. The summer Dogstar's "fiery rays" are fever weapons. They "burn the flesh," "shoot out burning rays of fire." This star is "the brightest, but an evil sign, bringing much fever [*pureton*, "burning"] on wretched mortals." The plague-bringing god is *purphoros*, "fire-bringing."[9] Words for "fever," *puretos*, *thermē*, are words for "burning," "heat."

Emotions burn. *Menos*, *cholos*, madness, desire, sometimes fear or hope, and supremely anger, "boil" in, or burn, innards. Hearts are "set on fire" with important news, love heats Zeus's heart. "*Phrēn*-beating madnesses" inflame Io within. Desire sets human beings on fire. "I saw inside his cloak

---

[5] *Il.* 5.697, 19.415, 23.201–4; Lucian *Dialogi deorum* 14. Boreas and Oreithuia: Pl. *Phdr.* 229C; A. fr. 281N. Mares and Harpies raped by wind: see Chapter 4, n. 65.

[6] *Tro.* 79, *Od.* 5.292–97.

[7] *Ant.* 137, 929; *Phoen.* 454; cf. above, pp. 90–91.

[8] Sappho 47V; *IA* 69; *Sept.* 63, 115; *Ba.* 1095.

[9] *Scut.* 397, *Hec.* 1102–3, *Il.* 22.30–31. *OT* 27–28, cf. *phloga*, 167.

and burst into flames," says Socrates, teasing the image. Flames flash from the eyes of those in love or mad with rage. Fire's "pointed rays" are an image for the even more powerful darts of Eros.[10] Burning fever distracts the mind to delirium. Burning passion inflames us inside and out. This is the violent end of the heat-spectrum. More moderate hope, and joy, "warm" innards in a comforting glow like that produced by wine.[11]

Like wind, fire is god with violent "breath." Heracles destroyed Troy "with fire's red breath." The breath of Hephaestus—divinity of fire, who is synonymous with his medium, like Dionysus—scorches fish in the Trojan river. The name "Hephaestus" by itself can mean "fire." "Made by Hephaestus" is "made by fire." His "starry" house on Olympus is made of glittery bronze. He is a giant, fast on his feet but lame. His twenty bellows blow on melting vats, "sending out a blast of every kind of force." "Fire" is divine violence, fast, asymmetrical in its movement, a multiple blast, destructively creative.[12] When love or rage "kindles" the heart, these associations are brought within it. That violent divine gift on which civilization rests, which burns cities, which makes and destroys, is inside you.

The in-dwelling divinity of elemental forces, used by gods as artillery, resonates in poets' images of passion as fire, wind, storm. The physiology of feeling as storm (Chapter 4) interacts with its theology. Civilization may begin with sheltering from elements outside, but feelings are an elemental divine force within. There is no shelter against them.

GOADS, WHIPS, PURSUIT

Emotion is also a punching blow. Hecuba is "struck with terror in her soul," bacchants "struck with fear" at an earthquake, Phaedra "struck by Eros's goads," the Thebans "struck out" with horror at the thought that

---

[10] Pl. *Charm.* 155D; cf. S. fr. 474 *thalpetai . . . autos*; Pi. *P.* 4.219 (affecting *phrenes*), Ar. *Lys.* 9 (affecting heart). Heart scorched by fear: *Sept.* 289–90. Fired with anxious hope: S. *El.* 888. Burning with *lussa*: Ar. *Thesm.* 680. Burning with grief: Ap. Rh. 3.773; with passion: *OC* 1695, Ar. *Nub.* 992. Recklessness makes one "hot," *thermos*, or "on fire," *aithōn: Sept.* 603, *Aj.* 222. *Splanchna* heated by *kotos*: Ar. *Ran.* 844. Fiery, swelling heat of *thumos*: Pl. *Ti.* 70C; cf. Arist. *De part. anim.* 650B35, "passion produces heat." Ares is a "burning" god: *Phoen.* 241, and martial rage the paradigm of fiery anger (see Chapter 2, nn. 52–53, the heat of *menos* and *cholos*). Cf. *Ag.* 480; *PV* 590, 879. Fire in the eyes: see Chapter 3, nn. 21, 32–35. At A. *Supp.* 1004 (cf. *Hipp.* 530), an imaginary admirer, "mastered by *himeros*," shoots an *ommatos thelktērion toxeuma* at girls he fancies.

[11] *Aj.* 478, E. *El.* 402; cf. *PV* 685. A longed-for son "heats the heart with love," Pi. *O.* 10.105. A highwayman "warms his *phrēn*" by killing and robbing, *Cho.* 1004. Glow of wine in *splanchna*: *Cyc.* 424, *Alc.* 758. Cf. the rarer "chill" of feeling: "an evil coldness falls around my heart," *Sept.* 834.

[12] Fire: *Tro.* 814; *Il.* 21.355, 2.426; *Ant.* 123, 1007; A. fr. 69N. Hephaestus: *Il.* 18.370, 410–11, 417, 470–71. Zeus's "flame" is lightning, *Theog.* 854–67, divine counterpart to the "far-seen ray of fire" stolen by Prometheus, which was originally divine. (Men pay an "evil" price for it, *Theog.* 566–70.) Dionysus as "wine": cf. *Cyc.* 519–27.

their king may be a murderer.[13] Like a Homeric spear—"Watch out or someone may stick a spear in your *metaphrenon* [midriff]"—emotion's target is innards. A warrior cowers in his chariot, "struck out in his *phrenes*." Another model is the divine blow. Zeus's thunderbolt sweeps down, "breathing out flame." Typhoeus is "struck out of his boasting words . . . thumped to the very *phrenes*, blasted in his strength." A "murderous knife of gods" strikes Oedipus's family. "Ate's bloody blow" strikes the *thumos*.[14]

This daemonic blow is a punitive lash, or a goading stimulus, or both at once. That which "goads" a mind to do something may also punish that mind for doing it. This principle underlies daemonic icons of madness like Erinyes and *atē*. Greek language of madness is constructed around images of a "struck" mind. In tragedy, madness incarnates the double bind of someone "struck" for doing something that a similar "blow" goaded them to do.[15] When the blow is a goad, the mind is "driven" like a panicked animal. The victim, or the victim's mind, is carried off out of control like a chariot. "You are carried away by fury," Electra tells her mother. Passion "drives" the mind as god "drives" a plague-ridden city. Ajax is "driven" by terrible grief. Desire "drives" Admetus to continue mourning his dead wife, when he is offered a new woman, veiled.[16]

"Driving" emotion or madness both is and is like a driving daemon. "Which *alastōr* [avenging daemon] drives him?" asks Clytemnestra when she hears Agamemnon plans to sacrifice their child. Erinyes "drive" their victim out of his mind, on through the world. "God drives towards disaster the *phrenes*" of those who think bad is good. Vase-painters represent Poinai (Punishers), Ananke (Necessity), Erinyes, and Lyssa (Madness) with goads in their hands.[17]

The word *mastix*, "whip," often darts through these contexts, but the supreme word is *kentron*, "ox-goad" (also an instrument of torture). It can mean an insect's "sting." *Kentra* of love "sting" the innards. Aphrodite applies "*mastix* of Peitho," "whip of Persuasion," to Medea's heart.[18] Reproach "strikes with its *kentron* under the *phrenes*," Io is "*kentron*-tortured"

---

[13] *Tro.* 182, *Ba.* 604, *Hipp.* 38, *OT* 922.

[14] *Il.* 8.95, 16.403–4; *PV* 363–64. *Ant.* 603 (with Lloyd-Jones 1990 i. 375); cf. *Cho.* 467, *Ant.* 1097.

[15] See Chapter 8, n. 11. Madness's "double bind," madness as mind struck aside: see Padel 1981:110–13.

[16] S. *El.* 628, cf. *Cho.* 1023; *OT* 28; *Aj.* 275; *Alc.* 1080, cf. *Andr.* 27 (*elpis m' aei prosēge*).

[17] Erinyes: *IA* 878, S. *El.* 1252–53; see pp. 176–78 below. *Atē* as "disaster" to which *phrenes* are driven: *Ant.* 622–23. Iconography: see Pickard-Cambridge 1946:945, and below, Chapter 8, n. 47.

[18] See Hdt. 3.130; Ar. *V.* 225, 40. *Kentra* of love: *Hipp.* 39, 1303 (Phaedra "bitten" or "stung" by them); Pl. *Rep.* 573A (*pothou*); Pi. *P.* 4.215 (see Buxton 1982 for Aphrodite's use of Peitho).

by Hera with the maddening gadfly. Grief, pity, and misery goad the heart.[19]

Sometimes emotion's blow is a perforation, as by an ankus. The chorus's *phrenes* are hurt by "piercing fear" for Prometheus. Fear "darts through the chest" of the enslaved Trojan women. When Theseus's mother weeps for the mothers of the dead, Theseus confesses, "Through me, too, something came." Pity, sympathy, fear, grief, "come through" the mind. The Erinyes feel pain "sink into their side." Blinded Oedipus cries out, both with physical pain and with realization: "The sting of these goads and the memory of evils sink into me together."[20] Emotion's impact on innards is a sword, like that which penetrates Ajax's *phrenes* at his suicide. Electra, seeing the lock of hair on her father's tomb, hopes it is her brother's, but fears he will never come: she throbs, "struck as with an enemy's weapon."[21] Armed emotion is both a driver and a hunter, hitting, stabbing, beating.

BITING, EATING

Sometimes emotion's assault not anthropomorphic but bestial. Passion mauls, bites, stings. *Daknein* is the important word here. It can mean "bite," like a dog, and "sting," like an insect. One can hear it in these contexts mainly as a bite: innards "bitten" by shame, love, grief. When Hector heard words that shamed and angered him, "the speech bit his *phrenes*." The guard asks Creon where the bad news "bites" him, in his ears or his psyche. The realization of other people's pain "bites human beings." Jason thinks Medea so shameless, "a lioness, not woman," that "I could not bite you with a thousand reproaches."[22]

This bite "hits" heart or *phrēn*.[23] When the chorus hears Cassandra cry, its members say in pity,

> I am struck by a deadly bite
> by your agonizing fortune,
> listening to your high, pitiful lament,
> shattering for me to hear.

Helen, inciting desire in others' innards, is a "*thumos*-biting flower of Eros." "Raw-biting desire" impels Eteocles to fight his brother. These are Homeric compounds. "*Thumos*-biting" insults spur Homer's Odysseus to

---

[19] *Eum*. 157, A. *Supp*. 563, cf. Wilamowitz *ad HF* 20. Grief and misery "come round the soul with a goad" in a textual crux at *PV* 671. Cf. Ajax's title *Mastigophoros*, in the *Argument* to *Aj*.: the word could be active or passive.

[20] *PV* 182, *Tro*. 156, E. *Supp*. 228, *Eum*. 842, *OT* 1318.

[21] Pi. *N*. 7.26, *Cho*. 185 (*belos*).

[22] *Il*. 5.493, *Ant*. 317, E. *El*. 291, *Med*. 1345; cf. *Trach*. 254, *Ag*. 791, E. *El*. 242.

[23] *PV* 437, *Alc*. 1100, *Rhes*. 596; *phrēn*: *Heraclid*. 483; cf. *Ag*. 1164.

the discus contest. In Sophocles, the spasm of pain in Philoctetes' foot is a
"*thumos*-biting *atē*."[24] Emotion and physical pain "bite" *thumos*, *phrēn*, or
kardia, like an animal.

Different verbs make this attack ferociously baroque. *Amussein*, "to lacerate, scratch, tear," is used of animal claws. Hawks chase vultures and "tear
them to pieces"; lion cubs in the womb "tear it to bits," for their claws are
"much sharper than those of other creatures." The verb is apt for skin
wounds. Mourning women "tear" their breasts with their nails. This, apparently, is what passion does to innards. "In your fury you'll maul your
thumos within," Achilles warns the Greeks. The Persian elders' *phrēn* is
"mauled with fear" for the army. Pain and worry lacerate the heart. When
Heracles, in an Alexandrian poem, loses his beloved, he goes wherever his
feet take him, maddened: "A tough god mauls his *hēpar* within." Eros's
madness tears the surface of the lover's inward parts.[25]

Biting emotion "devours." Conflict is *thumos*-eating. Heracles' fits of
madness are "raw-eating." Hope "wards *thumos*-eating grief from the
phrēn." Emotion's impact on innards is like that of disease on the body.
Several diseases had nicknames of carnivorous animals, like fox or lion. An
ulcer is *phagedaina*, "eater." Its "savage jaws" gnaw flesh. When the ulcer
throbs in Philoctetes' foot, he cries, "I am destroyed, I am devoured." Another animal model is the eagle devouring Prometheus's liver. Being open
to emotion is everlasting vulnerability to something that gnaws the innards, which grow again, to be devoured again.[26]

Oistros, Poison, Snakes, Dogs

The "sting" meaning in *daknein* shades into an idea of "biting" passion as
an insect. *Oistros*, "gadfly," is mating madness, the "fly" that torments cows
in heat. Homer's Athene "drives" Penelope's male suitors like a herd of
cows, "whom darting *oistros* whirls along in spring." This word "oestrus"
becomes the Western term for female animals "in heat."[27]

In tragedy, *oistros* often either means "madness" or is qualified by the

[24] *Ag.* 1164–66, 743. Lloyd-Jones (1990 i. 313) suggests that "flower" implies the fire of
erōs: it "stings" the *thumos*. See also *Sept.* 692, *Od.* 8.185, *Phil.* 703.

[25] Hdt. 3.76, 108; *Il.* 19.284, 1.243; *Pers.* 115, 161; Bacc. 16.19; Theoc. 13.71.

[26] *Il.* 19.58, *HF* 889; *Ag.* 103. See *Phil.* 745, *Cho.* 280–81. According to Arist. *Poet.*
1458B20, Euripides changed the verb from Aeschylus's *Philoctetes* ("the *phagedaina* that *esthiei* my flesh") to the rarer, more baroque verb *thoinatai*, "makes a meal off, banquets off."
Esthiein is standard in Hippocratic accounts of ulcers, cf. Silk 1974:54 n. 3. Animal names
for diseases: see Parker 1983:248 n. 68. Prometheus's eagle: see Chapter 2, n. 29.

[27] *Od.* 22.300. Hdt. 2.93 uses it of the mating "impulse" in fish. The *oistros* above all pursues Io, the *oistrodinētos korē*, wearied by *oistros*-driven fear (*PV* 566, 581–89). In *PV*, *oistros*
interacts with the hounding ghost of Argos. Io is *oistroplēx*, *oistrodonos*, *oistrodonētos* (*PV* 589,
681; S. *El.* 5; A. *Supp.* 16, 573).

adjective "mad."[28] It is thought of as stinging. Maybe it was thought to inject dementing poison. When Io is a cow, the *oistros chriei*, it "rubs" or "anoints" her: *chriein* is a verb used of poison "rubbed" on cloth or arrows. Its core sense seems to be frictional: "graze."[29] Its action may be implicitly pleasurable, or irritating, or maybe both. The verb may express male am- bivalence over female experience of sexual desire—desire as torment—as well as a Greek impulse to see female sexuality in terms of cows.

Oistros is strongly linked to the goddess Hera's cow-sexuality, central to her cult in the Argolid. The Argolid is also the site of the mythic daughters of Proetus. According to one, possibly two versions of their myth, Hera inflicted these girls with madness and a terrible repulsive itching. There is a vital erotic element in their plight. This, and their mad wandering, has fostered interpretation of their myth as a local rite in which girls passed from girlhood to womanhood. Cows, linked with sexuality, inform Hera's cult-titles, and her Homeric epithets. She is "Ox-Eyed," Zeuxidia ("Yoker"), Euboia ("Well-Cowed"). Her cow images proliferate.[30]

Io was "key-keeper" of Hera's shrine at Argos. In her ambivalent rela- tionship with Hera of victimization and identification (similar to that of Iphigeneia with Artemis), Io takes on, as it were, the cow-pain of Hera's sexual relationship with Zeus. In the *Prometheus*, Hera's relation to the *oistros* and to Io's cow-shape is ambiguous. In Aeschylus's *Suppliant Women*, it was Hera who changed Io to a cow. Elsewhere (in Sophocles' lost *Inachus*, for instance) Zeus apparently did it. Once Io is a cow, Hera sends on her the *muōps* ("fly") or *oistros*. "Fly" persecutes Io-as-cow. She is "*oistros*-struck," maddened, stung: by the fly, by her madness. Both "drive" her. They drive her innards mad, her limbs into wandering. The *oistros*- sting is image, accompaniment, symptom, and cause of her madness and wanderings. *Oistros* comes, ambiguously, from Zeus's frustrated desire and Hera's sexual jealousy. It embodies the sting of Io's position in the erotic crossfire between Zeus and Hera. Zeus's lust, Hera's hostility, Io's mad- ness, the *oistros*: all cease together when Zeus impregnates Io, "touching her only," with his hand.[31]

Elsewhere in tragedy, *oistros* is less specifically madness, mad desire, sting. Phaedra, stung by the *kentra*, "goads," of desire, is stung also by the mad *oistroi* of Eros. *Kentron*, too, had conscious erotic overtones in the fifth

[28] *Ant.* 1002, *Or.* 791, *Ba.* 665, *IA* 548.

[29] *PV* 566, cf. 675, 880; "anointing" arrows: *Trach.* 675 (see Jebb *ad* 832), 689; *Od.* 1.262; "rubbing" cloth: *Med.* 634.

[30] Hes. fr. 133; see Löffler 1963; Burkert 1983:168–74. Dowden (1989:77, 71–95, 117– 37, 144) fits Io into his initiation-rite argument as an "addition to the Proitid myth." Virgil simply links the two, *Ec.* 6.50. Hera's titles: see Farnell, 1:181–82; A. B. Cook 1914–40, 1:440–41.

[31] See A. *Supp.* 291, 299, 307–8, cf. *PV* 848–49. *Inachus*: see Sutton 1979:5.

century. It could mean "penis." *Kentein*, "to goad," could refer to modes of sexual intercourse. Centaur is "kentauros," and centaur activity recalls these resonances: centaurs paradigmatically rape, and "kentauros" could be used at Athens of an active homosexual. It is worth remembering the centaurs killed by Heracles' poisoned arrows. *Kentron* suits the complex erotic, maybe poisoning overtones of *oistros*. But *oistros* is also used for the nonerotic "madness" of Heracles and Orestes, and the Dionysiac "madness" of bacchants on the mountain, whose "desire" is to kill. An augur watches birds who have an ominous "raging desire" to attack each other. The thunderbolt's "sting" is less destructive than Madness's "dart" in Heracles' breast.[32]

The idea of a maddening sting is apt for an image of love as bee. Bee stings are proverbial. They linger even when the stinging agent dies. Socrates says he does not want to "leave my sting in you, like the bee, before I die." In the *Hippolytus*, love as bee is the climax of the ode to Eros. But it follows a sequence of raiding, barbed, murderous images for love: arrows of star and fire, a bolt thrown, ravaged land, sacked cities, the lightning that impregnated Semele "in murderous fate." The play itself opens with a double image: a young man keeps himself apart from sexual activity, correctly prefiguring its destructiveness, and a woman on a bed shivers with lust for him, faint from her self-cancelling attempt to fight desire. The bee image, following a pack of destructive images, brings us up against Eros's sudden sweetness, maybe Phaedra's would-be sexual virtue (bees were an image of purity too), but also Eros's stabbing, lingering, dementing pain.[33]

Love's "honey" interacts with poison imagery. Stings involve something "smeared," onto either the hurt flesh or the arrow, the stinging agent. Women or cows in the grip of sexual passion are "maddened." *Oistros*—whether used of erotic desire, of other mad desires, or of bacchic madness, especially female—has poisoning undertones. Poisoned arrows are known from Homer onwards, and figure in at least one extant tragedy. Heracles' arrows are tipped with the Hydra's poisonous blood.[34] Insect stings, like arrows, can inject. Maybe poison is the source of the madness. Maddening drugs seem to be mentioned in the *Bacchae*, a play whose background, and

---

[32] Phaedra: *Hipp.* 1300, cf. 1303; centaurs, *kentron*: see duBois 1982:31; Ar. *Nub.* 346, 350; Henderson 1975:122, 178–79, 202–3, 219. *Oistros* as unerotic madness or desire: see *IA* 548; *HF* 1144; *IT* 1456; *Or.* 791; *Ba.* 665, 1229; *Ant.* 1002; *HF* 862.

[33] Pl. *Phd.* 91. At *Hipp.* 563, Barrett takes the image only to mean that love flits from victim to victim, which is weak as a climax to 531, 533, 542, 558, 562. Bee as image of virtue, purity, sweetness: see Parker 1983:83 n. 37. Love's maddening power: cf. *hōste Bakchan*, *Hipp.* 550.

[34] *Od.* 1.262, *Trach.* 573–74 (with Long 1967:277 n. 4). Pearson (1910:257) collects "maddening" (see *IA* 548) arrows of love from *Hipp.* 533 onwards. Cypris's inescapable arrow is "anointed with desire," *Med.* 634. Is this "poisoned"? Cf. *ios*, "poison," used of the honey that snakes feed to Iamos, Pi. *O.* 6.47.

whose chorus, embodies female madness. "You are painfully mad," Teiresias tells Pentheus, "and no drugs will heal you, though you are sick because of them." This is a famous interpretive impasse, but whatever Teiresias is precisely suggesting, these words of his inject into the play the thought of dementing poisons.[35]

In the *Oresteia*, envious hatred is "a malignant poison, settled on the heart." The Erinyes' resentful thoughts

> will fall on the land, an everlasting,
> intolerable, unfading pestilence.

The Erinyes "spew out poison." Their poisonous, serpentine connections underlie the image of poison spilling from their passion onto human ground. It reflects back on an image earlier in the trilogy of poisoning hatred lodged in the heart.[36]

Snakes were believed to have poisonous teeth, tongue, and eyes. *Drakōn*, "snake," is connected to *derkesthai*, "to look, glare." Snakes were greedy for blood, and poisoned blood itself was poison, so serpentine associations with blood had complicated resonance.[37]

Fear of snakes was axiomatic in Greek poetry from Homer on:

> When a man in mountain gullies sees a snake
> he turns back. Trembling grips his limbs,
> he starts back, his cheeks pale over.

Several tragedies have snake death in their plot. The poison of the snake's bite or sting remains for ten years in Philoctetes' foot. Snakes infect, infiltrate with their poison through their teeth and eyes, as well as (in other myths) engulfing, constricting.[38]

Snakes (a normal part of Athenian domestic life) are a greedy, nonhuman, potentially draining force within a human structure. They are an image of threat to a city, to a head of house, or to a mind and soul. Creon, accusing Ismene of diminishing him within his house, compares her to a snake that "drinks out, drains":

[35] *Ba.* 326–27, see Dodds *ad loc.*

[36] *Ag.* 834; *Eum.* 479, 730.

[37] "Deadly" poisonous glare of snake's eyes: see *Pers.* 81, *Or.* 479–80, Bond *ad Hyps.* fr. 18.3. Cf. the Gorgon, and the basilisk whose glance Pliny (*NH* 8.32) compares to that of the *katoblepas* (the gnu?—surely not) and the wolf. *Drakōn* and *derkesthai*: Snell 1953:2. An inscription of unknown date connects snakebite with snakes' appetite for blood: "As a thirsty *echidna* bites, eating" (*IG* 4:620). Poisoned blood poisons: *Trach.* 717–18. Again, cf. Gorgo and her "deathly" blood, *Ion* 1015.

[38] *Il.* 3.33–35. Philoctetes "wastes away with a savage ailment, struck by the wild imprint (*charagma*) of man-killing *echidna*," *Phil.* 267. The most popular episode of Cadmus's life in fifth-century iconography was his fight with the Theban snake, see Prag 1985:46–47. Sophocles wrote a *Laocoon*; the snake that kills Opheltes was essential to Euripides' *Hypsipyle*.

> You, girl! have drunk me out in secret,
> hiding in my house like a snake.

Clytemnestra accuses her daughter (another unmarried girl living in the parental home) of the same thing. This time it is Clytemnestra's soul that has been drained. Electra

> lived in my house, always drinking out
> unmixed the blood of my soul.

She does not compare Electra directly to a snake, but the resemblance of her charge to Creon's suggests the audience might sense snake resonances in her words. In the *Choephoroe*, which influenced Sophocles' *Electra*, the snake-haired Erinyes "drink the unmixed blood," which snakes supposedly drink. The same word, "unmixed," figures in both passages. The house-rulers see Antigone and Electra, like snakes, "drain" prosperity and strength: from the house, from its ruler's mind. Snakes drain from within, poison, squeeze. Snake resonances are fundamental to Erinyes, whose function is to hurt the mind. Infiltrating poison, entering by barb or sting or tooth, settles within, shrivelling innards. Passion stings and diminishes the mind, like *oistros*, like snakes. Snakes and insects furnish basic images of poison forced in, poison that destroys or maddens. Plato tells us of people who claimed to enchant "vipers, spiders, scorpions, and other beasts [*thēria*] and plagues [*nosoi*, 'diseases,' 'pests']." Against these images of fear human beings can only pit "magic spells."[39]

Another animal shadow behind emotion's images in the assault on innards is a hound. Dog fidelity, important in British culture, is a faint image in ancient Greek. Yes, Homer has Odysseus's hound. In classical times dogs, familiar in life and sport, were represented as petted by children. But on the whole, Greek dogs are images of impure untrustworthiness. They eat the corpses of men who nurtured them. The dogs Priam fed in his halls will chew his genitals when he lies dead in those same halls. Hector will give Patroclus's headless corpse to Trojan dogs. Dogs infest battlefields.[40] "Dog" is an insult designating shamelessness, greed, treachery, something rotten yet superficially friendly. *Sainō*, "I fawn," a characteristic dog word, means "I gladden," but also "I cheat, deceive." Dogs fawn on human beings, then turn and rend them, as in the myth of Actaeon, staged by Aeschylus in his lost *Toxotides*. In Euripides' *Bacchae*, Cad-

[39] *Ant.* 531, S. *El.* 784. For *ekpinein* here, cf. *Trach.* 1050–56, where the corrosive poisoned robe "drains," "sucks," "drinks" flesh. Cf. Aristophanes' parodic *tēn psuchēn ekpinousin*, *Nub.* 712. Erinyes: see *Cho.* 578. Snake-charming: see Pl. *Euthyd.* 290A. *Merimnai* besiege the mind like (implicitly) snakes, *Sept.* 291–93; see Chapter 7, n. 21.

[40] *Od.* 17.291–304, 326–27. Petted: see Richter 1930:32ff. Eating corpses: *Il.* 22.70–75, 17.127, 272. Inhabitants of the battlefield, image of its impurity: see R. M. Cook 1952:35ff.; Redfield 1975:169, 193–99, 259 n. 67.

mus foreshadows Pentheus's fate by recalling Actaeon, torn to pieces by his own hounds. Pentheus will be torn to pieces by his own mother and aunts, by "hounds of Lyssa [Madness]," led by his mother "glorying in her prey."[41]

Dogs had a low place in the sacrificial system. They were offered to "marginal," "tainted" gods, like Eilithuia (Birth-Goddess), Ares, Hecate, and other chthonic powers. Natural guardians, they were mythic or cult protectors of dark, secret places, tombs, shrines, the underworld: of the threshold between living and dead, light and dark. Hermes, god of threshold, was "Dog-Strangler." Cerberus, guardian of Hades, is a "raw-eating, bronze-voiced dog."[42]

Daemonic power worked through dogs, as through all animals. The lick of temple dogs at Epidaurus could carry Asclepius's healing touch. The hound-imagery for daemons of mind indicates how divinity works through the most ordinary, unregarded elements of domestic life. The greeting at one's own door, the passion in one's own innards, becomes a tearing assault. In one vase-painting, Lyssa, Madness, wears a hound's head above her own. *Lussa*, it has been argued, means "rabies, dog-madness, wolfish rage." Even in people, madness is canine or lupine. Maddening Erinyes are like hunting dogs (Chapter 8). When Orestes sees them, he says, "Clearly these are my mother's furious hounds." Ate, the mind's maddening self-destructive impulse, also has a hounding role:

> Ate, fawning, friendly at first,
> drives a human being aside into nets
> where there is no escape.[43]

"No escape": from hunting, snapping passions, and madness within.

THE MOBILE ADVERSARY ONE CANNOT FIGHT

From images of a rabid female animal-daemon, hunting, driving, to passion as male-sounding humanoid enemy: a conqueror, a huntsman felling his prey, a master who binds and mounts. The image (so simple it is near-invisible) of emotion "coming upon" innards recalls a motif in medical imagery (see Chapter 3). Disease or swelling liquid "falls upon" innards

[41] Insults: see, e.g., *Il.* 13.623, where Menelaus insults the Trojans (cf. 8.299: Teucer calls Hector "this mad dog"—he has shot many Trojans but cannot hit this one). Treacherous greed: A. *Supp.* 758; cf. *Il.* 1.159, 3.180, 18.396; Ar. *Eq.* 1029–34. Actaeon: *Ba.* 337, 976, 1144; A. fr. 244.

[42] Marginal, tainted: see Parker 1983:357–58, with n. 6. Cerberus: *Theog.* 311. Cult: see Nilsson 1906:396, 399. Hermes "Dog-strangler": Masson 1962:104–5.

[43] *Cho.* 1054, *Pers.* 96–100. Temple dogs: see Dodds 1951:114, 128 n. 65; Schouten 1967: ch. 3. Lyssa as "wolf's rage": see Lincoln 1975; Redfield 1975:201–3.

with warlike overtones. *Empiptein*, "to fall on," used of warriors "attacking" enemies, suggests deliberate violence. Oedipus crashes into the doors and "bursts into" the bedroom; Polyneices shouts to his allies to "fall upon" the gates of Thebes.[44] Emotion, like disease, is an invasive enemy, bursting in upon a barred room, a closed city, the guarded camp of heart or mind. Physiological intermingles with military language (as in our "attack") for illness. Emotion's advent is physiological seizure and enemy assault. Clytemnestra untruthfully says she hopes that

> Some *erōs* to ravish what they should not touch
> may not attack the army.

A terrible pity "falls on" Neoptolemus watching Philoctetes. A terrible *erōs* for war "fell upon" Greece by the gods' will. Non-Greeks, terrified of Xenophon's army, ran away, and "we were afraid some kind of *lussa*, like that which attacks dogs, had fallen on us."[45]

These little phrases belong to a telling pattern. "Fear came up on me"[46]: the movement this describes is common to more lavish images involving emotion's mobile attack. "Great grief comes on the land," anguish "moves to the *hēpar*," nothing "comes to" people without disaster, disaster "comes" upon us.[47] Within this there seems at work the idea of god "coming" at you irresistibly. Safer, less wayward figures of tragedy—many choruses, for instance—often pray that an emotion or god will "come" calmly. The form of such prayer is kletic, "summoning." The singer calls god to come to her, as Sappho summons Aphrodite ("Come to me now," "come here to me from Crete to this holy temple"), asking the god physically to leave one place of worship, and to "come" to a particular worshipper, hoping divinity will be *euphrōn*, "kind-minded," when she comes.[48] "Do not come to me *arrhuthmos* [unrhythmical, disorderly]," sings the chorus to Eros, watching Phaedra blasted by Love. They trust music, the medium of their

---

[44] See Chapter 3, nn. 20–22. Warriors: *Aj.* 58, *Rhes.* 127, *Il.* 16.81, *Od.* 24.526; in prose, e.g., Hdt. 3.146. Bursting in: *OT* 1262, *Phoen.* 1146, cf. *IA* 443.

[45] *Ag.* 341–42, *Phil.* 965, *IA* 808, Xen. *An.* 5.7.26.

[46] *Hupēlthe moi phobos*, *Phil.* 1231, cf. S. *El.* 1112, *OC* 1465, *Med.* 57 (*himeros*), Hdt. 6.134. Some scholars think the *hupo-* prefix is "inceptive" only: that the emotion need not be coming "up." (What is the force of *hupo* at, e.g., *PV* 878: do *sphakelos* and madnesses "burn" Io "*again*"?) The *hupo-* may have had a force we cannot feel. *Hupesti moi tharsos*, says the chorus, S. *El.* 479.

[47] Cf. *eiserchomai* (*eisēlthe moi ti theion*, *Cyc.* 411, cf. *Or.* 1668), *erchomai* (*Or.* 968, *HF* 771). Homer uses *hikanō* in such places, e.g., *Il.* 1.254, 240, etc. Cf. *Aj.* 938; *Ant.* 615, 618, where the repetition of *herpei* carries the ode's burden of menace. *Ouden herpei ektos atas*, . . . *eidoti d'ouden herpei* expresses a pattern of relationship between what happens to people, and covertly mobile adversaries that cause it.

[48] Cf. *OT* 166 *elthete kai nun*; Fraenkel 1931; Norden 1956:148; Sappho frr. 1, 2V. Cf. *molon anax Apollon . . . emoi xuneiē*, *Aj.* 705; *Hupne . . . euaes hēmin elthois*, *Phil.* 828; cf. Nisbet and Hubbard *ad* Hor. *C.* 1.19.16 (*veniet lenior*).

prayer, to order daemonic, mobile passion. "Rhythm," and the political, mental, social, aesthetic order that "rhythm" represents, is the antithesis of god or emotion "approaching" with violence. Music patterns, and thereby opposes, is the antidote to, violent passion. Another chorus, appalled at Medea's violent feeling for Jason, sings of *erōtes* (passions) "coming too much," which "yield neither virtue nor good fame." If Aphrodite "should come" moderately, gently, no other god is so welcome. But—

> Lady, never send against me
> an arrow rubbed ["anointed"] with desire,
> inescapable, from your gold bow.[49]

This kletic conceit may seem ornately removed from small phrases like "fear came upon me," but the pattern is common to both. Emotion approaches inexorably. All we can do is hope it will be gentle when it comes.

Our own feelings, then, are our adversary, on campaign against us. Love, "unconquered in battle, goes out to war" on his victims. Aristophanes mocks this language. One of his characters explains his drunken drowsiness by saying, "A nod-compelling Persian sleep set out to war against me—against my eyelids." But Aristophanes is parodying something real. In tragedy, anything that alters consciousness is an alien conqueror.[50] Emotion is a pugilist, Eros a boxer, Fortune "comes bad to wrestle with," Orestes "struggles" with Erinyes. The mind's relation to emotions, fortune, daemons, resembles the mythic combat of Heracles and Old Age or Death on vase-paintings. This hero, strongest of all human beings, "wrestles" against human-looking daemonic adversaries:[51] an enduring iconography for the mind's struggle against its feelings, for human beings' struggle against their selves and their fate.

For this fight against god as tragedy embodies it is full of self-conflict. It is impossible, but necessary—and also wrong. When Deianeira suspects Heracles is in love with someone else, she asks the messenger for the truth. She promises she can take it:

> You'll speak to a woman who's not wicked,
> who knows men don't enjoy
> the same things all the time.
> Whoever stands against Eros, like a boxer
> putting up his hands, is not thinking sanely,
> for Eros rules even gods when he wants. And me.

[49] *Hipp.* 529, *Med.* 627–34. *Chriei*: cf. above, n. 29.

[50] Ar. *V.* 12, *Hipp.* 527, *Ant.* 781. The love conceit develops: Ovid's Eros becomes a consul "triumphing" over the chained lover-poet, *Amores*. 1.2.23–48.

[51] *Trach.* 442, *Alc.* 889, E. *Supp.* 550. *Examillasthai* (used for "struggling with" rivals in a chariot race, *Hel.* 387) of Erinyes with Orestes: *Or.* 38, 431. Heracles: see *Alc.* 846–49; Brommer 1952; G. Giglioli:1953.

She would be mad, she says, to blame her husband or the girl he loves. She is reassuring:

> I will not add an extra evil
> to my burdens, by fighting against gods.[52]

A scholiast in the margin here explained "extra evil" (*noson epakton*) by saying *tēn theomachian*, "battle against god." Against the second line he writes, "To engage in rivalry with *erōs* is outright *theomachia* [fighting with god]."

But *theomachia* is one way of describing what Deianeira in fact goes on to do. She does fight against Heracles' *erōs*. She tries to swivel it back to herself with what she thinks is love-ointment, but is really corrosive poison. It destroys him, and thereby her. The *theomachos* is paradigmatically destroyed. We know of many tragedies (some survive in fragments) that explicitly told the story of a *theomachos* who fought with god and lost.[53] Obvious *theomachia* is more than useless. It is impious, fatal.

Gods may send emotion, be in it, be it. Emotion is their weapon, habitation, manifestation, medium. Through it they control human beings, demonstrate their power, and enjoy their own honor. Fighting emotion—in oneself or in others—may therefore mean fighting god. Deianeira exemplifies *theomachia* against emotion in another; Phaedra fights her own. Her play does not insist on her *theomachia*, stressing rather the impiety—or the flawed astounding piety—of the man she loves. Hippolytus dishonored Love by avoiding feeling it. Nevertheless, Phaedra enacts a *theomachia* against emotion in herself. To fight god at work in others or self ends in destruction.

If emotion is sent by god (or is god), why fight it? Because, divine though it may be, emotion is also, as its tragic images insist, anarchically damaging. Passions goad us to destruction. Even gods are not necessarily good in Greek culture: not, at least, in the sense of directing or desiring what is good for individual human beings. Self-control, controlling one's own passions, was an explicit ideal in fifth-century Athenian public discourse. Tragedy is drawn to the paradox that we must try to fight destructive emotion, despite its divinity, and despite the fact that fighting divinity is both impossible and wrong.

The impossibility is underlined by images of emotion as conqueror. Fear "conquers" *phrenes*. We are "conquered" by joy, sleep, misfortune. Youthful passion "conquers" *noos*. Desire "conquers" beasts and human beings, "subdues" the *thumos*. In an age without contraception,

---

[52] *Trach.* 438–45, 448, 491–92. I follow Jebb at 439 (Deianeira is saying she knows that people's desires change; otherwise one reads "Joy is not always given by nature to the same people").

[53] See Kamerbeek 1948:275–76; Padel 1981:112.

> A woman may [try to] escape the pain of childbirth
> and swear to her resolution, but once free of pain
> she gets caught in these same nets [of Eros],
> conquered by instant desire.[54]

Sometimes the mind seems to be a trussed animal overmastered by emotion. Frenzied Phaedra is told, "Some god ropes you back and strikes your *phrenes* aside." Ajax, maddened by Athene, is "yoked to a terrible *atē*." The mind yoked or bound: this image is apt for madness inflicted by Erinyes, or by Hera on the Proetides.[55] But it also appears, paradoxically, in more rational, intellectual contexts. Parmenides pictures logical necessity as a bond that ties down (and so limits) what exists. Plato speaks of "binding down" correct opinions in the mind.[56] Are philosophers deliberately using a familiar image, the mind bound by passion, by god, by madness like a prisoner or tethered animal, and turning it onto the power of logic, thereby suggesting that logic, too, is a daemonic overmastering force?

THE AERIAL TERRORIST

The mind "flies" in passion. Feelings hover, flit, swoop, outside in the world, inside in the mind, like wind, like winged words, songs, dreams, curses, hopes, prophecies. "Omen-watching fear flies near the heart." Love flies "with variegated wing," "on swiftest wing," over earth and sea. He is "winged" and attacks all living things. His "wandering" role persists in tragic song: "Love loves to wander," sings the wounded traveller at the start of Schubert's *Winterreise*. From classical times onward, Love is anarchically, autonomously mobile; double-edged as Hope, who is "far-wandering" through the vulnerable human world.[57]

Emotion in its flight and swoop resembles misfortune, clouds of disaster, menacing diseases, gods. The Persians, despairing at the massacre, say "a Stygian cloud"—that is, a cloud of death—"flies" over them. Tragic figures apostrophize their own fate by saying, "O daemon, how heavily you swept upon us, with heavy feet!" The "heavy" swooping power may be fortune, *daimōn*, *theos*, Erinys. Its "feet" attack the "head." Gods are heavy.

---

[54] S. fr. 932R, *Cho.* 600, A. *Supp.* 1005, *Il.* 14.316 (*edamassen*: most of the others involve *nikaō*); *Eum.* 88, S. *El.* 1272, *Ag.* 291, *Med.* 1195; *Il.* 23.604.

[55] *Aj.* 123, *Hipp.* 237–38 (which might suggest Phaedra "lashed" to her sickbed, but her *psuchē* is "bound," 159, and *phrenes*, 238, suggests that the image of binding applies to her emotional state). Scholia compare *anaseiriazei* ("ropes back") to reining in horses. Cf. *Eum.* 345, *desmios phrenōn*; Bacc. 11.43–44, *paraplēgi phrenas karterai zeuxas' anankai*.

[56] See Parm. fr. 8DK; Pl. *Meno* 97D–E; Vlastos 1965:154–55 with n. 20.

[57] *Ag.* 976–77 (which is ambiguous, see Fraenkel *ad loc.*, but I am interested in *potatai*, see Chapter 4, n. 59: whatever else is going on, fear "flies"); *Hipp.* 1270–76; *Ant.* 615. See above, pp. 96–97.

People in disaster are "heavy-fortuned," "heavy in *daimōn*." God's anger "swoops down" from above. Fate, *potmos*, is what "falls" (*pitnei*) upon us.[58]

These figures of tragic language interact with wind images of passion, and also with iconography of winged creatures. Birds tear both animal flesh (an eagle tearing a hare was a popular device on coins and seals) and, in a culture intimate with battlefields, human flesh. Eagles, which eat live prey, were not generally distinguished from vultures, which eat dead flesh. Dogs were both associated with and used as metaphor for winged predators. Corpses left to "glut the dogs and birds with fat and flesh," an image repulsive with religious and physical pollution, epitomized human vulnerability to the nonhuman. Creon's impiety flowers in a fantasy of precisely this *miasma*, pollution: he will not weaken, not

> if Zeus's eagles want to carry the body up as food,
> snatching him up to Zeus's throne.

Even this worst of all thoughts (and to think it is itself a sacrilege) will not make him bury that corpse.[59]

In life, myth, and poetry, birds scavenged human flesh. The resonances of du Maurier's *The Birds* go back to Homer. Eagles, birds of Zeus, are aerial rapists, daemonic raiders snatching from the air. One devoured the liver of Prometheus, object of Zeus's hatred, another "raped" (from *rapere*, "to snatch") Ganymede, object of Zeus's sexual desire. A king soothing his suppliants promises to defend them against everything, even the worst imaginable, a winged rape:

> No, we shall not give you up
> even to the seizing of winged creatures.[60]

"Eagles," with dog implications, provide a mixed image of savage, impure, scavenging beaks and claws, aerial assault: embodiment of the nonhuman world's carnivorous, destructive relation to the human body.

Close to this image are those other aerial assailants, the winged daemons. Ate walks on human heads. The Sphinx swoops on Thebes. Erinyes

---

[58] See *Pers.* 668; *Hipp.* 819; *OT* 263; *Pers.* 515; *Ag.* 1175; *Eum.* 370–80; *Ant.* 1272–73; *barudaimōn* (*Alc.* 865, *Tro.* 112), *barupotmos* (*Hipp.* 826, *Phil.* 1096, *OC* 1449), Aphrodite's *orgai* "swooping" on Hippolytus, *Hipp.* 1418. *Potmos*: see Dietrich 1965:12. Jebb (*ad OT* 263, 1299) documents fate and *daimōn* "swooping" on the head.

[59] *Ant.* 1040–43, cf. 29; see *Il.* 13.831, 11.454, 16.836; *Od.* 3.271; *Phoen.* 1630. See further Redfield 1975:168–69, 184–89, 199. "Dog" for winged carnivores (griffons, eagles, harpies): see *PV* 803, 1022; *Ag.* 136; A. fr. 282N; Ap. Rh. 2.89. Eagle rending hare: see Richter 1930: figs. 187–88. Eagles and vultures: see Pollard 1948.

[60] A. *Supp.* 510. The Danaids have already been compared to doves chased by hawks. Prometheus's eagle: A. fr. 193 (Cicero's reworking): "On the third day he rends me. . . . Then, crammed full on my fat liver, he screams and flies aloft. . . . When my gnawed liver swells, renewed in growth, he greedily returns again to his terrible meal," *TD* 2.10.23–25.

rush down on Orestes. Winged Lyssa "sinks into" Heracles' house and breast. Their wings sometimes figure in the poetry, sometimes not, but often appear on vases.[61] Eaglelike wings are an external token of daemonic advantage over human victims, and *daimōn*'s superior mobility.

All this is a compacted image for emotions as they come, go, and attack. Tragic images for emotion invest it with the force of birds of prey, especially Zeus's eagle, and of winged, part-animal daemons, giving off a characteristic Greek sense of being under attack by one's own feelings. Emotions seize, hold, plunder.[62] Daemonic power bombards from above, inhabits the air over human heads. "All the air is full of souls. These, daemons, and heroes send signs of disease and health to human beings," writes one Pythagorean. Hesiod's vision of human life is of continuous aerial terrorism. Millions of *nousoi* (ills, plagues) escaped Pandora's jar. They flew out. Now, they

> wander the earth among human beings.
> The earth is full of evils, and the sea.
> *Nousoi* come on human beings in daytime and at night.
> They wander *automatoi* [moving of themselves]
> bringing evils to mortals.

This sense of myriad airborne hostility continued to direct Greek religious understanding into the Christian world. Fifth-century Athenians would have recognized the world from which Augustine wrote, "The nature of demons is such that, with the sense of their air-made body, they easily outstrip the sense of earth-made bodies. Also, because of their air-made body's superior mobility, they far outstrip in speed not only the running of men and beasts, but even the flight of birds."[63]

Olympian gods inhabit the *aithēr*, "upper air." Like dreams, heroes, emotions, diseases, gods use winged things to attack us. Wings are a sign, in Augustine's phrase, of their "superior mobility." In tragedy, when gods enter human action, they come from above. The stage could represent this by a higher level: the roof of the stage building, a flying machine. Even a sea-goddess appears from above. Chthonic daemons may be "children of earth," but their feet hurt human heads. They, too, attack from air, just as Homeric gods fly down to the human world, sometimes on their own,

[61] Ate on men's heads: *Il.* 19.94–95. Winged, aerial Lyssa: see fourth-century illustrations of *Edoni*, Trendall and Webster 1971:III, 1.15; *HF* 864. Sphinx: see *Phoen.* 805. Winged figures on vases: see Ellinger 1953.

[62] E.g., *Il.* 16.599, *Phil.* 766 (*lambanein*), *Ba.* 828, *Or.* 460, *Phoen.* 622 (*echein*). Fear seizes (*harpazei*) the tongue in *apsuchia*, *Sept.* 259. Capture: see *Aj.* 216 (*maniai halous*); cf. *Hel.* 669 (*daimōn* or *potmos* "plunders people of their homeland"), *IT* 157 (*daimōn* "plunders me of my brother").

[63] D.L. 8.32, *Erg.* 100–104, Aug. *De div. daem.* 3.7.

sometimes on winged transport.[64] The stage conventions, like Homer's flying chariots for gods, express Greek culture's instinct that divinity penetrates human action especially sharply from above.

THESE INNER WOUNDS ARE REAL

Wings, teeth, claws, running and kicking feet, goads, ropes, stings, poison, arrows: animals and *daimones* together created a spectrum of assault. All the ingredients of science fiction start here: insects, carnivorous grotesque pursuit, invisible enemies and masters, cosmic rays. Western technological imagination has added a bit to this arsenal, but mainly it glosses and rearranges these essentially Greek ingredients. The images assembled physically what people were afraid of and found their way, through verbal translation and assimilation, through architectural and painterly influence, into our own European architecture (gargoyles, for instance), art, and languages.

It may be that the continuing hold of these images comes partly from the fact that they are used so early and cumulatively in tragedy, which was the first Western genre to stage the assault on human interiors by daemonic human passion. Daemon attacks the outside of the human being, what we think of as body, but also, more significantly, the inside. They attack that which (in our terms) conjures them up. In mediaeval imagination, the visual iconography, differently expressed but with the same basic ingredients, interacted with the attack of demons and devils on the soul. In the fifth century, it interacted with tragedy's evocation of emotion at war with innards.

We still use these shapes of fear. Science fiction, especially on screen, reactivates tragedy's gargoyle inheritance, the monstrous assault by the invasive alien. But our continuing use of these shapes can get in the way of our seeing them in a Greek context, with specific Greek (rather than universal) significances. As with physiological imagery of feeling, perception, and thought (Chapters 3, 4), we see more freshly if we try to separate our particular categories and preconceptions from the Greek material. For example, our assumption that emotion, sleep, misfortune, and gods are different sorts of thing is challenged by patterns of tragic language, which imply that all these act on the self in the same way.

Of course, there are vital questions here, especially about the "reality" of metaphor. We have met in other contexts the problem of metaphor's alien status in the fifth-century linguistic world. I go into this more fully else-

---

[64] Gods from machines, on roof: see Taplin 1977:440; Padel 1990:362 n. 96. Gods flying in Homer: e.g., *Il.* 5.366, 769. Thetis: *Andr.* 1228–30. Attack from above, Erinyes: *Eum.* 373; Eros treading like Homer's Ate on human heads: Pl. *Symp.* 195D; cf. above, pp. 83 (n. 23) and 129.

where.[65] Here I want to concentrate simply on the composite tragic picture of emotions lacerating innards, which is completed and fulfilled in tragedy by the actions, the result of passion's aggressively imaged activity. Concrete damage done within, to innards, is realized on stage in torn bodies, torn families. Hippolytus, horse-tamer, huntsman, active lord of animal bodies, has his own "young flesh" and blonde head mangled:

> Through my head dart sharp pains
> and a spasm of agony leaps through my brain.

He is torn apart by a dramatic action that began with the lacerating passion he inspired. Heracles, too, conquered the deadliest animals. Now his body is convulsed with burning pain:

> Look, all of you, at this miserable body. . . .
> Alas, a spasm of *atē* burns me now again,
> it shoots through my flanks:
> the terrible disease eats through me,
> will never let me rest.[66]

He, too, mastered animals. He, too, inspired passion. Now pain masters his body. The relation of pain to body evokes the biting animals, the stabbing, burning, shooting, leaping diseases, fires, and enemies familiar from tragic imagery of passion in its relations with innards. These two broken bodies are the consequence of action directed by torn-up minds.

But not their own minds. Part of tragedy's horror is the indissoluble linkage between different human beings, as well as between passion and action. The one whose body ends up torn may not be the one whose mind was torn in the first place. *Thumos* masters Medea; but it is not *her* body that is burned and stabbed. Hippolytus's torn body at the end of his play images the wounded *phrenes* of Phaedra at the beginning. Heracles' writhing body incarnates the internal writhing of Deianeira, who is "struck out"; who knows she is "warring with gods," yet who cannot bear to share Heracles; whose son will crown her pain by praying that "Justice in revenge and Erinys punish you."[67] Like Pentheus, like his cousin torn by dogs, Thebes' royal house will suffer *sparagmos* (tearing apart) in punishment for Pentheus's mad boasts.[68] In many tragedies, savage physical and familial destruction fulfils, results from, and is a concrete image of some earlier laceration of a mind. "There is no escape" from what savage passion, animal and daemonic at once, like Ate, will "drive" people to do, to themselves and each other.

---

[65] See above, pp. 10, 34–40; Padel (forthcoming).
[66] *Hipp.* 1342, 1351–52; *Trach.* 1079–83.
[67] *Hipp.* 239, 241, 248, 279; *Trach.* 386, 492, 441, 546, 808.
[68] See *Ba.* 268, 327, 332, 339, 359, 1352–80.

THE ALTERNATIVE: GROWTH WITHIN

Most daemonic metaphors of emotion represent it as animate onslaught. Emotion's daemonic relation to innards carries out the overall pattern expressed in physiological imagery of innards: something "comes in" from outside, vessel-like innards receive, are hurt and invaded, as women are perceived to be in sexual and social roles.

But, as with physiological imagery, there is an alternative. Something already in the mind comes out. In these images, something within—feelings, attitudes, or pain—is a growth, a harvest.

There is an odd slippage here, characteristic of archaic Greek but carrying on into tragic poetry, between flowering or vegetable growth on the one hand, and daemons personified through this imagery on the other. It is common in moral and political nouns that we ourselves might call abstract. *Hubris*, arrogant violence, "reaps a crop of *atē*," "flowers and withers among the young," and "plants" (that is, "engenders") a tyrant. *Eunomiē*, good rule, "withers *atē*'s growing flowers." These images figure in the late sixth and early fifth centuries in allegory-like explanations of moral change. The beginning of some feeling or attitude within an individual mind or a community grows, has harvest, withers away.[69]

Other more concrete images remind us that this moral burgeoning happens within an individual, as well as among and between people. It is inward and private as well as political. *Kear*, "heart," is "fed on laments," *thumos* "is fattened in gladness," the wise man "reaps a deep furrow through his *phrēn*, from which lofty counsels grow," suffering "flowers for the one who awaits it."[70] The innards are a flowering-place: of sadness, gladness, wise advice.

Inward harvest is connected also with images of emotion as a liquid bubbling in the mind. The froth or surface-scum of liquid is its "flower." This can be a foul image: pus, a herpetic poisoned bubbling. *Exanthein*, "to flower out," is used of boils and ulcers erupting. "Bloody foam" from murdered cows "flowers" on the sea. Blood "grown around" the centaur's wound is *thremma hudras*, poisonous "growth from the Hydra."[71] But Homeric phrases also put the bubbling overfroth of wine in flowering terms. "Mixing bowls were wreathed [or crowned] with drink." Men "set up mixing bowls wreathed [or crowned] with wine."

Are these flowers "real" garlands decorating the bowls? Or are they met-

---

[69] *Pers.* 821, S. fr. 718N, *OT* 873 (famously ambiguous, cf. Müller 1967; Winnington-Ingram 1980:188–93 with n. 30, Lloyd-Jones and Wilson 1990:100); Sol. fr. 4.36.

[70] *Cho.* 26, *PV* 539, *Sept.* 593–94, *Cho.* 1009.

[71] Th. 2.49, *IT* 300 (cf. Ar. *Lys.* 1257, foam "flowers" round Spartan teeth; the Aegean "flowers" with corpses, *Ag.* 659); see *Trach.* 572–74 with Long 1967:277; cf. Gal. 11.628; cf. *halos anthea* of sea, *AP* 6.206.

aphorical (as we would put it) liquid? Nearly a millennium later, Athenaeus, in the second century A.D., explains that bowls filled to the brim
seem "crowned" with wine. The swollen surface-tension, or overspill, is
crownlike, and wreathing means completion: "Fullness is completeness
and wreathing means a kind of fullness." What the Homeric words in fact
mean we cannot say, but these famous phrases worked in the Greek poetic
tradition to ensure that the idea of something filled with liquid was linked
with that of wreathing and flowers.[72] The Hippocratic author of *Humors*
begins his treatise by comparing the colors of the inner liquids (black bile,
yellow bile, blood, phlegm) touchingly to "the color of flowers." Aristotle
glosses Thales' idea that everything comes from water by explaining that
he got this idea from the dampness of seed. Moisture—water, semen—is
source of life and growth.[73]

Growth, flowering, harvest are connected in various Greek contexts,
therefore, with liquid. This has a strong bearing on ideas of innards, and
emotion in them. Inner liquids move along *poroi* (Chapters 3, 4). Sometimes it seems as if the *poroi* are hollow stalks containing generative liquid,
a growing vegetable tangle within us. Here, for instance, is Aeschylus's
image of Zeus's unknowable *prapides* ("understanding," "mind," a word
used rather like *phrenes*, but more sparsely, see Chapter 2):

> The desire of Zeus is not easily tracked;
> the *poroi* of his *prapides* stretch thick and shaggy,
> impossible to guess at or see.

Words that qualify Zeus's *prapides* here ("thick," "shaggy") are used elsewhere of bodily hair and of forests.[74]

This seems to be a double picture: an obscure mind (especially impenetrable because it belongs to Zeus) and an impenetrable forest. These two
ideas meet in Zeus's oak-forested center of prophecy, Dodona. One tragedy links Zeus's tree-shadowed prophecies with the future of his own son
Heracles. Heracles calls the oracle "my father's many-tongued oak." It
prophesied his moment of death. Death comes when he is marking out
"altars to his father Zeus and a sacred grove." Both Zeus's prophecy and
its fulfillment happen among his sacred trees. Dodona's trees are central to
Zeus's prophetic persona. Pausanias says that the title Zeus Skotitas, "Zeus
of Darkness," came from the shadowy forest surrounding his shrine.[75]

[72] Athen. 1.13D, 15.674F; cf. *Il.* 4.70, *Od.* 2.431.

[73] *Hum.* 1 (Loeb 4:62), Arist. *Metaph.* 983 B25.

[74] A. *Supp.* 87–90. *Prapides*: see Chapter 2, n. 30. *Daulos* of body hair: A. fr. 27; cf. *daskios*,
Pers. 316, *Trach.* 13. Strabo 9.3.13 (Casaubon 423) says the name Daulis came from *daulos*,
used for forests. "The place-name comes from the *dasos*. For they call *dasē daulous*." *Daskios* for
forest or wooded mountain: *Od.* 5.470, *Ba.* 218.

[75] See *Trach.* 171–74, 1167–68, 753–54; Paus. 3.10.6.

When Zeus's unimaginable interior and understanding are represented through forest-language, a Dodona-like shadowiness of trees expresses his mind and meanings, which are intricate, and to human beings obscure. *Poroi*, therefore, may have the force of both inner channels and of forest paths. "Impossible to guess" is *aphrastoi*: "unseen," "impenetrable," "impossible to understand." Human beings try to track what Zeus intends but cannot see it clearly. One never sees clearly what is in anybody's *splanchna* (Chapter 3), especially not in those of the supreme god, whose place of prophecy is shadowy but growing.

This passage shows us again, I think, that profound connections are at work in the anatomical assumptions (often, to us, absurd) underlying Greek imagery of feeling. Liquid and air flow along *poroi*, nourishing heart and mind as plants are nourished by rain and wind, fattening them with thought, with feeling. "Valued counsels" grow from a well-tilled "deep furrow" in the *phrēn*. *Thumos* is fattened "in festivities," the heart nourished by laments. The mind bears "fruit."[76]

Many passions are represented as liquid (Chapter 4), but the ones that particularly foam and flower, that burst out and die away, are madness and sexual passion. If Heracles had never seen the altar where he received the poisoned robe, he would never have "looked upon this flower of madness, impossible to soothe." Lycurgus, who insulted Dionysus, was imprisoned in a cave:

> In this way the terrible flowering force (*menos*)
> of madness trickled away.

Helen seems the "heart-biting flower of *erōs*," a flower of heart-stinging liquid.[77] Overspilling frenzy "flowers," then "trickles away." Passion is something within that is ex-pressed, pressed out.

It would be simple to say this strand of imagery, like the out-swelling liquids in physiological images, represents the minor partner in that doubleness with which, I have argued, the fifth century images the mind. Instead of an external cause or force, here is something within coming out: emotion, madness, *hubris*, an innate growth. But it is not so simple when we remember ambiguities contemporary with tragedy: about women's role in reproduction, which is one basis of this growth image, and about the mind's creativity (Chapter 5). Faced with images of innards or emotion as a harvest, another image we must bring into play is mind as earth. If emotions are a vegetable growth within, the mind is their field, their soil,

---

[76] *Sept.* 593–94, *PV* 539 (cf. *Od.* 6.156), *Cho.* 26, Pi. fr. 211 Snell. The Erinyes' song "withers" (*Eum.* 332) as if the *phrenes* it damages are a growing thing.

[77] *Ant.* 959–60 (where Jebb compares Pl. *Polit.* 310D, *teleutōsa exanthein pantapasi maniais*, and *Trach.* 998). Cf. *Ag.* 742 (though Lloyd-Jones [1990 i. 313] suggests this means a "flowering" flame, see above, n. 24).

home to all the ambiguous resonances that this image itself entails. "Female" earth is sometimes not the creator, merely the receiver of the seed.[78] If mind has harvest, if agony and madness flower in it, the absent question is, who plants it there? Where does the seed come from?

Tragic vegetation images of mind are inevitably linked with images of divinity. Gods plant things in innards. When Homer's Ithacan poet pleads with Odysseus for his life, he says he is "self-taught,"

> but god planted all kinds of paths of song
> in my *phrenes*.

His phrase sites planting images of mind within the idea of intimate daemonic incursion into *splanchna*. Aeschylus says something similar in a fragment of his *Niobe*:

> When god wants to destroy a house completely
> he plants the cause in [or "for"] human beings.

This image bears upon the entire tragic nosology of pain. Prometheus says he helped human beings because he stopped them foreseeing their death: "I settled [established, planted, colonized] blind hopes within them."[79]

Is this good or bad? Do we owe even the ways in which we face our destructive impulses and the fact of our ultimate destruction to seeding from outside? Phrases that look as if emotion might be homegrown, a flowering-out from the mind rather than daemonic intrusion into it, are not a true alternative to the overall pattern that emotion comes in from outside. They turn out to suggest—maybe—that same daemonic intrusion, at a deeper, prior level. The root may be in the mind, but where did the seed come from? Deep fifth-century ambivalences over male and female roles in procreation (Chapter 5) are carried through into the growth imagery of feelings in the mind. There is no escape from *daimōn* in tragic innards. Even when they are thought of as plants.

[78] See above, pp. 58–59.

[79] *Od.* 22.347–48, A. fr. 156N, *PV* 252 (*katoikizein*: cf. *OC* 637, where Theseus will "settle" Oedipus in the *chora*, and *Ant.* 1069, where Creon "implanted" a living soul in the tomb).

Chapter 7

ANIMAL, *DAIMŌN*: BRINGERS OF DEATH AND DEFINITION

Nonhuman: What We Defend Ourselves Against

I have smelt them, the death-bringers . . . have seen at noon
Scaly wings slanting over, huge and ridiculous. . . . I have felt
The horn of the beetle, the scale of the viper . . .
In the mews in the barn in the byre in the market-place
In our veins our bowels our skulls.·
　　　　—T. S. Eliot, *Murder in the Cathedral*

TRAGEDY IS a hunted world. Human beings walk in, over, and through multiple hostile forces, on the defensive against the nonhuman. I assume this reflects how most of tragedy's audience saw themselves in their own world, some (but not all) of the time. We do not think all the time of the multiple chemical and viral forces we know are attacking us. If someone not professionally concerned with these forces (not an immunologist or a radiation expert) worries about them incessantly, we use words like paranoid, phobic, neurotic, superstitious, obsessed. The late fourth century B.C. had a different word for such a person: *deisidaimōn*, "*daimōn*-fearful." Daemons, like AIDS, were truly to be feared. But they had to be lived with, just as we have to live with radioactivity, carcinogens in our food, and a thinning ozone layer. It seems mad to put up with a world like ours. It was no madder—less mad, perhaps—to live in a world in which similar threats were daemonic, and out of human control.

To approach tragedy's thought-world, we should remember how we knowingly face unknowable chemical damage, and transmute this into animate and malign form. In the fifth, fourth, and third centuries at Athens, the shared awareness of animate nonhuman menace was an ordinary part of life. Within this framework, everyone was fluctuatingly aware of different specific threats. To be afraid constantly was a bit odd. It was, says Theophrastus, "a sort of cowardice in relation to *to daimonion* [the daemonic]." A *deisidaimōn* will consult professionals—the exegetes of sacred law, the board to which ceremonial questions were referred—on the most trivial portents. If mice gnaw his meal sack, he ignores practical advice like "Mend the bag" and demands expiatory rites. If "the red snake" appears in his house, he calls on the god Sabazius. If he sees "the sacred snake," he makes a shrine on the spot.[1] The *deisidaimōn* takes normal daemonic fears to ridiculous extremes. But this shows us, the outsiders, normal arenas of Greek fear.

For most people, the daemonic, like snakes in the house, was a basic fact of life, unexamined, shared by all in their own way while they got on with living. Plato complains that personal shrine-making, especially by women, is choking every house and village with altars (like, presumably, that which the *deisidaimōn* erects on seeing the snake). Nervous people in trouble, or after nightmares, "promise seats to divinities." They "fill every house, every quarter of the city, with their foundations." These shrines were little monuments to local anxieties. In our own century, archaeology has turned up the massive and complex fundamental fears underlying Greek cult. Twentieth-century readings of myth have also stressed these underlying—or overlying—insecurities. Our epoch has specialized in this note in Greek culture: in the Greek sense of human helplessness that, as E. R. Dodds said in his influential book, "has its religious correlate in the feeling of divine hostility."[2]

We are products of our own epoch, culturally predetermined to perceive the anxieties of Greek culture. That does not mean we have created them, merely that we are good at noticing them (and probably correspondingly bad at noticing others). Many Greek rites in which the human tries to manipulate the nonhuman articulate both a Greek need to control the nonhuman and perceptions of its uncontrollabilty. Tragedy, I think, was one of the deepest expressions of this need and this perception.

In our lives, we might expect to divide "nonhuman" into two categories, animal and divine, or natural and supernatural. These divisions will not do for fifth-century experience. The fifth-century world is "naturally" charged with gods (Chapter 6), as radically as ours is with pollutant chemicals, radioactivity, bacteria, electricity, television waves. We do not think continuously of these forces in the world around and in us, yet we know they are there. They are invisible, but we acknowledge their power to excite, benefit, and hurt us. For fifth-century Greeks, gods are active in every part of the environment: wells, trees, wine cups, street corners, shadows, the hearth, the door hinge. They are in every activity: running races, ploughing fields, throwing a pot, falling ill, making love, giving birth, crossing the threshold, giving presents, singing songs, sharing the last drink at sup-

---

[1] See Thphr. *Char.* 16 (below, n. 15), Plu. *De deis.*
[2] See Pl. *Legg.* 909E; Dodds 1951:29; J. Harrison 1962:1–11; above, Chapter 1.

per. They lurk in every relationship: with parent, guest, spouse, child, stranger, head of the tribe, lover, enemy, friend, athletic rival, or commercial partner.

Surrealism creates something like this world: "The things that surround us, usually quiet, domesticated and invisible, are seen suddenly as strange. . . . The real sea is cold and black, full of creatures." Carlo Levi in *Christ Stopped at Eboli* observed, perhaps, its lingering counterpart in that isolated South Italian community of the 1930s: a world where "everything has a double meaning. The cow-woman, the werewolf, the lion-baron, and the goat-devil are only notorious and striking examples. People, trees, animals, even objects and words have a double life." His representations of this life match the thorough penetration of lived experience in fifth-century Greece by divinity. There is "no room for religion, because everything participates in divinity, everything is actually, not merely symbolically, divine: Christ and the goat; the heavens above, and the beasts of the fields below." In Levi's village, this attitude coexisted with Christian practice. Even church ceremonies became "pagan rites celebrating the existence of inanimate things which the peasants endow with a soul," deeply interwoven with "innumerable earthy divinities of the village." As in early mediaeval Europe, the supernatural watched every human move from every corner.[3]

The way in which tragedy's first audiences experienced the world might well strike us, I think, as surreal. Or more accurately, as super-real. A world crackling with temperamental, potentially malevolent, divinity. Personal, particular gods, permeating and disturbing all things, acting through the world's solid fabric, in "natural" elements (Chapter 6), and in animate nature, in the animals. Imagine the possibility of car crash or plane crash, which we live with all the time, personified as a whimsical, amoral, easily angered nonhuman being, invisible and loose beside us on the road. Picture sudden impossible cruelty in family relationships as an animate unpredictable presence in the house, or incarnate in the family dog who suddenly—no one knows why—bites a child.

The chorus of Sophocles' *Ajax* wonders why Ajax went mad. "He would never had gone 'to the left' from his own *phrēn*," that is, he would not have done such mad, bad things by himself. Which god has he offended? Did he shoot a deer belonging to Artemis? Or fail to give a thank-offering to Ares? The sailors are on the right track, but pick the wrong gods. It is Athene's anger that will destroy Ajax. His offense was telling her he could do without her. Sudden destruction, sudden abnormal destructive passion, is most "naturally" explained by previous offense to divinity, inadvertent or unnoticed at the time. This, a basic feature in the landscape of Homeric

---

[3] See Murdoch 1953:16, on Sartre's *La Nausée*; Huizinga 1955:148–51; Levi 1947: ch. 12.

myths, is the backdrop to tragedy. But it is recognizable also in anthropological reportage of other polytheistic religions and communities.[4]

There are so many gods. You may offend any without knowing. From a Western, loosely atheistic, materialist perspective, this seems an uncomfortable way of being in the world, comparable in our own society to mental disturbance. But such comparison is misleading. It points only to what we might feel if we, with our present intellectual and imaginative baggage, were suddenly removed to that world. In any definition of madness, an essential condition is that the outlook labelled "mad" must deviate from the culture's agreed horizons of normality. But in the fifth century, everyone, except possibly a few intellectuals, shared this way of seeing. Though the outlook sounds uncomfortable, it clearly had enduring, even comforting aspects. We cannot compare it to obsessive experience within a Christian framework, like that which led to witch-hunts in Puritan New England. It could have obsessive expression, but in practice it was a socially stable, adaptive mentality, with emotional and imaginative advantages. Despite its premise of nonhuman hostility (whose most obvious expressions I shall chart in this chapter), this mentality seems to have provided many different effective communities with a safe, flexible, interesting basis for an extraordinarily long time.

ANIMAL WEAPONRY

Fears of the nonhuman are crystallized in its aggressive tokens, the weapons of animal and *daimōn*. As we have seen, the word *daimōn* covers Olympian gods but also many other forces, some less iconographically precise than Olympians, and many of them chthonic, "of earth." Animal and this hold-all concept "daemon" belong together in a fifth-century world, though they are generally distinct in ours. Keeping to our categories, I start with animals. But they lead to daemon, all the same.

Specific animals provide the Greeks, as they provide all preindustrial cultures, with most of their basic images of things to fear. Aristotle says men in passionate and morbid states, prone to illusions, "mistake figures on the wall for animals and make bodily movements to escape them." Raw fear takes animal form. Basic tools by which nonhuman hurts human are animal. Dogs, eagles, vultures, snakes, insects, teeth, beaks, airborne claws, scavenging, raiding, persecutory, impure; earth-born blood-drinking tongues, poisoning eyes, injected poison, stings or bites that madden and enflame: these are the metonyms and media of animal aggression (Chapter 6). In pursuit as in attack, animals have an unfair advantage. Their feet run

---

[4] *Aj.* 171–81, cf. *Il.* 9.534–40: Oeneus forgot Artemis's offering and was punished by the boar that killed his son. Cf. the Dinka thought-world described in Lienhardt 1961:147–58.

faster than human feet and can tear and squeeze their prey. Wings put them above their quarry; they can remove us to a different level, as Zeus's eagle carries off Ganymede. From early times, metalwork, sculpture, pottery, and poetry use wings as a cardinal emblem of all the advantages over defensive humanity possessed by the nonhuman: by the animal world, by gods, and by daemonized personifications and diseases.[5]

Horses and bulls add to this arsenal. Horses, larger, faster, stronger than human beings, suggest uncontrollable physical violence. They kick, they bite, and they provide men (not, in normal life, women) with their fastest transport. Hippolytus's name means something like "Releaser of [or, Released by] Horses": a hieroglyph suggestive of his life and death. Horses "nourished at his own mangers" destroyed him. Mythical horses sometimes eat people, as in the story used by Aeschylus in his lost *Glaucus Potnieus*. These mares were fed on human flesh to keep them fierce in battle and eventually ate their master. Medea glares like a bull at her children, "as if she would do something to them." Glaring, snorting, bellowing, "violent bulls" are "angry in their horns," and again, myth goes further than life: the bulls that Jason yokes also breathe fire. The struggle of man against bull—Heracles and the Cretan bull, Theseus and the bull of Marathon—was a favorite theme of sculptors, or of those who commissioned them, and figured, for instance, on the metopes of the Athenian treasury at Delphi.[6]

Huge emblems of uncontrolled male aggression, paradigms of frightening violence, horses and bulls swell the range of nonhuman weapons with hooves, fiery breath, horns, enormous heavy teeth, physical superiority in strength and size, and a precarious temper that men may not be able to control. Women are not pitted against them in Greek myth, though Medea's drug saves Jason against the fiery breath.

Already here we must add in the daemonic. These weapons which their animal possessors use on the human body are also, in tragic imagery, the main ways in which daemons, and daemonized personifications, attack the human interior (Chapters 6, 8). And in the fifth century, animals are not only animals, as they are mostly for us. They also embody daemonic violence working through the everyday world. Human beings apprehend divinity through its manifestations here, around them. Any animal, at any moment, might be alive with *daimōn*. A god might be manifest in an animal in the woodshed or kitchen. Animal epiphanies were a normal part of imaginative and lived experience. That is why the *deisidaimōn* rushes off to

---

[5] See Arist. *De insom.* 3.460B3. Ganymede: see Burkert 1985:399 n. 29. In Homer, *theoi* "snatched him up [*anēreipsanto*] to pour wine for Zeus," *Il.* 20.234. Wings of personifications: Körte 1874:49ff. Cf. Chapter 6, nn. 57–63.

[6] Horses: *Hipp.* 1241–42, 1355; A. frr. 36–39. Bulls: *Ba.* 743; *Med.* 92, 278. See, e.g., Richter 1930:20–21.

the board of sacred interpreters when he sees mice or snakes at home, where we might call the pest-control officer. Animal epiphany is standard in Greek myth, in cult, and in representation of innumerable gods. Gods took animal disguises. They had animal familiars and ancient animal-epithets.[7]

An extra, specifically Greek reason to fear animals, therefore, is that they are part of the unpredictable physical fabric through which gods express their power. Horses, for instance, are a standard (though expensive) part of human war, sport, and sacrifice. When men think they are controlling them, horses may in fact be responding to divine will. Most great race-tracks have a shrine to Taraxippos, daemonic "Horse-Disturber," a "hero" who makes horses shy and stumble. Presumably competitors try to buy him off before the race.[8] But none of this means the human arts of horse-manship and horse-training are not needed. Humans must do what they can, despite acknowledged possibilities of divine interference.

Horses' violence is inseparable from their violent divine associations. They, as well as bulls, are the right sacrifice to Poseidon. Aristophanes' horse-mad boy swears by Poseidon. Horses are linked with other chthonic gods, too, and with earthquakes, floods, sea, winds: any heaving violence of land, water and air, as an earthquake culture knows it. In Sophocles' "Colonus ode," Athens is blessed in being "well-horsed, well-oceaned." She has Poseidon's loving beneficence rather than fury:

> Cronus's son, lord Poseidon, you gave us this boast:
> first in our roads you made the rein
> that tames [or "heals"] horses,
> and the flying oar. . . .

Poseidon's blessings are bit, rein, oar. With these frail instruments, and by his grace, human hands control the violence of his horses and his sea. Horses also appear on gravestones, reminding us (though like all signs they are open to multiple interpretation) of their links to *chthōn*, "earth," and death.[9]

Bulls and horses belong with earth and sea, on which human beings walk and sail and which they temporarily furrow, but which outlive and can

---

[7] See Vernant 1980:121. Animal epiphanies: see Harrison 1927:447–50; Burkert 1985:64; cf. Dionysus Melanaigis: Vidal-Naquet 1986:112. Bird-gods: see Harrison 1927:101–17; Detienne 1981b:20. Some gods had animal foster-parents, see Preller 1887–94, 1:351; Dietrich 1974:109 n. 230.

[8] See Rohde 1925:127, 147 n. 59. Paus. 10.37.4 suggests Delphi was unusual in having no race-course shrine to Taraxippos.

[9] Ar. *Nub.* 83, *OC* 711–18. Horses' chthonic resonances: see Farnell, 4:59, 15–23; Halliday 1913:104; Dietrich 1965:106, 361–68; cf. Kirk 1970:155; below, n. 12; Vernant 1985:53. Nilsson changed his interpretation of horses on graves from chthonic death-symbols (1906:66–72) to emblems of aristocratic status ([1925] 1940:104 n. 1).

overwhelm them. Poseidon sends the bull, the "monster from the sea," to panic Hippolytus's horses. Other male gods, too, even Zeus, may be "in" a bull. Pentheus sees the Dionysiac stranger as a bull. Cows belong with "ox-eyed" Hera (Chapter 6).[10] The bull's possibilities of violence sum up the diverse divinity, chthonic and Olympian, within it.

USING ANIMAL IS USING *DAIMŌN*

Tragedy stresses nonhuman aggression and humanity's defensive vulnerability to the nonhuman. But like the world outside it, tragedy also assumes that human can, up to a point, tame and manipulate nonhuman. Here is the balance we met in the causality of medical writers. What is outside intrudes, damagingly, but human can fight back, can try to control the stuff and forces of damage, and send in its own forces. What is in human beings does ex-press itself into the world.

From the Bronze Age onwards, art and poetry reflect the confident, controlling side of human relations with animals. Like us, Greeks used the nonhuman qualities of animals, especially their self-protective or aggressive powers, to make up human deficiencies, as we use police horses and guide dogs. Bronze Age boars-tusk helmets survive in our museums. We hear of hide shields, horn bows. The bow with which Pandarus breaks the truce is made from the horn of an ibex he shot. Classical Greeks used war dogs and war horses, wore and slept under animal skins, ate animal meat, used animal strength and warmth in agriculture, sport, hunting, war.[11]

The extra daemonic dimension to relations with the "natural" world meant that Greeks also used animals, or parts of them, for getting in touch with gods, just as gods used animals as emissaries or instruments in contacting human beings. Most cultures "treat animals with reverence similar to that we show the gods." Urban, agnostic Western culture is historically anomalous in its generally nonreligious attitude to animals. We do not normally think there is divine power in them. But the tragic audience was familiar with animals in an infinite number of cult roles.[12] Since animals were an inevitable aspect of human relations with gods, their daemonic contact was another "natural" nonhuman quality that humanity could tap. In many magic and ritual ceremonies, animal fleeces, skins, blood, or flesh were central. From Pindar onwards, we hear of the "wryneck" spell, the

[10] *Hipp.* 1214, *Ba.* 920, cf. 1159 (Dodds *ad loc.*); see Nilsson 1906:80ff.; Farnell, 1:56–58; A. B. Cook 1914–40, 1:430ff., 3:590ff.; Harrison 1962:431–36.

[11] *Il.* 4.105–11, see Snodgrass 1967:19, 24, 88, 140 (war dogs); see further Keller 1913; Rahn 1967; Toynbee 1973.

[12] See Bergson 1935:153–57; and among many discussions, Bodson 1978; Burkert 1983:84–93, 136–43, 204–12, 1985:64–66; Detienne 1977:37–58 (with Vernant 1980:130–67).

bird tied on a wheel, beak, legs, and wings, to recall a lost lover. Aphrodite brought this magical, "maddening," erotic bird from Olympus. Crows' eggs and bats' eyes feature in erotic spells. Dogs and snakes in healing temples were instruments of, or embodied, the god's touch. Dogs appear in many other Greek magic rites. Puppies were especially popular in purificatory rites.[13] I suppose they were cheap.

Snakes, however, are the most important animal in Greek magic and cult. They were not used as sacrifices but were interpreted as messengers. The double meaning of *pharmakon*, both "healing drug" and "poison," sums up the ambiguity of Greek snake-power. Snakes guard dark divine places and hidden objects against human beings. Maybe they also protect human beings from the defiling darkness of earth. Snakes crystallize the double-edgedness of *pharmaka*.[14] They were an emblem of fear, potent in poisonous glances and bites (Chapter 6), but they were also healers. Asclepius's sign and incarnation was a snake. Several species were sacred to him, including the two that Theophrastus's *deisidaimōn* meets in his house: the so-called "sacred snake" (Aristotle in another context mentions a snake "some call sacred," a small kind "of which the larger kinds are afraid," and when it bites "the flesh mortifies at once all round"), and "the red snake," which Aelian says did not have a dangerous bite, was gentle, and was sacred to Asclepius. This one appeared in temples of Asclepius and also Dionysus.[15] It must have been hard, in fact, to get rid of any snake that had moved into, or under, a temple.

Snakes supposedly knew healing herbs. The Epidauran records illustrate many snake-healings: the dumb girl who recovered her voice, crying out when she saw a snake; the woman cured of barrenness when she dreamed of a snake coiled on her stomach. By 430 B.C., twenty-five years before Sophocles and Euripides stopped work, Asclepius's snake was in place at Athens, both in the city and in the terrified imagination of the plague-struck citizens.[16]

---

[13] Fleeces: Pley 1911; Harrison 1962:23–28. Cf. Melanaigis: Vidal-Naquet 1986:112. Wryneck: Pi. *P.* 4.214, *N.* 4.35; Xen. *Mem.* 3.11.17; Theoc. 2.17; Hor. *Ep.* 7.7; Gow 1934; Vernant 1980:143; Sourvinou-Inwood 1979:245 n. 76. Birds in ritual, esp. erotic spells: see Dodds 1951:290, 304 n. 63; Pollard 1977:130ff.; Moke 1984; Winkler 1990:81. Snakes and dogs in healing temples: Dodds 1951:114, 128 nn. 63–64; Majno 1975:154, 165–66; above, Chapter 6, n. 43. Dogs in magic: Scholz 1937. Puppies: see Plu. *QR* 68; Thphr. *Char.* 16.36.

[14] Snake-guardians of, e.g., Golden Fleece, cities, first Delphic shrine: see Ap. Rh. 4.128–60; Mitropoulos 1978: pt. 1, 49ff.; Fontenrose 1959: chs. 1, 5. At Trophonios's shrine: Halliday 1913:822, 244. Snakes and *pharmaka*: see Nicander *Theriaca* 31ff., cf. Derrida 1972, on the ambiguities of *pharmaka* in Plato.

[15] Thphr. *Char.* 16; Arist. *HA* 607A30; Ael. *NA* 8.12; schol. Ar. *Pl.* 690. Snakes and healing generally: see Apollod. 3.1.77; Halliday 1913:88–89; Dodds 1951:275; Mitropoulos 1978: pt. 2, ch. 13.

[16] See Herzog 1931; Wilamowitz 1931–32, 2:222; Dodds 1951:193; Lloyd-Jones 1983: 212 n. 13.

Snakes are also linked with prophecy. In some cults, snakes were themselves prophetic. In some myths, snakes lick the eyes of seers, such as Melampus, Cassandra, and Helenus, empowering them to foresee the future
or understand birds' speech.[17] Snakes, the most obvious chthonic creature
to emerge in our surface-world, are the prime animal intermediary between
this world and its underneath. They are "children of earth" like Erinyes or
Madness (see Chapter 5). They incorporate multiple messages and connections between human and divine, a ubiquitous presence in hero and healing cults, prophecy myths, and cults of the dead. Human beings had to put
up with snakes anyway, and used the earth-power with which they invested
snakes to exploit daemonic contact for, as they thought, human good.[18]

Snakes also figure in Olympian cult. Certain cults of Zeus, Ares, and
Athene, for instance, gave snakes an important role. Artemidorus says that
a snake in a dream "signifies all the gods to whom it is sacred, namely Zeus,
Sabazius, Helius, Demeter, Kore, Hecate, Asclepius, and the heroes." Zeus
may appear, or be represented, as a snake. Gods "send" snakes, as they send
other destructive animals, against human beings.[19]

The spectators, leaving a tragic performance, went home to snakes in
their houses. The *orophias* lived in their roofs. Presumably it kept down
mice, but it would have been hard to keep out anyway. As in India, house
snakes were propitiated, given milk, honey-cakes, and shrines. The snake
might be, or might be the familiar of, an ancestor or a hero. Tragic audiences lived with snakes, venerated them, watched specialists handle them
for show or magic. They took snakes' healing power for granted.[20] But
they also lived with the possibility that gods might turn the snake's power
against them at any moment. The fact that snakes might be divine did not
make them any less dangerous. Snakes represent a multivalent threat to
humanity, which matches their ambiguous mythic links with divine punishment and death: an image of lightning-quick, invisible menace in one's
own house.

In one play, besieging armies are like snakes attacking a bird's nest.
Later, one of the leaders of this army "cries out like a snake with noonday
hissing." In between these two images, the frightened women of the cho-

[17] Melampus, Cassandra, Helenus: see Porphyry *De abstinentia* 3.4; Pliny *NH* 10.49, cf.
76, 136; Bouché-Leclerq 1879–82, 2:12–20; Löffler 1963; Dowden 1989:100–102. Prophetic snake given honey-cakes: see Suda s.v. *melitounta*.

[18] See Lloyd 1983:10–11 n. 14; Artemid. 22.13.103. For chthonic power generally, see
Burkert 1985:199–203. Snakes in cults of the dead: see Mitropoulos 1978: pt. 1, chs. 2–3.
Further snake associations: see Chapter 6, nn. 36–39; Nilsson [1925] 1940: ch. 4.

[19] Zeus cults: see Nilsson 1906:25, 401; Burkert 1985:201. Athene, Ares: see Farnell
1:290, 5:401. Gods "sending" animals: below, n. 46.

[20] Schol. Ar. *V.* 206; Hesych. s.v. *orophias*; Eustathius *ad Od.* 2.337. Snake-charming: Pl.
Euthyd. 290A (cf. Chapter 6, n. 39); Tibullus 1.8.20; cf. *V. Ec.* 8.71. Snake-handling: see
Plu. *Alex.* 2.4–6; Hamilton *ad loc.*

rus say their minds are besieged by *merimnai*, "cares": the mind is a target for besieging activity simultaneous with the siege on their city, already compared to a snake's attack on a nest.[21] Snakes threaten human beings and their houses, in which they are an inevitable, mostly unseen presence: a tight, perfect image of the daemonic within.

Other animals, too, remind us, as they must have reminded fifth-century Greeks, so aware that an animal might be under divine control rather than their own, that the human grasp upon or ordering of the nonhuman is fragile. Bird wings and bird song, for instance, incarnate what is out of human reach. The human desire to see meaning in the world is drawn above all to the birds, to decipher their flight, behavior, and calls. "Bird omen," *oiōnos*, is a general word for "omen." "You call every kind of omen a bird," chants Aristophanes' bird-chorus. The birds in this play go on strike, cutting communication between human beings and gods. Human prophets read *oiōnoi* and their patterns, like animal entrails, as a transmission of divine will. One mark of the prophet, in Greek as other cultures, is understanding "speech of birds." Augury, one of the most basic Greek forms of divination, is an attempt to see pattern in, and thereby control, the unreachably nonhuman.[22]

In areas of experience we do share with the Greeks (like agriculture, war, sport, and domestic life), but also in important aspects of their experience we cannot share (like cult), Greeks made intimate, physical use of animals to supplement their own powers, to give themselves, materially or symbolically, nonhuman strength. But in using animals, the Greeks were handling, uninsulated, material charged with energy to which our own imaginations are essentially immune. Divine power could seep through animals and rush into human life. Taming or using any member of the animal world was dangerous, both because of its private animal violence and because of its daemonic affinities. All the more cause for pride, therefore, when humans (usually men) do master animals.

NONHUMAN DEFINITION OF THE HUMAN

The Greeks, like other cultures, also used animals to think with. Especially about human nature. They did this in two main ways. One is through "animal semantics." From Homer onwards, animals provided a familiar

[21] *Sept.* 290–94, 381. These images, close together, contribute to the atmosphere of siege in this part of the play. The *merimnai* passage does not mention snakes, but lies between the two snake images, which resonate in this play with the Theban *drakōn*. But see also A. *Supp.* 989, where the evil herald, a "two-footed snake," "bites like an *echidna*."

[22] See Ar. *Av.* 719 (with Gould 1985:18); Halliday 1913:248–71; Bouché-Leclerq 1879–82, 1:142–44; Lindsay 1965:252; Pollard 1977:116. "Speech of birds" motif: see Halliday 1913:82, 249 n. 3. *Oiōnos* can mean "bird" (*Il.* 24.293) or "omen" (*Il.* 2.859, *Hel.* 1051).

"code" to articulate thoughts about human qualities and behavior. The early poet Semonides classified types of wife by sorting women into animal categories. The animal fable and animal comparison provided a critical typology of human nature. In Homer, warriors are like boars or lions, "whose strength is not slight." In Semonides, a "bee-woman" makes a better wife than a "weasel-woman." Aristophanes' animal choruses draw on this tradition. So does the Hellenistic Greek *Anthology*, whose animals make it, paradoxically, "a human document."[23]

Work on the animal code of tragedy has to consider each play's preoccupations. The culture's overall code interacts with that of a particular drama, and with its myths, deities, images, and plotting. Each animal comparison is active in, and is energized by, the play's specific atmosphere and motifs. In one play, for instance, women escaping suitors are compared to a heifer running lost on the mountain. Not an isolate image: these women are descendents of Zeus's union with the "heifer" Io who ran from him. In another play, dancing women celebrate the "delight" of galloping "like a colt in flight with its mother." The same women will later urge a mother on to take delight in killing her human child. In a third play Helen, Zeus's child, is part-seen as a lion cub, initially gentle, friendly to children, "fawning to the hand in its belly's need," ultimately violent, manifesting "its *ethos* [moral nature] from its parents." Through the play, the image develops an oblique relation to Aegisthus, who avenges the murder of his brothers as children, on behalf of his "wretched father." Aegisthus is a "cowardly lion rolling in his bed." "Lion" becomes a vicious presence, gathering complexity within the relationship of children to parents, a double-edged emblem of treachery hiding in blood relationships that ends in blood let from opening family wounds.[24]

But to say human is "like" animal is also to say it is *not* animal. For us, at least, "like" implies "is not." Here is a second conceptual use of animals, which we might think covertly contradicted the first. While operating an inherited animal semantics to categorize human beings and behavior, Greek thought also stresses the difference between human and animal. Fifth-century and fourth-century thinkers use the nonhuman as something to define themselves against, to establish what human beings are by distinguishing them from what they are not.[25]

[23] For the general point, see Foucault 1970:129; Tambiah 1969. In Greek thought: Lloyd 1983:8–12, 24–26, 53. In other cultures: Bleibtreu 1968:223ff.; Needham 1978:55; Ladner 1979:223–26. In Homer: see Fränkel 1921; Redfield 1975:193–99; Dierauer 1977:6ff. Lionlike, boarlike heroes: e.g., *Il.* 5.782–83, 7.257, 11.548–55, 24.572. Semonides: see Lloyd-Jones 1975; Loraux 1978. Aristophanes: see Taillardat 1962:371; Sifakis 1971:78ff. *Anthology*: see N. Douglas 1928:3.

[24] A. *Supp.* 351, 17, 44; *Ba.* 164, 982; *Ag.* 721–28, 1605, 1224.

[25] See Lloyd 1983:25.

This strand of Greek thinking was absorbed into and used forcefully by Christianity. "He that hath well learned wherein a man doth differ from a brute," says Richard Baxter, the late seventeenth-century Nonconformist divine, "hath laid such a foundation for a holy life, as all the reason in the world is never able to overthrow." Cardinal to this originally Greek pulse of thought is a wish to separate beast from "man." ("Man," in these discussions, represents humanity.) This historically compounded vision acknowledges that "men" do share animal nature, but differ from animals because they also share in what is divine: reason. "Man" stands "between beasts and gods": an image crystallized by Pope (born towards the end of Baxter's life) in his *Essay on Man*:

> He hangs between; in doubt to act, or rest;
> In doubt to deem himself a God, or Beast;
> In doubt his Mind or Body to prefer. . . .
> Created half to rise, and half to fall;
> Great Lord of all things, yet a prey to all. . . .[26]

Some seed of this vision of an essential distinction between human and nonhuman is certainly fifth-century, and Athenian. But it is easy to be overinfluenced here by the powerful schematizing of the century that came after. The most enriching and sophisticated approach of our own time to these issues in Greek thought is structuralism. Transformative, pioneering, alert to elements in Greek thought that were passed over before, structuralism made monumentally clear, in many different contexts, that Greek cult, myth, and society stressed what divides human from animal and what divides human from god, and illuminated in new and profound ways the coherence in Greek views of divinity.[27]

But structuralism's early model for Greek approaches to the nonhuman was implicitly, and I think anachronistically as far as the fifth century is concerned, taxonomic. Taxonomy is dear, in the fourth century, to Aristotle's heart. But even he had to abandon it at some points. His taxonomy had antecedents in, for example, the early Hippocratics. Once one thinks taxonomically, one can see where Aristotle is coming at things from. But no taxonomic classification of animals, gods, and human beings before the fourth century is anything more than implicit.[28]

It is natural for us, heirs of Aristotle and the great taxonomic tradition, and of our own century, which has illuminated liminality, to speak of "boundaries" between human and animal, human and divine. The "boundary" image has been a revelatory heuristic tool in our age. It has made

---

[26] See Pope, *Essay on Man* 2.7–16; Foucault 1970; Thomas 1984:36–41.

[27] The founding work here is that of Vernant 1980:92–67; Vidal-Naquet 1975, 1981, 1986; Detienne 1977, 1981a; and Burkert 1972, 1977, etc.

[28] See Lloyd 1983:14–15, 25.

sense, for instance, of Hermes' persona as boundary-marker, master of thresholds (Chapter 1). But if the image is used to categorize all fifth-century experience and representations of the nonhuman, it distortingly implies a coherent spatial and vertical topography: "man between the beasts and gods," humanity subverted "from below" by animals, "from above" by gods.[29] The fifth century is too mixed and fluid *vis à vis* the nonhuman, and humanity's relation to it, for this. Would Erinyes, for instance, subvert from "below" or "above"? That "insight into the disunity" of emotional experience, which is so vivid in Homer (see Chapter 2), is alive in the fifth century also. It marks not only emotional experience, but also its mirror-image, the nonhuman world, which is the prime source of disturbing passions in human beings. We should beware, I think, of superimposing later, taxonomic, worked-out models of relationships on fifth-century mentality, with its essentially unworked-out, disunited, kaleidoscopic vision of the nonhuman.

As far as tragedy is concerned, humanity's vision of itself is of something invaded at all points—above, below, outside, inside, by beasts acting for daemons, daemons acting through beasts, beasts that may be *daimōn*, daemons that have beastly attributes, and emotions that may be all at once. Nonhumanity, the surreal or super-real anarchic inseparability of animal and daemonic, besieges the definition of humanity on every side. Animal life, daemonic life, is threatening, negative, upsetting, uncontrollable. Human is its opposite.[30]

Further, tragic mentality, like that of Homer and Hesiod, uses animals both to distinguish and to relate divine and human. Tragic characters become beastlike and godlike simultaneously: like late Shakespearian tragic heroes who destroy their humanity in their search for an "absolute mode of behavior," becoming beastlike, godlike, where they want to be most human.[31] The experience in which this most often happens is characteristic of tragedy in Dionysus's theater: mad passion, madness. Dionysus is a specialist in madness. In his rites, human wears animal skin, eats animal flesh, is mad, like the "mad" god. Tragedy, another Dionysian ceremony, is deeply drawn to madness as a manifestation of both divinity and animality.[32]

[29] See, e.g., Thomas 1984:36–41. "Boundary" images came into prominence with the work of Van Gennep [1909] 1977, and have been impelled by developments both in world history and within anthropology. Hermes: see Vernant 1983:127–60; L. Kahn 1978 (above, Chapter 1). "Below," "above": see Detienne 1981a:220; Vernant 1980:130ff.

[30] See Bleibtreu 1968:118; Foucault 1971:77ff. On Aristotle (e.g., *EN* 1145A18–25), see Lloyd 1983:35, 49–50.

[31] For Hesiod, see Lloyd 1983:11–12. For Shakespeare, see Hunter 1978:261.

[32] Dodds 1951:277; cf. Burkert 1983:84–93. Madness in Dionysus's theater: see Padel 1981, 1990:336, 365.

Heracles is the "supreme benefactor of humankind," because he rid the world of deadly animal menace:

> Through his suffering labor he destroyed fearful beasts,
> and gave untroubled life to mortal beings.

But then he is made mad and madness makes him like what he once conquered, makes him animal. He snorts and bellows "like a bull about to charge." Afterwards, distraught, he wants to kill himself. His father says, "Control your wild lion's *thumos*." As with other mad figures in tragedy, the distinction between human and nonhuman—which Heracles, above all others, fought to uphold—dissolves. He is animal, *daimōn*. Lyssa acted through him. The audience heard her say she would enter his breast, heard her say what she would make him do, and he has done it. She who was like a Gorgon made his eyes glare like Gorgon's. He "rolls his wild Gorgon's eye" while killing the second child. When he wakes and wants to know who killed his children, his father tells him "You, your bow, and whichever god was responsible."[33]

Ajax's madness also manifests a *daimōn* who acts through the human while the human becomes animal. Ajax seemed to Tecmessa to converse "with some shadow." The audience knows this was Athene. In madness, he attacks bulls, "falling on animals . . . as if they were people." Afterwards he cries and groans "like a bull," a sign that "he'll do something bad." His dealings with animals and gods are incomprehensible to the sane. Distraught in madness's aftermath, he foreshadows some terrible deed of passionate animality.[34] Animality, intermingled with the daemonic, defines humanity by contrast and simultaneously threatens to invade and mar it, as animal features mar the human form in persecutory daemons such as Sphinx or Harpy. In tragedy, this threat is realized in the interior. Passions, which drive human beings to do horrific deeds, act on innards as animals and daemons act on the body. Emotions are nonself and come from outside, not within.

Part of the comfort in this way of seeing is a clean self-image. Human beings may live surrounded by invasive, hostile nonhumanity. But the source of human destructiveness is not human, not inside them. Wicked people have animal in them, "tempers of reasonless, unhallowed beasts." Plato, using this inheritance, will represent the passionate part of the human soul as animal. It has a nature like Scylla or Cerberus, "many forms grown together in one," and must be starved. The human part of the soul

---

[33] *HF* 698–700. *Euergetēs*, *mochthos* and related verb, *sōtēria*, and *ōphelein* (see, e.g., 1309, 22, 54, 80, 84, 265) are the play's key words for Heracles before madness, and they mark him as the archetypal laboring savior of (Greek) humankind. Heracles in and after madness: see *HF* 869, 1211. Lyssa in him: see 861–73, 883, 990, 1135.

[34] *Aj.* 301, 91–117, 297, 300, 317–22, 326.

must be nourished and capable of controlling the animal within.[35] Before Plato, the fifth-century norm places the nonhuman outside, a temporary, unwelcome, disturbing visitor to innards.

While tragic passion is savagely animal and daemonic (Chapter 6), tragic acts (like the murder of one's own child) are so numbingly destructive that they must be impelled, even perhaps performed, not by a human but by animal or daemonic agents, or by human beings "driven" by animal and daemonic passion. Clytemnestra seems to claim that an avenging daemon in her own shape killed her husband. Medea glares like a bull, is like a mad bull or lioness. Touching and smelling her children, overwhelmed by their physical sweetness, she says she understands "what sort of evils I shall do," but *thumos*, "anger" (Chapter 2), which is "responsible" for the greatest evils, is "stronger" than she. After the murder, Jason calls her "lioness, not woman." She accepts this. Call me Scylla, too, she says. She finally appears, like a *deus ex machina*, in a dragon-chariot that incarnates her daemonic inheritance, given her "by my father's father Helios." When Pentheus stands out against the god, endangering his house, he demonstrates his chthonic lineage, the race of the *drakōn* (serpent, dragon), "whom chthonic Echion bore . . . like a giant who fought with gods."[36] Exploring the invasion of humanity by the nonhuman, tragedy stages human beings becoming that which they are normally defined against, and which both impels and punishes them.

GODS' WEAPONS

The Olympian gods, humanity's most well-lit nonhuman assailants, are armed with specific weapons. Like animal tusks and stings, these have a metonymic, iconic quality, marking daemonic advantage over the human: that power to hurt, that aggressiveness. These weapons, an emblematic explanation of humanity's need to defend itself against the nonhuman, are essential to the iconographic code by which contemporary Greeks identify representations of each god. As Christian saints are defined visually by their instruments of martyrdom, Greek gods are defined by their instruments of power: power to change (Hermes' staff, Demeter's flail, Bacchus's thyrsus), power to stir the elements (Poseidon's trident), power, above all, to hurt.

Apart, perhaps, from Artemis's arrows, which can also symbolize her hunting of animals and the "release" she brings to women in childbirth, the purpose of divine weapons is the control and punishment of human beings. Except once. The Titanomachy and Gigantomachy, "battle with

---

[35] A. *Supp.* 762; Pl. *Rep.* 588C–589B.
[36] *Ag.* 1500; *Med.* 90–92, 187–88, 1077–80, 1342, 1407, 1359, 1321; *Ba.* 539–41.

Titans," "battle with giants," popular themes in archaic sculpture, stage the far-off story of gods' battles against creatures that were not quite human, when manlike giants challenged Olympian rule. Gods' weapons were then turned against what was neither human nor divine. Gods even enlisted a human hero, Heracles, to fight on their side. But ever since, they have used those weapons on humankind. Human beings here represent divinity armed. At the heart of Greek experience of divinity, as of Greek politics, is armor and power.

The gods are "many-named." Manufactured weapons are built into their varied titles, and form part of each god's "plastic being" in art. Epithets of Apollo and Artemis include "Silver-Bowed," "Golden-Bowed," "Conqueror-by-Bow," "Bow-Bearer."[37] Artemis's arrows kill women. They are ambiguous: a "painless" release in labor, but also the labor's pain, and death in labor. Their user is the one who brings women through that pain. One female chorus remembers calling on Artemis "who wields the bow" when the wind of pain "pierced through my womb." Artemis's arrows strike down sinful Coronis for infidelity to Apollo before she bore his son: "and many neighbors were destroyed with her." Artemis, huntress, "Mistress of Animals," lives in the spilling of women's blood, the ending of their lives.[38] Her arrows are aggressive, multiple signifiers of this persona.

Apollo's arrows are the plague that strikes the Greek camp before Troy. When his priest prays to him as "Far-Shooter," the arrows clatter on his shoulder as he comes. But like his sister Artemis, Apollo can use his arrows simply to shoot, rather than as disease-bearers. With Artemis, he shoots the children of Niobe, who boasted she had more children than their own mother. "Apollo killed the sons," says Homer, "with his silver bow. Artemis, Arrow-Pourer, shot the daughters." Sophocles staged these murders in a play whose surviving fragments show the two gods above the palace, picking out the children down below.[39]

Poseidon, "Lord of the Golden Trident," stirred storms and earthquakes with this weapon, which Aeschylus seems to call a *nosos*, "plague." In Homer, his "terrible sword" has

> a long edge, like lightning.
> It is not *themis* [right] to meet it in war.
> *Deos* [fear] stops men.

[37] Cf. Chapter 1, n. 9. Divine epithets in literature: see Bruchmann 1893. "Plastic being" of Olympians: Burkert 1985:103. Apollo and Artemis: see *Il.* 1.37; Pi. *O.* 14.10; *Sept.* 970; *Hipp.* 1451. "Gold-helmeted" Ares: *Sept.* 106; cf. *toxodamnos*, *Pers.* 86.

[38] *Hipp.* 164–68 (cf. the prayer that Artemis-Hecate will watch over childbirth at Argos, A. *Supp.* 676); Pi. *P.* 3.10, 36. See King 1983:120 and passim; Lloyd-Jones 1983:99.

[39] Apollo's arrows: *Il.* 1.48–56, 37–45. Niobe's children: *Il.* 24.605–6; S. fr. 401 with Barrett's reconstruction, see Carden 1974:176–86.

Athene, who "delights in battle," normally appears fully armed, as she was born, with helmet, spear, shield, and her own particular armor, the aegis, trimmed with snakes and Gorgon-head. When she arms for battle in Homer, she drops her "soft robe" on the floor, throws on the "tasseled aegis," adds a horned helmet, and grasps her huge spear. She is exchanging soft for hard, a robe for complex weaponry whose tassels, the only possible softness, are (by implication) lethally animal.[40]

Athene and Ares are professionally concerned with war. But at Sparta, even Aphrodite was worshipped "Armed." Eros, her son, engages human beings in perennial "war" (Chapter 6). His arrows are "unconquerable in battle."[41] Apparently unwarlike gods can incorporate weaponed aggression. In some sites, Demeter was worshipped as Demeter-Erinys, Black Demeter, or with a horse's head. A fourth-century coin from Thelpousa shows a Demeter-head of wild hair rising like crested snakes. Her flail is not only for corn. Dionysus's title at Tenedos was "Man-Hammerer" (as Death, in the *Iliad*, is "*thumos*-hammerer").[42] The gods' forged weapons articulate the violence that all gods can turn on human beings. Above all stands Zeus, "holding a flaming thunderbolt" that blasts the impious besiegers of Thebes and always hits its mark. Disaster is the "stroke of Zeus." The fate of Paris is summed up in the statement that Zeus "stretched his bow" against him.[43]

In tragedy, the gods' weapons are a presence especially in the choral lyrics, which draw heavily on contemporary religious song. These hymnlike songs use the weapons as a verbal correlative of visual iconography depicting armed gods. None of this is empty decoration. Gods' epithets do as much work in tragic lyric as any other word. Epithets and addresses remind listeners of divine armory in complicated compound titles and descriptions. They are part of the code of hostility, a small but significant element in the tragic representation of divinity in its aggressive relation to human beings. The Theban women under siege call on all the "gods who guard the city" to "come" and "see" them in their peril and mention the gods' weapons, which they wish to be turned against the besiegers:

> Ares, *daimōn* of the gold helmet,
> will you betray your land . . .?
> Pallas, Zeus-born battle-loving power,
> be helper-of-the-city;

---

[40] Ar. *Eq.* 559, cf. *Sept.* 131, *PV* 924 (uncertain text). Cf. *Il.* 14.385–87. Athene: see *Sept.* 128; *Il.* 5.734–46, 430; cf. Warner 1985:104–26 on aegis symbolism in the post-Greek tradition.

[41] Armed Aphrodite: see Farnell 2:700–703. Eros: see Chapter 6, n. 50.

[42] Black Demeter, Demeter-Erinys: Farnell 3:50–68, 221. Dionysus Anthroporaistes: Ael. *NA* 12.34; Farnell 5:156; cf. *Thanatos thumoraistēs*, *Il.* 13.544, 16.580.

[43] *Sept.* 514, *Ant.* 131, *Ag.* 362–67; see Chapter 6, nn. 2–4, 14, 34.

Poseidon with fish-striking weapon,
bring release from terror. . . .
Maiden, Leto-born, prepare your bow!

When the Theban elders (the chorus of *Oedipus Rex*) hear that Apollo's anger with Laius's murderer has caused the plague, they call on three gods, Athene, Artemis, and Apollo. Here, at the start of their journey of understanding, they invoke Apollo in his weapons, as "Phoebus, Far-Shooter." They call on other gods, too—Ares the furious, Zeus who wields the thunderbolt—to strike the unknown murderer. But they lavish their attention most intricately on Apollo. Each word here has a deadly fulfill-able weight. Apollo must shoot down the sinner, with "unconquered darts from a gold-twisted bent bowstring." The play answers their prayer in a characteristically tragic, double-edged way when Oedipus, so the messenger says, strikes his eyes with "gold-driven brooches." This word, *chrusē-latos*, "of beaten gold," is a compound of "gold" and *elaunein*, "to drive." It had been used by Aeschylus of the gold-armed warrior on the shield of Oedipus's son Polynices. It will reappear qualifying Jocasta's brooch in Euripides' *Phoenician Women*, where another Jocasta faces her warring sons. In Sophocles, the violence in the compound—"driven"—could suggest the driving force that rams the pin into Oedipus's eyes:

Not once, but often, and at each stroke
his eyes wet his beard, not with light drops of blood
but a whole black downpour of bloody hail.

So Apollo "strikes" the murderer. The chorus's loyal prayer, in Apollo's fulfillment, boomerangs. The singers did not realize that they were invoking Apollo against the king. Yet the very word *ankulē*, which they used for Apollo's "bow," suggests torsion. It means something bent back on itself, like an elbow. Apollo's crooked bow and "twisted" gold bowstring re-emerge in the play's language as the violent gold brooch-pin. When the chorus sees Oedipus's bloody eyes, the king says, simply,

Apollo was these things, fulfilling my pain.
But the hand that struck the blow
was none other than my own.

If this blow created "bloody hail," well, one of Apollo's epithets at Thebes was supposedly "lord of hail."[44] Apollo is what happens to and in Oedipus. In all the poetic encrustations of the chorus's initial summoning ode, imaging Apollo's weapons in decorative prayer, each word has weight and

[44] *Sept.* 104–48; *OT* 162, 190–206, 1268–79; *Sept.* 644; *Phoen.* 62; *OT* 1329. Apollo Chalazius: see Phot. *Bibl.* 321B31.

will be reified. His weapons violently fulfil that prayer, twisting it back on itself, to reach annihilation of the light brought about by the lord of light.

Gods' manufactured weapons blur into divine use of the elements as weapons (see Chapter 6). What we think of as the natural world was for the fifth century a divine arsenal. Gods "send" animals, as Zeus "sends" thunderbolts, or as Apollo, Eros, and Artemis "send" arrows.[45] Gods send animals sometimes as signs, like Zeus's eagles, interpreted as an omen of victory for the Greeks, but often as an instrument of destruction: a plague of snakes, a boar or hind that devastates the country. Hera tries to destroy the baby Heracles by sending snakes to his cradle.[46]

Gods throw at human beings the whole environment, not only weather, elements, animals, but also other daemons. Zeus sends Hephaestus, Power, and Force to nail Prometheus to the rock. Hera sends Iris and Lyssa to madden Heracles. Zeus, Fate, and Erinys send Ate against Agamemnon. In the *Oresteia*, Zeus has an intense, conflicted relation to the Erinyes, but they are—somehow—agents of his will.[47]

In the same way, the gods also "send" emotion. Tragedy's dominant images of emotion see it as a mobile, unconquerable, daemonic, or animal-like adversary (Chapter 6), an apt weapon against humanity. Sometimes a god's own emotions are hurled at human beings. Gods are easily roused to bitterness against us. Aphrodite's angers "swept down on" Phaedra, on Hippolytus's "body." *Phthonos*, "envy," can be felt by gods as well as by other people. Divinity, says Herodotus in a famous phrase, is "*phthoneron* [grudging, jealous] and disturbing." Divinity "creeps up on" human beings. Emotions themselves are *phthonera*. "*Phthonos* creeps up on the man who has," on the wealthy and successful.[48]

But more often, emotion felt by the human being—the victim's own passion, as we would see it—is the god's weapon. When Hera sends Madness to Heracles, this is far more effective than the snakes she sent at him when he was a baby. The Erinyes have physical weapons like whips and snakes. In Aeschylus, their attack includes physical disease, skin ulcers. They appear entwined with snakes. Vase-painters show Erinyes in hunting costume, Erinyes waving snakes, Lyssa (Madness) with a goad in her hand and snake round her arm. But their essential weapons are their victim's feelings: madness, terror, nightmare fear. Their song paralyzes the mind. Euripides' Orestes in delirium demands the bow that Apollo gave him to

---

[45] See Chapter 6, nn. 2–3.

[46] Animals sent as sign: *Ag.* 114–30, 135; as punishment: A. *Supp.* 267 (snakes), *HF* 376 (hind), *Il.* 9.539–46 (boar); Hera's snakes to Heracles: *HF* 1266–67, *N.* 1.37–47, Theoc. 24.

[47] *PV* 1–53, *HF* 823–61, *Il.* 19.87–88, cf. Winnington-Ingram 1983:154–74.

[48] *Hipp.* 438, 1418; Hdt. 1.32, cf. 7.46. "Jealous" emotions: see *elpides*, Pi. *I.* 2.43; *algos*, *Ag.* 450; *odunē*, *Phil.* 1141. *Phthonos*: see *Aj.* 157; Dodds 1951:30–31; Eitrem 1953.

defend himself against Erinyes, when they "frighten me with their raving madnesses." His weapon is useless against theirs: the madness and fear they send. Emotions are daemon, animal. Like Pandora's ills in Hesiod, they may act *automatoi*, of themselves. But like any *daimōn*, they may be "sent" by god. Phaedra saw Hippolytus, says Aphrodite, and "by my plotting, terrible lust possessed her heart."[49] What we think of as our "own" emotions: these are the gods' best weapon against us.

PERSONIFICATIONS

Tragic emotion is represented essentially, therefore, as other in self. A destructive other, sent to change and hurt innards; a god's most effective weapon.

Emotions belong within the general Greek urge to externalize (as we see it): to personify and daemonize everything, especially conditions of the human mind and body. Modern Western ways of seeing emotion are not the only ones possible. If fifth-century Athenians were to turn back on us the fundamental anthropological project—of describing another culture, in its terms but their language—they might well remark our idiosyncratic "urge" to internalize, and our odd assumption that the emotions we feel are "ours."

From the earliest poetry, personification is a basic feature of Greek imagination and language. Hesiod's *Theogony*, "Birth of Gods," describes the birth of gods, yes; but also the birth of forces like Fear and Terror. These are the "terrible" children of Ares. The children of Styx are Emulation, Victory, Strength, Force. Zeus marries Themis (Right) and Metis (Cunning Thought), whom he later swallows. Such personifications are pervasive in classical Greek, too, and a strong presence in visual art contemporary with tragedy.[50] They are multiple, just as there are multiple Greek words for innards, multiple representations of feelings that affect innards (Chapters 4, 6), and multiple images of divinity. Multiplicity is the essence of Greek ideas of consciousness, divinity, and states of mind.[51]

How real were these figures of language and paint? Painters easily label a winged figure with an emotion's name, poets easily ornament a song with titles of lively abstractions. Is this personification a facile, promiscuous con-

---

[49] Heracles: *HF* 825–59. Erinyes: *Cho.* 1050; *Eum.* 344–47, see Trendall and Webster 1971:III, 3.41, 1.11, 1.15–16; *Or.* 269–70; *Cho.* 283–88. Pandora: *Erg.* 103. Aphrodite: *Hipp.* 28–29.

[50] See Burkert 1985:184–85, 422 n. 16; *Theog.* 934–36, 383–85, 901, 886, 925–35; Detienne and Vernant 1978.

[51] See Chapter 1, n. 9 ("many-named" gods, and many of them); Chapter 2, n. 23 (multiple innards).

vention? Are tragic personifications "figures" only of speech with no solidity in the lived world of the speakers?

We come back here to the status of metaphor in the fifth-century world, so different from its high profile in our own.[52] Fifth-century listeners did not have our option of saying that something is metaphorical, "therefore not real." Personification, as the fifth century inherited and used it, was not an isolatable trick of language, but part of explaining what happened to and inside people. Lived reality was air filled with nonhuman forces. There were good reasons to think of these as the main source of human feeling and experience: a style of thought that continued into Augustine's vision of demons and beyond. In the fifth century, Aristophanes flirts constantly and provocatively with his own language. But he is teasing something live. When he speaks of libations poured "to Dullness," this is not absurd in the way we feel it is. It tickles because both libations and personified "abstractions" are part of everyday experience. Euripides says, "Recognizing friends is god." "Force" appears on the tragic stage, arguing with Hephaestus. "Force" forces the god of technology to nail Prometheus to the rock.[53] Personified emotion is part of the nonhuman arsenal surrounding the human.

Vase-painters paint what the tragedies speak of, and sometimes (as with "Force") what they stage: daemonized emotions who attend, and may well cause, the destructive tragic action. One early fourth-century illustrator of Euripides' lost *Meleager* puts a winged figure beside Aphrodite. The figure is labelled Phthonos (Jealousy). This is similar to the myriad figures on vases labelled with names like "Desire," "Old Age," "Yearning." When the painters represent a drama, such figures are as much "there" as the personae whom the dramatist did bring on stage, like the Erinyes of Aeschylus.[54]

This suggests a relation between emotion and innards, self and its conditions, that is seriously different from any we might own to. Emotion inflicts "real" wounds (Chapter 6). Eros's poison really enters *kardia*. Erinyes really goad *phrenes*. Fear, anger, pity, really are out there in the world, ready to rush damagingly into *splanchna*. We cannot call this metaphor or allegory. It has a weight in the fifth century quite different from later ages' appropriation of Greek personificatory impulses.

For example, La Navigation and L'Electricité, personified sculptures erected on the Gare de Lyon by nineteenth-century Parisians, had mean-

52 See Chapter 1, n. 19; and above, pp. 33–40 and 132.

53 See Webster 1954; Dover 1974:141–44; Ar. *Eq.* 221; *Hel.* 560; *PV* 1–87 (see Kratos's persecutory imperatives, 58); Chapter 6, n. 63.

54 Trendall and Webster 1971:98 (III, 3.40). See Burkert 1985:184–85. R. M. Cook (1972:278), refusing to "see daimonic forces on pots," beautifully exemplifies resistance to the daemonic realities of Greek life, and to any significant differences between "us" and "them."

ings that belonged to their specific social context and the history of how their state had used the personificatory mode. The image of La République as woman had developed from 1789 to 1848, often becoming a key political issue. By 1848, allegorizing statues of Justice, Shipping, and others were borrowing from the related core images of La Liberté, La France, La Marseillaise. By 1851, everything is personified and monumental. By 1900, part of the importance of such personifications is their history of re-use.[55] Each Western city and state has its own history of mainly female personification: monuments, poetry, and rhetoric with overlapping layers of meaning that vary between different individuals and groups, in the poetic and political discourses of different societies. Later ages re-create Greek monumental and linguistic habits for their own purposes, driven by their own ways of looking at women, architecture, and politics—or the mind. This personifying mode can be used emptily. Our inheritance of baroque allegory predisposes us to feel it must be empty whenever used: a stylizing shell, a formal convention. But living things have—indeed, they make—shells. Personification is not always empty.[56] Its belated possibilities are worlds away from fifth-century Athens, where it was embedded in ways of explaining one's own experience of, and other people's behavior in, emotion.

Personification was part of Greek religious life. Cult, above all, tells us that the personifying mode answers to lived fifth-century reality. The communities in which poets and painters worked invested in daemonic personifications, and built them altars and temples. Sometimes the personifications were satellite figures in a central cult-divinity. Persuasion and Urging (Peitho, Paregoros) were worshipped in, as it were, side-chapels at cult sites of Aphrodite. But personifications were also worshipped alone. At Thespiae, Eros was worshipped as a stone. At Rhamnous on the Attic coast were expensive temples to Nemesis (Indignation) and Themis (Right). Personified emotions had not only iconographic status, but sometimes cult status, like other daemons.[57] Emotions are the nonhuman outside the human self that are only visible at work within it, as real, autonomous, animate, and destructive as snakes or thunderbolts.

STATES OF MIND: MULTIPLE, DAEMONIC, FEMALE

Emotions are also, often, female. Greek personifications generally are mainly female. The case that brings this home is a condition more of body than mind: the most prized condition of the male physique, *hēbē*, "lusty

---

[55] See Warner 1985:86, 346 n. 88; Agulhon 1981:12–22, 48, 52–53, 70–71, 101, 115.

[56] See Fletcher 1970:25–69 on "the daimonic agent"; Burkert 1985:184.

[57] See Burkert 1985:185, 422 nn. 16–20; Usener 1948:364–75; Hamdorf 1964; Buxton 1982:31–36; Farnell 1:75, 2:487, 5:44; Wilamowitz 1931–32, 1:267–69.

youthfulness." Hebe's personification is the ultimate man-made female. As a goddess, she shared the bed of Heracles, who throughout the Greek world (except Crete) crystallized ideals of maleness in a divine presence in every home. Words over the door said, "The fair conquering Heracles lives here: no evil may come in." Presumably he was a vital presence, a persona to be identified with, in every male self-image, too. Every man would like to be this god who had been man: appetitive, large, beautiful, sexually and militarily all-conquering, the boss of perfect *hēbē*, who possessed, carnally and eternally, the personification of his own physical peak. Hebe's other role was to pour the gods' drinks. As the Homeric lexicon has it, "In the *Iliad* she always appears as goddess performing some manual service for other divinities." She is the ideal facilitator, for the male. In life, every *ephēbēs*—man who had *hēbē*—was her possessor. His physique temporarily gave him imaginative access to immortal, "golden," "lusty" bloom, personified as servile female mate.[58]

"Female" imagery dominates tragic representation of innards (Chapter 5), and innards are described in an intensely concrete way (Chapter 2). Appropriately, the personification of the most treasured, concretely physical male condition is also female. It matches the general Greek trend towards personifying other conditions and experiences as female, like the "Hours" or "Procession."[59] If we take the personifications seriously, we must take their predominant femaleness seriously too. Some—like Old Age or Eros—are male. But most are female. Why?

The question can be answered at a general level: the ways in which men in the West have used women include using them to represent aspects of themselves. This explanation is fine as far as it goes. But it depends on material later than, and ultimately deriving from, ancient Greece. It does not solve questions raised by Greek material itself.

In relation to Greek, it used to be argued that in the Indo-European language, from which Greek derived, the abstract nouns that tended to be personified tended also to be feminine. Hence Greek personified nouns tended to be female.[60] This argument itself tended to abstraction. Usener argued that the idea of the image must have "come before" the condition: "The first creation of the word must have been inspired by some idea of a living, personal being. . . . The feminine adjective only became an abstraction after it had denoted a female personage." Cassirer pointed out that the opposite impulse, from the abstraction to the image, is always operating at the same time. As in other areas of argument over word-meanings and thought-processes, the idea of priority, "first" one thing, "then" another,

[58] Heracles: see Burkert 1985:211. Female images of mind: see Chapter 5, nn. 1–6, 41–42. Ephebes: see Vidal-Naquet 1986:106–58.

[59] See Burkert 1985:184–85.

[60] Dietrich 1965:62 (with n. 6 on *moira*), 358–60; Warner 1985:66–70.

is a heuristic strategy. "Priority"—does language come before myth or myth before language?—was a nineteenth-century battle. But it patterned the field of debate over how Greek abstract nouns were formed, and what the relations were between linguistic gender and representations of femaleness in Greek-influenced societies.[61]

At best, "priority" pushes back the issue to some unreachable society where Indo-European linguistic forms evolved a tendency to use nouns of a feminine gender for emotions and abstracts. But languages evolve where people with specific ideas—about femaleness, and about femaleness in relation to other things—are speaking them. Language both influences and is influenced by the culture that uses it.[62] Either the Greeks, or some other dimly defined culture we cannot get back to, attributed animate multiple femininity to abstract conditions of mind and body. What I am concerned with is fifth-century tragic expression of the Greek end of things. "Priority" ducks the important question here, which is how the female gender of these abstract nouns interacted with other features of Athenian experience. Female personifications in classical Greek are a living part of a precise imaginative landscape.

This landscape concentrated daemonic danger in female forms, such as Sirens (Chapter 3) and tragedy's talismanic daemons, the Erinyes (Chapter 8). The tragic thought-world was biassed to expect forces that threatened human life to be mainly female. Within overall daemonic multiplicity, it tends to be mainly (not only) female divinities like nymphs who are plural, especially destructive daemons like Gorgons or Harpies. Animate, chthonic, dangerous female multiplicity is the background for destructive tragic passion, and underlines by gender tragedy's general implication that the forces disturbing the tragic self, the male self, are not self, that human passion is nonhuman.

[61] See Usener 1948:375; Cassirer 1946:43, 86. Cf. Chapter 2, nn. 86–90.

[62] See Steiner 1972:66–134 on modern developments in understanding relations between language and thought. For specific psycholinguistic and anthropological bearings on this question, see P. P. Giglioli 1972:110; M. Douglas 1975:173–80.

Chapter 8

BLOOD IN THE MIND

ATE, LYSSA: MADNESS PERSONIFIED

IF INNER VIOLENCE is generally female and not-self, madness, its most extreme example, inevitably has a female form and source.

Homer and tragedy have two nouns for madness, both feminine, both daemonically personified: *Atē* and *Lyssa*. *Atē*, the older personification, means in Homer a disastrous state of mind: inner confusion, delusion, ruinous recklessness, shading into "disaster," which this recklessness can cause. Ate is Zeus's eldest daughter. Her feet are "delicate":

> She does not tread the ground
> but walks on men's heads, harming them.
> This one or that one she binds.

Strong, quick, she runs through the world damaging human beings, blinding them mentally and morally. Ate has Olympian origins but does not operate there now. Long ago she blinded Zeus. He made a reckless vow that bound his son Heracles, intended to be king, to serve another man. When Zeus realized what had happened, he could not undo the vow, but he made sure Ate would never trouble gods again. He took her

> by her shining locks,
> and swore she should never come back
> to Olympus and the starry sky.

He threw her out, and

> she soon reached the works of men:
> Ate, who blinds all.

Ate now is in "works of men." Homer's Agamemnon mentions her to explain his mistake in offending his best warrior. "Savage *atē*," damaging his *phrenes*, made him misjudge things. Since even Zeus was damaged by her once, Agamemnon's error in insulting Achilles has a divine royal precedent.[1]

Tragedy does not personify Ate in this way. No more delicate, quick feet. Aeschylus does once sketch her as a dim daemonic hound:

---

[1] *Il.* 9.505–7, 19.91–95, 113, 126–30, 86–87. See Doyle 1984, Stallmach 1968.

Fawning Ate, welcoming,
draws a mortal astray, into nets
from which there is no escape.

But otherwise tragedy increasingly uses the word *atē* more of the "disaster," rather than of the mental blindness that causes it.[2] No tragedy brings Ate onstage, personified. No vase-painter gives her a body or label. The fifth century, especially tragedy, seems to replace *atē* with madness itself.

Madness is central to tragedy. "Tragedy" is painted as a maenad in Dionysus's train.[3] Lyssa, "Madness," is the fifth century's personification of madness, especially in tragedy and in vase-paintings of tragedy. She has speaking parts in one surviving Euripidean tragedy and at least one lost play by Aeschylus, possibly more. Illustrations of other lost plays show her attacking men with a goad, like Erinyes, and urging on destruction. She has a canine aspect, which matches Aeschylus's houndlike sketch of Ate. An Attic vase of around 440 B.C., representing Aeschylus's *Toxotides*, gives Lyssa a dog's head. It fits like a hat over her own, as she urges Actaeon's hounds to kill their master. Is this dog-head like a "defining genitive" in grammar, saying, "This is *lussa* 'of dogs' "? ("Even dogs have Erinyes," went one Greek proverb.) Other contexts suggest that *lussa* generally had mad-dog overtones. Lyssa is "madness," but also "rabies." Lyssa, it seems, is "wolfish rage" personified, raging and destructive.[4] Ate and Lyssa epitomize epic and tragic representation of psychic disintegration. Chthonic, exterior to self, swift, shining-haired, snake-wreathed, houndlike, female, they site madness in the Erinys territory, which tragedy makes its own.

Lyssa, like Erinys, is a winged wielder of snakes. Two fourth-century Italian illustrations of Aeschylus's *Edoni* show her winged. In one, a snake is coiled round her arm, and she hits at Lycurgus with a goad. Euripides in *The Madness of Heracles* says she is "like Erinyes," a "child of Night," an "unwed virgin" born like them from Ouranos's blood. She is also Gorgon-like. Her victim's eyes glare like Gorgon eyes. She is a Gorgon hissing with "a hundred snake-heads."[5]

---

[2] *Pers.* 112–14. See Stallmach 1968; and Dawe 1968, where the author argues that tragedy replaces Homeric *atē* by misjudgment and error: which drew Aristotle to develop his ideas of *hamartia*.

[3] Madness in tragedy: see Padel 1981, 1990:336. Tragedy as maenad: see Burkert 1985:185.

[4] See *HF* 815–73. A. fr. 169 (*Xantriai*) is spoken by Lyssa, who may have appeared in *Toxotides*, urged on by Artemis (as Iris urges her in *HF*): see Trendall and Webster 1971:62, III, 1.28. Lupine, canine Lyssa: see Lincoln 1975; Trendall and Webster *loc. cit.*; above, p. 126.

[5] See Trendall and Webster 1971: III, 1.15; *HF* 822, 834, 844, 868, 883–84 (cf. *Theog.* 183–85, where the blood of Ouranos gushes from his castration wound). Winged Lyssa: see Chapter 6, n. 61.

Homer's personified Ate stands rather within Erinys's gift, her agent, not her double. In the *Odyssey*, Melampus is imprisoned,

> because of Neleus's daughter and heavy *atē*,
> which the goddess, heavy-hitting Erinys,
> sent on his *phrenes*. But he escaped *kēr* [fate, i.e., death].

Trying to win a girl by stealing cattle, Melampus is caught and jailed (not killed) by her father. There is too little here to know what it means, that Erinys sends *atē* on Melampus's *phrenes*. It may explain his rash attempt at rustling. Erinys's ruinous disposal of *atē* is clearer in Agamemnon's case, as Agamemnon reports it. *Aērophoitis Erinus*, "Erinys who wanders in air, walks in mist" (or, on another reading, who "sucks blood"), with Zeus and Fate, "sent" *atē* to his mind, making him insult Achilles.[6]

EPIC ERINYES

> Caesar's spirit, ranging for revenge,
> With Ate by his side come hot from hell,
> Shall in these confines with a monarch's voice
> Cry "Havoc!" and let slip the dogs of war.
> —Shakespeare, *Julius Caesar*

To understand tragic Erinyes, we need their epic background. Epic Erinyes monitor anger in crucial personal relationships, above all the relationship between parent and child. Telemachus cannot send his mother back to her father: she would call down on him "hateful Erinyes." When Epikaste dies (Homer's Jocasta), she leaves Oedipus "many sufferings, as many as the Erinyes of a mother bring to pass." In the *Thebais*, Oedipus realizes his sons are mocking him:

> He cursed them. The gods' Erinys watched.
> Oedipus prayed they might not divide
> their father's heritage in friendship.

The name "Erinys" here is tucked between the verb of cursing and the curse itself. Grammatical imagery enacts Erinys's lodging in the parent's relationship with his children, his legacy to them. She lurks between utterance and content, direct narrative ("he cursed") and indirect speech ("that they might not divide"). As precisely as a grammatical rule, she will influence following events, affecting relations between those children. In another family, Phoenix, acting on his mother's request, seduces his father's girlfriend. His father calls "on loathly Erinyes" to ensure Phoenix will

---

[6] *Od*. 15.234, see Walcot 1979; cf. Dowden 1989:99 (who is interested mainly in stories about Melampus that might express disguised initiation rites); *Il*. 19.86–87.

never beget a son of his own. "The gods fulfilled his curse, Zeus Katach-thonios ['Below-Earth'] and dread Persephone."[7] "Lower Zeus" and Per-sephone fulfil prayers to Erinyes. They have the royal backing of the underworld. They are the retributive force within the ground of a parent-child relationship and appear if its rules are broken.

Erinyes inhabit sibling relationships, too, "following the elder," sup-porting the older's brother's rights. And Meleager's mother curses her own son when he accidentally kills her brother:

> She beat many times on all-nurturing earth with her hands,
> kneeling, her pleated breast sodden with tears,
> calling on Hades, on awesome Persephone,
> to give her own son death. Erinys who walks in darkness
> heard her with an ungentle heart, from Erebos.[8]

Here it is the other way round: Erinys listens when Persephone is ad-dressed.

Erinyes are summoned in other relationships where jealousy lurks, and anger. Odysseus prays that Antinous, who threw a stool at him, may die before marrying, "if there are gods and Erinyes of beggars." His words are a curse disguised as an apparently helpless prayer, their speaker a king dis-guised as an apparently powerless beggar. Antinous wants to marry Odys-seus's wife. When Odysseus kills him, he fulfils the curse. Listeners might well feel retrospectively that Erinys, hidden loss-adjustor of relationships, inhabited those words which hinted that even a stripped, wandering, un-considered self may have Erinys-guaranteed claims on others.[9]

Erinyes live in the tension that makes oaths needed and monitor the oath when made. Hesiod says they were present when Conflict bore Oath, who troubles false oath-makers. Erinyes punish "false oath-makers" in Hades.[10] Having or summoning Erinyes means possessing or calling up power to hurt someone who was bound not to hurt you, and did. It is not a gentle or sociable thought. Erinys and Erinyes, these singular and plural figures, are not wholesome. Homer's Erinys is "heavy-hitting." Aeschylus's Erinyes are physically repulsive. Erinys is as strong a fact of life as rotting food: a power in human relationships and the world's daemonic electricity.

Relationships bonded by blood or promises are the Homeric Erinys's sphere. All Greek divinities destroy in that territory which they protect. Divinity is part of the contradiction and conflict of the world. "The one who gave the blow will heal," said the Delphic oracle, according to the lost

---

[7] Phoenix: *Il.* 9.451–57; Telemachus: *Od.* 2.135; Oedipus: *Theb.* fr. 2 (Hes., Loeb ed., p. 484).

[8] Meleager's mother: *Il.* 9.568–72; "follow the elder": *Il.* 15.204.

[9] *Od.* 17.475, 22.15.

[10] *Erg.* 804, *Il.* 19.418.

epic the *Cypria*, which tells of Telephus, incurably wounded by Achilles' lance. Like the Dolorous Stroke in Arthurian epic, only the lance that made the wound could cure it. Euripides, and possibly Aeschylus, made a tragedy out of Telephus's story. The principle is reversible. The one who is the proper healer may give the ruinous blow. This principle is at work in every Greek divine persona, both ways round. Hermes has power to lead from silence to language, dark to light, as well as from light to dark, language to silence. In the *Iliad*, Zeus has a truce sworn in his name, and sends Athene to break it, but is also the one who is angered by its break.[11] Zeus Horkios ("Of Oaths") is present in the swearing and the breaking of a truce. He also punishes its violation. In accordance with this principle, Erinyes who guard bonded relationships also send *atē*, to brutalize self's sense of other's rights, and make self savage the relationship. By sending *atē*, Erinys made Agamemnon insult Achilles, damaging their relationship and Achilles' sense of his self.

Further Homeric glimpses of Erinyes involve them obscurely with death. The obscurity is probably part of the point. Erinyes seem to control what lies beyond death. At the close of book 19 of the *Iliad*, where the poem concentrates most of its Erinyes, Achilles' horse prophesies his death and the Erinyes stop it talking. Achilles and death are polar opposites. In the *Odyssey*, his ghost expresses his everlasting bitterness at death:

> Don't speak glancingly to me of death, Odysseus.
> I'd rather be someone else's slave on earth,
> some unallotted man whose living's not rich,
> than lord of all the dead. Tell me of my son.

Achilles stands for living male glory won through bodily power. This now exists for him on earth only through his son.[12]

In another passage, Pandareus's daughters are kidnapped by storm-winds and given to Erinyes. It is uncertain what the text means. Either they will be the Erinyes' servants or (more likely, I think) Erinyes will "deal with" them in Hades.[13] Erinyes deal in Hades with people who disappear,

[11] See *Il.* 3.276–80, 298 (cf. 107, 302), 4.71–72, 168, 235. Cf. Menelaus's prayer to Zeus for vengeance on Paris, and his anger with Zeus ("no other god more destructive") when his sword shatters, 3.351, 365. For the general principle, see Dodds 1951:98 n. 100; Aeschylus, Loeb ed., 2:461; Vernant 1980:103.

[12] See Agamemnon's use of Erinys and *atē* to explain his insult to Achilles, *Il.* 19.87; Dodds 1951:3–8. Achilles' horse and ghost: see below, n. 15.

[13] See *amphipoleuein*, *Od.* 20.78, and Monro *ad loc*. The verb may mean they will "serve" Erinyes, or that Erinyes will "attend to," "deal with" them. One ancient commentator on *Od.* 19.518 says that Pandareus stole Zeus's golden dog and was punished, theft for theft. If the girls were kidnapped to punish their father, this is a possible common feature with Melampus's story (above, n. 6). Alternatively, Pandareus's story is a broken oath, avenged by a winged figure stealing his daughters (Harrison 1922:226–28).

or prevent people knowing what will happen there. They are where the dead are, divinity of the fact that death is central to the bond between present and future, present and past. They make death matter in living relationships. They embody death, the permanent future, within a present relationship, and the power of the past, of the dead, over the experience and minds of the living.

All this is crystallized in the way Erinyes hear curses. They are activated by harm-wishing words spoken within a relationship, which change the future. Oedipus's curse transforms his sons' future. The curse shouted by Meleager's mother ensures his death. Erinys "hears," and punishes Meleager. She would "hear" Penelope if Telemachus banished her, and punish him. She "hears" Oedipus's curse on his sons, and punishes them. Erinys hearing such words makes them self-fulfilling. Erinyes make the wish for other's destruction, spoken by the hurt self, come irrevocably true.

As one might expect, given Homeric "insight into the disunity" of emotional experience (Chapter 2), Homeric Erinyes have multiple roles. They attend specific relationships but are also free-floating, called "from Erebos" by destructive anger and words that express it. They lurk in darkness, in the human potential for anger, and in glimpses of death.

Thirty years before the first extant tragedy comes Heraclitus's ambiguous allusion to Erinyes: "Sun will not overstep his measures, otherwise the Erinyes, helpers of Justice, will find him out." This has been read to suggest that the Erinyes' basic role was to preserve cosmic order. But the one thing we know for certain about Heraclitus's messages is that they were regarded as unusual. One could even assume that if Heraclitus says something, it is likely that no other Greek thought it. Whatever Heraclitus says is precisely the opposite of evidence for what the culture as a whole normally believed.[14]

Heraclitus is policing the cosmos, even its "ruler," with regulating forces, Erinyes, which are both resident in and destructive of human relationships. Heraclitus works by paradox. He also calls justice "conflict." The idea of cosmic order as "justice" was a philosophical creation, which deliberately used human relationships to describe the workings of the universe. It would not be odd if Heraclitus were enlisting, in a way that may have sounded outrageously inappropriate to his contemporaries, powers characteristically resident in *personal*, especially family, relationships, to convey an unorthodox vision of *cosmic* order. He may be the exception that proves

[14] See C. Kahn 1979:155–56. Cosmic justice: see Vlastos 1947. In another fragment, supposedly also by Heraclitus, sun is the seasons' "overseer." See Heraclitus frr. 94 and 100DK. So when Heraclitus calls the Erinyes "Justice's aides," he may be suggesting (among other things) that even the world's ruler must respect the rights and existence of everything else, must respect the terms of his relation with the rest of the world—as Agamemnon, Greek commander, should have respected Achilles' rights.

the rule that in the early fifth-century thought-world, Erinyes inhabit relationships between self and other.

In those relationships, death has a fundamental role. Achilles' horse used to be linked with Heraclitus's pronouncement to suggest that the world order that Erinyes supposedly supported was one in which horses do not talk. But supporting world order is not what Erinyes do elsewhere in Homer, except that like all gods—Zeus Xenios, for instance, or Aphrodite—they have a precinct of human operation whose rules they jealously protect. To read the horse passage fully, one would take it in relation to every word in *Iliad* book 19, and to questions about the kind of magical event kept out of the poem. It is Hera who gives the horse speech. The way the narrative sets this up implies that talking horses are not shocking in themselves. What "should not" happen, I think, is the prophecy of, specifically, death. Erinyes inhere not in speechless horses or world order, but in Achilles' relationship with his self and his death.

Iliad 19 makes reparation for some of Achilles' rights but ends by menacing others, reminding him of his future. Paradoxically, Achilles, antithesis of death, for most of the poem has functioned like a dead person whose removed "anger" (*mēnis*, the poem's first word) affects everyone. *Iliad* 19 brings him to active life again, but before setting him loose it reminds him that he is soon truly to die: to be where he can no longer act. He is "deeply grieved" at the reminder. The horse "ought not" or "did not need" (the words could mean either) to say *that*. The speech, not the speaker, upsets. Achilles knows he will die here, "far from" home. "All the same," he "will not stop." He drives into battle. Death prophecy intrudes on his relationship with himself. Erinyes let it go far enough, not beyond what he already knew. The future to which he is driving, and which his ghost lastingly resents in the *Odyssey*, is Hades.[15]

TRAGIC ERINYES: DAMAGE "FROM THE GROUND"

> Absolute tragedy makes implicit or explicit the intuition that there can be . . . [no] reparation. . . . Each absolute tragedy . . . re-enacts the mystery and outrage of innate evil, of a compulsion towards blindness and self-destruction incised irreparably in men and women.
> —George Steiner, "A Note on Absolute Tragedy"

Tragic Erinyes come from a different world. Their Homeric roles (involvement with cursing, punishment of the person cursed) are still active, but now there are new dimensions and a different balance. The power to "send" destructive blindness is still there, but not so explicit. Erinyes may

[15] Horse and Achilles: *Il.* 19.410–17, 407, 420. Achilles in Hades: *Od.* 11.488–92.

be present in the damaging moment, but they are now supremely concerned with the punitive consequence.

We know practically nothing about the lived experience of pre-*Oresteia* Erinyes.[16] It used to be argued, mainly from Oresteian evidence, that Erinyes "were originally" the vengeance of the dead, the snake-embodiment of a murdered person's spirit or dying curse.[17] This argument was being dismantled by 1955, starting from the obvious point that Homer's Erinyes are not invested in murder. (Melampus, for instance, is jailed but not killed.) Pervasive snake imagery in the *Oresteia* does not mean that Erinyes "were originally" snakes.[18]

That formulation begs the question of for whom Erinyes supposedly "were" snakes or curses. Whose consciousness is the target of such a claim? We have no evidence for anyone believing that Erinyes "were" snakes. Scattered remarks tell us that Erinyes were potentially involved in contexts unconnected with murder. One Pythagorean prohibition, for instance, forbids looking back at the start of a journey, "for Erinyes are following."[19] It has been too easy to make a modern myth of snake origins for Erinyes, forgetting how little we know about the pre-tragedy minds to whom this belief was attributed.

Scholars have also argued an opposite case, that Erinyes were not part of cult or lived imagination, and belonged in the fifth century only to the tragic stage, living, in effect, only off the impact of the *Oresteia*.[20]

It is true that our evidence for the Erinyes' connection with *daimones* of cult—like the Semnai Theai ("Holy Goddesses") on the Areopagus, Eumenides ("Kindly Ones," euphemistically named) at Colonus and elsewhere, or Mnamones ("Rememberers")—is later than the *Oresteia*.[21] But it seems freakish to suppose that Erinyes, alone of all the daemons in trag-

[16] See Winnington-Ingram 1980:206–7.

[17] See Rohde 1925:178–79; Harrison 1922:234–35. Snake pursuing man is a common sixth-century motif in sculpture. Some interpreters suggest that such a snake "is," or "is seen as," Erinys pursuing a murderer: that Erinys was first a snake or "simple snake-Fury," then developed into a "female figure with snake-attributes." This style of explanation depends on the "development" model from simple to complex, so often invoked in "searches for origins" (see Chapter 2, n. 87), and forgets that the earliest literary Erinyes are not involved with murder. The motif of snake chasing man is not evidence for early ideas of Erinyes. But its existence did mean that after the *Oresteia* with its wealth of snake imagery, painters newly inspired to represent Orestes' encounter with Erinyes could "think with" ready-made "man meets snake" iconography. (I am arguing here against very minor points in Prag 1985:44, 117 n. 41, a rich and important work that the author kindly let me see before publication.)

[18] *Oresteia*'s snake imagery: see Lebeck 1971:14. Dodds (1951:21 n. 37) and Winnington-Ingram (1983:156) firmly and gracefully demolished the idea of Erinys originating as "embodiment of dying curse."

[19] See Burkert 1972:173 n. 58.

[20] See Dover 1974:145; Parker 1983:14–15.

[21] For cults of Erinys-like figures, see Farnell 5:474 (n. 213), 471–74 (nn. 206–14).

edy, were a fiction of the genre, unconnected to wholesale fifth-century expectations of daemonic presence in the world and the mind (see Chapters 2, 5, 7). I argued (Chapter 1) that whatever the darkness of tragedy's unknowable distortions, tragedy does reflect important patterns in the imaginative world of its audience. It would be irresponsible to suppose that Erinyes were decoration with no correspondence in lived experience. I assume that Erinyes were an effective part of tragedy because they were a part of life, relationships, consciousness, of which the audience was intermittently aware. When I say "Erinyes were," I am making a claim about the imagination and experience of fifth-century tragic audiences.

Tragedy made Erinyes very much its own. Their cluster of roles suited the genre. After the *Oresteia*, Erinyes were connected profoundly, but not only, with tragedy, whose subject matter was central to their daemonic province. They were particularly connected with the matricide Orestes, and there were specific Athenian reasons, which we shall come to later, why this was so. The *Oresteia*'s impact was part of it. Erinyes do not appear directly in other tragedies of family bloodshed. One might ask why Erinyes do not attack Sophocles' Oedipus, for instance, for murdering his father. They turn up in his story in another place. At Colonus, he comes to them. It is relief when he gets there. They do not follow him. Separated from Orestes, Erinyes have different resonances, glancing mentions. Sophocles' Electra is the victim and, peculiarly, the agent of a deeply interior Erinys, "hiding" in ambush-places: the house, the minds of its family, the underworld.[22] Orestes is a very special case.

Vase-painters of tragedy are freer. They show Erinyes round Orestes, but also paint a single Erinys attending other tragic figures. She turns up everywhere in vase-paintings of tragedy, especially at scenes of vengeance summoned (like the *Choephoroe*'s grave scene) or fulfilled. Euripides' *Meleager* (416 B.C.) staged Althaea's curse on her son. Erinys heard that curse in Homer, but she did not figure on stage in Euripides' play. One vase-painting of this play has Erinys with torch and sword beside Meleager, illustrating, presumably, the messenger-speech describing his death, which must have mentioned the curse. Erinys is there at the curse's fulfillment. Another messenger-speech painting shows Erinys beside Hippolytus's bull from the sea, an icon of that "father's curse" remembered repeatedly by Hippolytus in the text. A fourth-century painting of another tragedy (probably Chaeremon's *Achilles Thersiktonos*) labels an Erinys standing over the corpse as Poina, "Vengeance."[23]

---

[22] See Farnell 5:437, 440; Harrison 1962:222–23, 228; Prag 1985:26–47. Electra's Erinys: see Chapter 4, n. 11.

[23] See Trendall and Webster 1971: III, 1.6, 3.24, 4.2; cf. III, 1.27, 3.33, 3.39, 3.41, 3.44. "Father's curse": Poseidon promised his son Theseus "three curses"—traditional number of

Tragedy explores damage within bonded relationships that is worked out by Erinys, daemon of the lasting reality of remembered hurt, of self's self-destructive awareness of other's anger. "Menis [Anger] and Erinyes belong together." In some Greek states, Erinys-like *Mnamones*, "Rememberers," had a legal role. Aeschylus's Erinyes say, "We are called Arai [Curses] in the house of earth.[24] The damage and relationships vary. Eteocles insulted his father, whose Erinys is now inescapable. The chorus hopes "Erinys of the house" will leave when gods are propitiated. Eteocles knows better. His father's curse made the *daimōn* of his house "boil." This damage was not murder. Fifty years later, spectators of Sophocles' *Oedipus at Colonus* will see this curse replayed, as Oedipus renews it, calling on Erinyes. Sophocles' Electra says Clytemnestra lived with her accursed lover, "fearing no Erinys." Electra summons Erinyes who "look on when people die unjustly and when beds are secretly dishonored," implying that Erinys monitors the marriage bond as well as murder. In Aeschylus, dead Clytemnestra stirs the Erinyes against her son. Here, they are Erinyes "of the mother." They did not persecute her for killing her husband. "Erinyes" express a perception of the world in which conflicting relationships are at work in the self. Erinys may punish you for punishing an act that "other" Erinyes, Erinyes invoked in a different context, might themselves have punished. These Erinyes summoned by Clytemnestra concentrate exclusively on Clytemnestra's injury.[25] Erinyes are as variable as relationships and the damage that can be done in them within a complex life webbed with relationships. They work punitively in the inner world, in the mind of a person who has hurt someone else. They are activated from the external inner world, the underworld.

An Erinys-sense of underworld, underground anger suited the fifth-century theater's consciousness of its own underground. The mid- and late fifth-century stage had some kind of underground channel through which an actor playing a ghost, for instance, might crawl up. Unseen underground space, where the dead lie in resentment, was present in tragic language and staging. It was a truth both of the stage and of relationships in tragic family and society that something might rise "from below" at any moment.[26]

Tragedy insists on the irrevocableness of action and word, the power for

---

the Erinyes—and Hippolytus remembers his father's curse continuously, before, during, and after the catastrophe. It "killed" him, *Hipp.* 888, 1315, 1378, 1241, 1324.

[24] See *Eum.* 417; Fraenkel *ad Ag.* 154–55; Dodds 1951:21 n. 37; Winnington-Ingram 1983:161, 171 (with n. 59).

[25] See *OC* 421–56, 1377, 1375–91. S. *El.* 275, 113–14 (which connects Erinyes with damage other than murder, a connection excluded by *Eum.* 212 and 605, but see Jebb *ad loc.*); *Sept.* 695, 700–709.

[26] See Padel 1990:345. Angers "from the ground": cf. *Cho.* 278.

lasting damage that inheres in one act, one word, performed or uttered under an entirely impermanent passion, even though (and this is one of tragedy's cruellest revelations) that passion may not "belong to" that person. It may never visit that person again. "I wish it had never come to my mouth," says Theseus to his dying son, of his curse uttered "in error." "I wish I could be a corpse instead of you."[27] This sense of damage through words, and an answering violence snapping back "from underground," is Erinys's province in human lives and minds. Tragedy's vision of inner experience assumes a mass of multiple external forces, which concretely assault self's concretely conceived interior. Erinyes sum them all up. Erinys was tragedy's ideal daemon. Aeschylus lays claim to her as tragedy's defining icon.

BLOOD, MURDER, MADNESS

The *Oresteia* is crucial to any attempt at unpacking the Erinyes' iconic power in Athenian imagination. A feel for earth and what is under it energizes its central play. *Choephoroe* begins with the son's prayer to "Chthonic Hermes" who "watches over fathers' rights." Chthonic Hermes has power to send souls down under earth to death, and to release them from the underworld, to the light (see Chapter 1). His name is the keynote of this play. Later, Clytemnestra sends libations to be poured to dead Agamemnon, to limit the retributive damage of "blood fallen to ground." To further their revenge, Agamemnon's divided children summon him separately from the earth. Their footprints meet and match in this same earth. Earth drinks Electra's offering, then offers hope: the lock found in earth, the print made in earth, are the first signs that Chthonic Hermes *will* help avenge the dead, will work "for dear ones under earth" and ensure that "the dead kill the living."[28]

Bloodshed is not the only damage possible in a close relationship, but it is one of the most dramatic, and it is the coinage of the *Oresteia*. Two of tragedy's most frequent words mean "blood." But they mean it in different ways. *Haima* means the physical stuff. *Phonos* can mean this too, but it has to be shed blood. *Phonos* also means "murder," and sometimes "death." As Aeschylus handles them, both *haima* and *phonos* are the point of the Erinyes' existence. Blood soaks down to earth and calls them up. They are angered by it, avenge it, lap it, call for more. "Blood-drinking Tiso sits on

---

[27] *Hipp.* 1410–12, 1363.
[28] "Ground" and "underworld" in *Cho.*: e.g., 1, 3, 15, 17, 66, 96, 124, 164. Electra's libation to earth, the footprints: see 164, 207–8. Hermes: 1, 811. "Dead killing the living": 886, cf. 833.

high," says one Sophocles fragment.[29] *Tisis*, revenge, is written into the name of the Erinys titled Tisiphone, "Blood-Avenger."

In other contexts, too, Erinyes haunt possibilities of family bloodshed, or blood shed in relationships bonded by oath. Heracles' mortal father fears that Heracles in his madness will kill him and acquire *haima sungonon pros Erinusi*: "blood [spilled by] a blood relation, apt for Erinyes." "Assaults of Erinyes" come "out of" such blood. They bind and stir the killer's *splanchna*, sucking *his* blood out. When Iphigeneia nearly kills her brother, both are appalled at what she would have suffered if she had. Ajax, about to kill *himself*, regarding himself as destroyed by the Greeks with whom he is bound, calls on Erinyes to avenge him:

> I call as helpers the immortal, always virgin,
> watchers of all sufferings among mortals,
> the holy, quick-footed Erinyes, to learn
> how I suffer from the sons of Atreus,
> that they may swoop together on them. . . .
> Go, O you swift, punishing Erinyes,
> taste! Don't spare the army!

When Orestes asks why the Erinyes chasing him did not chase Clytemnestra for killing her husband, they answer, "She was not *homaimos* [of the same blood with] the man she killed." They are Erinyes of, specifically, her blood.[30]

The Erinyes' instant reponse to blood is snakelike, doglike. As often, dogs merge with snakes into a compact image of an animate force eating liquid, living matter from the human body (see Chapters 6, 7). They eat Orestes' blood. In the *Oresteia*, Cassandra says they were summoned by the first family bloodshed (presumably Thyestes' children). They "strengthened" themselves by that first "drink" and wait in the house for more. "Not gorged with *phonos*, Erinys will drink a third draught" at the next murder. They track Orestes by blood-drops like a wounded fawn, his "mother's furious hounds." Laughing at the smell of blood, they "drain off *phonos*," chase their victim "because of the fresh blood." Their attack will "come from fathers' blood," if Orestes does not avenge it. One vase, painted soon after the *Oresteia* was staged, shows an Erinys with a snake round her hair like a spotted band, holding two other snakes. Beside her is the word "Eat!" in dual form, clearly addressed to the two snakes she holds. In a Theban play, the dead bodies of Jocasta and her sons who killed each other are "objects of delight to Erinyes."[31]

---

[29] S. fr. 743R. Pfeiffer (1966) argued the name here was Tiso (not Pearson's Tisis), short for Tisiphone.

[30] *HF* 1076, cf. 1265, 46; *Cho.* 36, 46, 278, 283–84; *IT* 866; *Aj.* 836–44; *Eum.* 604–6.

[31] *Ag.* 1188, 1192; *Cho.* 577–78, 1054; *Eum.* 184, 248, 253, 359; *Cho.* 283–84; see fur-

Shed blood connects the inside and outside of a person. When "black blood" flows from a wound, what was inside other's innards is let out, by intentions hidden in self's innards. One person's *phrenes* have in them the possibility of destroying another's, of spilling what is within. Tragic language speaks of what is unseen in *splanchna*. One person must divine whether another's *splanchna* hold hostility or not.[32] Those alien *splanchna*, which self cannot see, may hide the intention of spilling the blood inside self.

When what belongs within comes out, Erinyes "rise." They incarnate horror at blood and desire for more. Murder makes blood visible. When it falls, Erinyes rise and follow the killer to drink blood from *his* innards. They drink what is inside, once murder lets it out. Children's universal horror at seeing blood is a recurrent reminder that blood is the sign and proof of hurt. Nightmarishly, in pain, what was in comes out. What ought to stay unseen is seen.

Blood is also the link between family members. They are *homaimoi*, "same-blooded," that word on which Aeschylus's Erinyes hang their case. *Homaimoi* are bound by stuff that rages, blackens, swells *splanchna* (Chapters 2, 3), and impels one to irreversible acts and words from which disaster flows. The ultimate evil is to let out of other the blood that binds other to self. Blood that falls is black. Anger is the blackening passion. Erinyes live in anger, in blood putrified, the good bond gone rotten, the stuff inside innards where we feel and think—stuff that binds a family—made visible, poured away, fouled. The sleeping Erinyes "breathe with unapproachably fetid blasts" says Delphi's priestess. "Shrivel him with vapor from your womb," Clytemnestra's ghost tells them.[33]

Once forcibly made visible, blood falls to the ground. But ground is not neutral. Ground is she who drinks blood, who nurtured the metal that castrated heaven, who sends forth dark children, holds the dead. In Hesiod, Erinyes are "born" from the spilt "blood" of Ouranos, male "Sky." Earth encouraged her son (child also of Ouranos) to cut off his father's genitals, creating in her body the weapon for her son to use. Erinyes were born from that blood. Earth drinks blood of dying warriors. *Psuchē* pours from their wounds. Blood poured into earth is libation to the dead. Earth and the dead in her drink blood, as Earth "received the bloody drops" after

---

ther A. L. Brown 1983:14. Cf. *Phoen.* 1503. Dog and snake resonances: see Chapter 6, nn. 39–45. Vases of Erinys with snakes: see E. Simon and G. Neumann in Berger and Lullies 1979:164–65 n. 60, 231 figs. 1, 3, 232–34, 237–38; Prag 1985:117 n. 41.

[32] See Chapter 2, nn. 8–9, 18.

[33] *Thumos* and *menos* as bloodlike, see Chapter 2, nn. 52–56, 69. Erinyes' foul breath: *Eum.* 53, 138; cf. pp. 28 and 102–3 above. Blood fallen to ground is black, see Chapter 2, n. 59.

Ouranos's castration. Thought and feeling are at work in blood. When it falls to earth, it is altered by earth and has dangerous power. One cannot call back a voiced word, nor make good spilled blood. In both, the power to harm is irreversible.[34]

Erinyes operate within this earth-nexus of blood, darkness (see Chapter 3), good turned bad, fertility made barren (see Chapter 5). Earth-born Erinys is dark and female, like Earth. She is the possibility of a powerful relationship gone powerfully wrong.

She is also the sender and apparition of madness. Spilt blood is the Erinys connection between murder and madness. The *Oresteia*, establishing murder as the paramount interest of Orestes' Erinyes, also established their punishment as madness. From the *Oresteia* on, Erinyes incarnate a link between murder and the madness that both punishes and fosters it. Greek imagination speaks of madness and rabid rage in terms of black liquid moving and turbulent within. Blackness qualifies blood, madness, and, we shall see, Erinyes.[35] Black madness and the blood of murder are henceforth inseparable in Western tragedy. The deepest roots of Dostoevsky's vision are Aeschylean and, beyond that, fifth-century Athenian.

Erinyes, center of the *Oresteia*'s pattern of blood, murder, guilt, crime, punishment, are also where the trilogy is heading. What to do with them once they are out in the open becomes its concern. The *Oresteia* clarifies Erinyes as the concrete, daemonic horror in the human potential for violence. The knowledge that self can damage other, that this force for damage is unlimited, mad, an aberration in the universe that goes on damaging self and others afterwards, is tragedy's heart. We know only three of the many tragedies that predated the *Oresteia*. For us, at least, it is through the *Oresteia* that tragedy, making Erinyes its own, added madness so clearly to the areas of human experience they claim.

Tragedy represents violence both in relationships and in *phrenes*. Its presiding god is another divinity of madness. Madness was perceived, of course, as diverse. Several Greek gods had power through it, and Dionysus's madness operates in a different context from that of Erinyes. But it is an important aspect of tragedy that its presentation of passion as violent inner movement, expressed in violent outward action, should happen in Dionysus's precinct. His persona links extreme outer violence, murder, to extreme inner violence, madness.[36] This link is central to tragedy even

[34] *Theog.* 183–85; see Chapter 5, n. 8. Earth drinking blood, souls of dead receiving blood running into earth: see Alexiou 1974:8, 209 n. 43; Pearson *ad* S. fr. 743. Bloodlike soul: see Chapter 2, n. 69. Thought and feeling in blood: see Chapter 4, n. 13.

[35] See Chapter 2, nn. 46–48; Chapter 3, nn. 66–71; Padel 1981:109–10.

[36] See Padel 1981:128–29, 1990:336, 365; pp. 65–68 above.

when the areas of experience and mind explored by an individual plot are not those normally monitored by Dionysus.

The Erinyes madden. They look "*phonos.*" "Blood" is the object of their gaze as well as their existence. In Aeschylus, it drips from their eyes. A Euripidean Orestes sees them as "blood-eyed." Madness and *phonos* collide in the idea that mad people have bloodshot eyes.[37] Erinys-madness, blood in the eyes, ex-presses the mad awareness that self has shed other's blood. When Orestes "sees" Erinyes, they are (we might say) the projected image of and from his blood-filled vision of the world as he now madly inhabits it. "Following," "remembering" Erinyes destroy him by keeping in his eyes (and all that "eyes" can stand for, see Chapter 3) the fact of having destroyed other. Other destroyed becomes the polluted center of self's consciousness.

Aeschylus describes the Erinyes' madness as a bloodsucking onslaught:

> From your living body
> we lap red thick liquid.

They "dry up Orestes while still alive." His existence is hemorrhage. They "drag him down to requite his murdered mother." He exists drivenly, in a place "where joy is absent," "not knowing where joy can be in his *phrenes.*" The Erinyes "unselve" him, bleed off joy in self or world. Embodying his sense of his victim's anger, they sap his life from within, make *him* victim, drink "from his limbs," suck his healthy inwardness. All this is his madness. Even apart from Orestes, tragic madness is typically described as inner wandering, wounding, twisting, dislocation, and is associated with the outward violence of murder.[38]

Orestes' somatic condition is constant vulnerability to these attacks in which he, and no one else (until the audience of *Eumenides*), sees Erinyes: sees female daemons, wielding weapons. Tragic language implies that the Erinyes' victim's "own" emotion, his madness, is a weapon, especially a "goad." "Driving," "goading" images, characteristic of tragic passion (see Chapters 6, 7), qualify the madness and fear that Erinyes inflict. They "rack" Orestes "*with* fear," "drive" him "*with* fits of madness." Madness and fear are in the "instrumental," dative case. One Euripidean Orestes sees Erinyes attacking with changing weapons:

> Look at this one, a dragon of Hades, wanting to kill me,
> open-mouthed with terrible snakes! And this one
> breathing fire and *phonos* from her clothes,

[37] Mad bloodshot eyes: see Chapter 3, nn. 31, 36. Erinyes' bloody eyes in Orestes' vision: *Or.* 256. Cf. above, n. 29.

[38] See Padel 1981:106–12; *Eum.* 264–65, 267, 268, 302, 422, 301.

> flapping wings, holding my mother in her arms,
> a heavy rock to throw at me—she'll kill me!
> Where can I run?

Hera's best weapon against Heracles is Lyssa (Chapter 7). The Erinyes' weapons include whips and skin disease, often associated with madness in Greek myth. They torture the body's outside. But their supreme instruments are madness and terror: violence within. The madness is the whip; the whip the madness.[39]

On vases, Erinyes carry torches, swords, goads, whips, snakes. Euripidean Erinyes "drive" Orestes. In the *Oresteia*, they have also a hunting "net." Their first word, spoken in sleep, repeated four times, is "Grab!" They wither their victim "with pursuit," drive a murderer from his mind, and from his place of origin and stability, the place where he should rule. Their appearance is itself pursuit, a lash or goad. They put a "bloody bridle" in Orestes' mouth. They hide in "ambush-places." Some painters reflect tragic imagery by giving them hunting dress or painting them as hunting maenads.[40]

Madness exemplifies tragic disintegration.[41] In Greek tragic plots, madness had two functions—to cause crime and to punish it—which reflect the two weightings of Homeric and tragic Erinyes. Homeric Erinyes fulfil curses, but also "send *atē* on *phrenes*," causing crime, causing damage, whereas tragic Erinyes, like tragic madness, are primarily punitive.[42]

These two roles interlock, of course, and this causes interpretive ambiguities. In a fourth-century text, Aeschines the orator tells a defendant, "Don't suppose that Erinyes with burning torches, as on the tragic stage, nag and punish the impious." What does he mean, "punish the impious"? "Make the impious do worse crimes which will be punished," perhaps? That interpretation accentuates Erinyes' Homeric involvement with *atē*, madness that makes one do a bad thing in the first place. Aeschines goes on: "The unbridled pleasures of the flesh, the inability ever to be satisfied,

[39] See *HF* 881; A. fr. 169 (of Lyssa); *PV* 598; *Aj.* 59; *HF* 837; *IT* 931 (*deima Erinuōn*); *Or.* 37–38, 270 (*maniaisin, phoboi, maniasin lussēmasin*); *Cho.* 283–88; *IT* 285–91. Skin disease and madness: see Parker 1983:214, 220.

[40] Scourges, etc.: see Harrison 1962:235 (fig. 51); Prag 1985:48. Cf. "blazing torches": Aeschin. 1.190. *El.* 1252, *Or.* 36, *IT* 32. Cf. *examillasthai*: citizens will "drive" Orestes from the land, Erinyes will "drive him out" of his mind, *Or.* 431, 38 (see Chapter 6, n. 51). Their net: see *Ag.* 1579, *Eum.* 147 (cf. *atē, Pers.* 112). Their hunting role in the *Oresteia*: see *Eum.* 130, 139, 210, 421; Vernant and Vidal-Naquet 1981:150–74. "Goading," "hunting" emotion: see above, pp. 117–19. Erinyes as hunting maenads: see Prag 1985:27 n. 42, 30–32. Bridle, ambush: see *IT* 935, S. *El.* 490.

[41] Madness is central to tragedy (see Padel 1981:199–201), as it evolved in the "mad god's" precinct (see Padel 1990:336); cf. above, pp. 48, 68, 150, 163, and 175.

[42] Padel 1981:110.

man the dens of robbers, fill the pirate ships. These pleasures are each man's Erinys. They incite him to kill his fellow citizens, enslave himself to tyrants, and join conspiracies against democracy." All this sounds as if Aeschines' idea of Erinys punishment is indeed incitement to further crime.[43]

But an imagination formed by the *Oresteia* and its legacy would also remember the external punishments involving skin and flesh on which *Eumenides* insists, and which contemporary vase-painters stress in their whips and torches: physical tortures that image also the inward, equally concrete (see Chapter 2) disintegration of innards in tragic madness. Erinys punishment, in Aeschines' day, may well be madness itself, concretely imaged as a harrowing of the flesh. Aeschines in public polemic may freight tragic Erinyes with sophisticated ironies of detachment, but this does not mean they are not alive in his audience's imagination, that no one in the fourth century feared them; nor, of course, that the ways in which fifth-century tragedy and its painters represented Erinyes had no relation to lived imagination. Our own journalists and cartoonists use irony about nuclear weapons. Their irony does not mean these weapons do not exist. It deals momentarily with things whose power we live with and silently fear. Aeschines' career was built at a time when medicine was modelling its cures on magic. Medicine as well as magic assumed the power of daemons over human interiors.[44] Madness and delirium were familiar, and associated (as we can see from Hippocratic case histories) with death. One would be mad, in that society, to ignore madness, or consistently to ignore divinities known to use it as punishment.

The *Oresteia*'s Erinyes inflict punitive madness. They do not force Orestes to murder. Apollo does that. (Euripides, we shall see, picks this up.) In Aeschylus, Apollo's oracle reminds Orestes of his father's "angers," Erinyes coming from father's blood. These would punish him for not avenging his father's death. Even so, they do not command murder. Orestes does not murder under the influence of Erinys-sent madness, but by Apollo's order. Erinyes wait round unseen, "hard to be sent out," wanting more blood. When they appear, the blood they demand is the murderer's own. They do not cause but gloatingly punish his crime.[45]

Aeschines rhetorically invokes their punishment, but does not say in what he thinks it consists. His unclarity derives from the doubleness of tragic madness endemic in the imagination of his time. Tragedy's madness is particularly (but not only) used to punish crime. Yet the "lash" that

[43] Aeschin. 1.190; see Dover 1974:146. Homeric, Erinys-sent *atē* in *phrenes*: see *Od.* 15.234.
[44] See Chapter 3, nn. 1, 71.
[45] *Cho.* 277–83, *Ag.* 1190, *Cho.* 403, *Eum.* 264–65.

"goads" one to do something also punishes one for doing it.[46] In the case of Aeschylus's Orestes, punishment consists in the way Erinyes alchemize his past murder to a madness that continually and concretely mangles the innards remembering it.

The Erinyes' role in tragedy, as the *Oresteia* sets it up, expresses tragedy's balance, and the balance of fifth-century nosology, between internal and external cause (see Chapter 4). Evil is both in us and outside us. But tragedy, like its society, accentuates the external. Evil is more in the world than in human beings. It enters from outside. On balance, harm is the world's violence penetrating the human interior (see Chapter 3). Erinyes, like perception and diseases, are *esionta*, coming in from outside. But they may also be "in" somewhere already. Either way, once there they incarnate damage within.

ERINYES SEEN

Aeschylus set up an Erinys iconography for tragedy and its painters. Homer and Hesiod do not say what Erinyes look like. Pausanias says Aeschylus was the first to show them as women with snakes in their hands or hair. Out of the daemon-discourse of epic, popular cult, and the visual arts, Aeschylus summoned the part-human, threatening female figures of late archaic art. As he describes them, and as vase-painters immediately portrayed them, Erinyes resemble visual representations of Gorgons or Harpies. They were played, of course, by male actors dressed as female. In *Oresteia*-inspired paintings, they sometimes resemble contemporary representations of maenads: women, sometimes with wings, often with snakes in their hair or hands.[47] The poetry stresses their blackness. The *Oresteia*'s Erinyes speak of their "black-clothed attacks. Tragedians describe them as black-robed, black-skinned.[48] Erinyes are an important part of Greek discourse of darkness about mind and its disturbance (Chapter 3).

Their feet are also important. Aeschylus's Erinyes sing of their "hostile dances of foot":

> Leaping from above
> I bring down the strength of my foot.
> My legs make men fall however hard they run:
> an irresistible destruction.

[46] See Chapter 6, nn. 14–15.

[47] *Eum.* 48–51; see Chapter 5, nn. 14–16. Vase-painters' response to the *Oresteia*, especially to its Erinyes' resemblance to Gorgons and Harpies (cf. *Cho.* 1048, Ar. *Pax* 810): see Prag 1985:26–47, esp. 28. Aeschylus's influence: see Paus. 1.28.6, cf. *IT* 286, *Or.* 256.

[48] See *Sept.* 699, 979; *Eum.* 370–71, 372–76; *Or.* 321.

Because their feet are often mentioned (delicate, bronze, multiple, swift), some scholars suggest that they derived from a horse-daemon. But Ate, who "walks on human heads, harming them," has important feet, too, and most emotions swoop down on human heads (see Chapters 4, 6). Erinyes have much in common with passions and daemons attacking from above. Sometimes a running Gorgon (Medusa's sisters run after Perseus when he kills her) is horselike and winged. Rather than looking to unprovable origins in horse-daemons, we might take the Erinyes' swift feet as a detail that suggests the immediacy of their response to crime. They appear instantly after murder, running after the killer.[49]

Erinyes also tend to have wings. The *Eumenides'* priestess says they look like wingless Harpies. Winglessness is easier to stage. Vase-painters, however, representing this play and others, give Erinyes wings, which are presumably fun to paint, and also truer to the language's sense of daemonic aerial attack. One of Euripides' Orestes figures does not know where to turn: the Erinyes he sees are "rowing with wings." Another Orestes shoots at Erinyes flying "to uppermost sky on their wings."[50] Their assault resembles tragic passion's attack on innards (see Chapter 6): a collage of animal and human weaponry, houndlike, overmastering, leaping, kicking, goading, pursuing, swooping.

What Erinyes see, how they are seen, is part of what they do—goad, drink blood, madden—and part of the madness they wield. "Staging and conception are inseparable."[51] Standing for other's rights within self, they are both inside and outside the mind. They are hunting maenads, pursuant, repellant, blood-lusting, embodying all that tragic language intuits passion does to *splanchna*. In Aeschylus's third play, there they are onstage, threatening, seen by everyone, the distilled blackness of underworld and inner world out in the open. Their ultimate target is innards and the blood in them. The center of their persona is self's *awareness* of other's anger. How they look is also how and what the mind that is threatened by them sees. They embody a self-and-otherness, an inside-and-outsideness, in tragedy's vision of the mind.

Innards are the center, in human beings, of gods' interest (see Chapter 2). Innards flow and swell with passion, with liquid (Chapter 4). Erinyes are daemons apart. They want to destroy all this. "Living, you'll be our feast," they tell Orestes. Their song binds and withers *phrenes*. Their victim thinks and feels nothing but their assault. Their attack is a constant mobile

[49] Daemon-horse Arion, born from Poseidon's rape of Demeter-Erinys, as possible "origin" of Erinys: Dietrich 1965:106; cf. Burkert 1985:38. Feet: see *Il.* 19.93–94. *Aj.* 837, S. *El.* 489–91. Aerial daemonic attack on the head: see pp. 129–32 above.

[50] Winglessness: see *Eum.* 51 (and above, p. 103), Harrison 1922:228; cf. *IT* 289, *Or.* 277.

[51] A. L. Brown 1983:29.

prison, draining innards, making outer limbs run. They "feed" until their victim is "bloodless food for daemons, a shadow" who "does not know where in his *phrenes* is the possibility of joy." Simply to see them is to be mad, is the sign and moment of madness.[52]

Seeing and not seeing Erinyes is crucial to tragedy. It is madness to see them. It may be madder not to. Their madness, like their persons, is both outside and in. They assault the mind; they are not born in it. Yet mind is where they live and operate.

This challenges both audience and dramatist. As daemons of personal relationships, Erinyes madden and appear to one person at a time: the one who did the damage. They are worshipped in isolation, as Clytemnestra's ghost recalls:

> You've lapped many things of mine,
> many wineless *choas* [libations]. . . .
> I've sacrificed banquets on a hearth of fire
> at night, an hour shared by none of the gods.

Their sort of festival is hated by other gods, says Apollo. They are divinities apart, unshared. They have the lone blackness of the goddess Night. Seeing them, having them appear to oneself alone, is part of being punished. The vision isolates. That is how they are seen, by one person at a time, in the *Oresteia*'s first two plays. First by Cassandra, no one else. Then by Orestes, no one else. In the third play, too, they are seen by the priestess of Delphi, no one else. These are the sort of people—the seers, the mad—whom tragedy expects to see what others cannot see.[53]

But differences between these seers stage a shift between Erinyes and audience. Erinyes move closer to home. A foreign mad priestess of Apollo, a mad Greek prince, a sane priestess of Apollo at the center of the Greek world: these figures are progressively closer to the Athenian spectators. Aeschylus's staging made visible to an enormous audience that which is normally invisible: other people's innards and blood, the emissions of Hades and of an individual mind.

Erinyes are the chief medium through which the trilogy moves (as many tragedies move) from invisibility to visibility, dark to light. The spectators, the last to see Erinyes, have put in front of them what the trilogy has been invisibly "about." They see what has lain "under its ground." Taken into the city and its land, Erinyes are received into the consciousness of the fictive citizens in solid view of real citizens. Are these real citizens now mad? Or polluted? Orestes' Erinyes have become everyone's.

[52] *Eum.* 299–306, 329–33, 376; *Cho.* 1048; *IT* 282–91; *Or.* 251.

[53] People who see Erinyes: *Ag.* 1190, *Cho.* 1048, *Eum.* 34; Padel 1981:109. Clytemnestra's lone offerings, Apollo's version of their "feast": *Eum.* 106–9, 191. Night's lonely blackness: see above, pp. 100–101.

The Most Polluted Day

Precisely this scenario was evaded annually at Athens at another famous Dionysus festival. On the "most polluted day" of the Athenian year, "all Athenians are Oresteioi," as a fragment of an Alexandrian poet puts it. This was the second day of a three-day Athenian festival of Dionysus called Anthesteria, also called the "Older Dionysia" to distinguish it from the Greater Dionysia, tragedy's main festival. The day was Choes, day of "jugs."[54]

On the day before Choes, the year's new wine was carried to Athens's most ancient Dionysian precinct, "Dionysus-in-the-Marsh." The first day must have had a touch of the atmosphere of "Le Beaujolais Nouveau est arrivé." But the precinct was opened only at the beginning of the Choes, after sunset on that first day (for the Greek day, like the Jewish, began at sunset). Choes began more somber and sinister associations. All sanctuaries in Athens were closed except this one. House doors were varnished with black pitch. Behind those newly black doors, in the house of the head of each family, the Athenian extended families drank that new wine, in company but without talking. It was competitive drinking, a contest with a prize for the first to finish. Most important, everyone drank from a separate Chous, "wine-jug."

The story that was used to explain this practice locally was that moment in Orestes' myth staged by the *Eumenides*. Orestes supposedly arrived at Athens during the Anthesteria. How could Athenians honor hospitality while keeping themselves and their temples free of his pollution? Answer: close the precincts, make everyone drink from a separate jug, and prohibit talking. Incorporate and simultaneously exclude Orestes.

Euripides, like all male Athenians, must have shared this hour of communal inclusion and exclusion, of drinking to ward off Orestes' Erinyes, from the age of three. In one play, he imagines what it felt like *to Orestes*:

> At first no host received me willingly.
> I was hated by gods. Some had respect and pity,
> and set a table for me as their guest:
> a separate table, alone, under the same roof as them.
> By their silence they built up the feeling
> I couldn't be spoken to [or, "that I might not speak"],
> so I was apart from them in food and drink.
> Each had pleasure of Bacchus [i.e., wine],
> filling an equal amount for all, but into private cups.
> I didn't think it right to question them, my hosts.

[54] Call. fr. 178.2; see Phot. *Lex.* s.v. *Choes*; Burkert 1983:218 n. 11, 1985:238–39.

> I was my mother's killer. I hurt in silence,
> pretending not to notice. I cried.
> I hear my sufferings became a festival
> for the Athenians. And still the custom stays:
> Athene's people honor a bowl made for the Choes.

After this party of apartness, Orestes was tried, confronting "the eldest of the Erinyes." Euripides brings out the paradox of isolation and community in that drinking session, of people (family members, in the festival) who both were and were not in touch.[55]

This day was so important in the calendar that "Birth, Choes, adolescence, and marriage" were the stages of a young Athenian's life. It must have a formative day for young imaginations. Children themselves were important. Miniature Choes, painted with pictures of children, were mass-produced. The spirits of the dead were abroad. There was a Halloween atmosphere. Food was cooked for Hermes Chthonios on behalf of the dead. The garlands worn while drinking could not be hung in sanctuaries (which anyway were shut), since they had been under the same roof as Orestes. They were hung round each Chous and given to the priestess of Dionysus-in-the-Marsh.[56]

This "most polluted day," the day the house door went newly black, began in a precinct of Dionysus that was closed for the rest of the year. This hour of domestic enactment on a day of Dionysian isolation staged in the home a paradox—about the isolation of being connected to others—to which the Erinyes' persona was crucial. The proper sacrifices to Erinyes, in contrast to Dionysus, were wineless. The festival states some tension of privacy and community, drinking and winelessness, contact and separation, to which only the combination of Erinyes, Dionysus, and the potential for guilt between people connected by blood could give Athenian meaning.

Tragedy itself happened at a festival and in a precinct of Dionysus. The *Oresteia* is concerned with the story of the Choes: how Orestes came to Athens. Like the Choes, it weaves a pattern of warding off and calling up the dead. Associations to the Choes run deep through the *Choephoroe*. The play's name is "*Choai*-Bearers." *Choai* means "libations." Like *choes*, "jugs," it comes from *cheō*, "I pour." Choes was the second day of a three-day festival, *Choephoroe* the second play of a trilogy. The play's first words are "Hermes Chthonios," who was honored on the Choes. It has a potent ghost-raising song; ghosts were abroad on the Choes. The song, like the day, repeatedly stresses children:

[55] *IT* 947–60. See Th. 2.15, 4; [Dem.] 59.73ff.; Burkert 1983:218–22.
[56] See Burkert 1983:221 n. 28; 1985:238–39.

> Children are savior voices to a man who has died.
> Like bobbing corks they draw up the net,
> saving the flax cord from the deep.[57]

Children, buoyant relics of those who sink without trace, draw the dead soul to the surface: the passage reflects the Choes's combination of children and the dead.

In the *Choephoroe*, Aeschylus brings to the stage resonances of that "polluted day." In the *Eumenides*, he stages it, making the nightmare behind Choes—that Orestes' blood-guilt and Erinyes might spread to Athens—come nearly, even apparently, true. *Choai-Bearers*, the libation play, begins with Clytemnestra's *choai* to Agamemnon and ends with her blood shed. After this, the first pouring images in *Eumenides* are the hands of Orestes "dripping with blood" on the Delphic altar. Foul liquid oozes from the Erinyes' eyes. This play's first *choai* are those which Clytemnestra's ghost remembers pouring to Erinyes. Her earlier *choai* were sent to soothe Agamemnon. The remembered *choai* here rewake the whole notion of libation rites. Libation is liquid poured away, as blood is poured in murder. Pouring away can mean things going wrong as well as right. In the *Choephoroe*, Electra carried Clytemnestra's *choai* unwillingly, not knowing what to do with these offerings from a killer to her murdered husband. Should she pour them out,

> in silence with dishonor, the way my father died?
> And then walk back, like someone throwing out
> waste-matter from a rite, chucking the vessel away,
> my eyes averted?

Libations and offerings were not inert matter (the way we ourselves think of them), but dangerous. The chorus advises Electra to turn Clytemnestra's libation into a prayer for herself and Orestes. The rite becomes bad turned good.[58]

This, then, is the previous play's image-basis for the lapping, the liquid blood falling to ground, which is such a feature of Erinys-songs in the *Eumenides*. Erinyes are the polluting waste-matter that waits, normally unseen, round people who are and are not in touch, individuals of the same blood, parents, children, brothers, with power to bring grief to one another. That ceremony of communal liquid kept private under Dionysus's auspice averted danger in these relationships. Athenians did it every year, behind black doors, and starting very young. The *Eumenides* made them collectively see what this festival kept out. The Choes must, I think, be the

---

[57] *Cho.* 334, 349, 379, 477, 501, 505–7.

[58] Images of pouring, *choai*: *Eum.* 42, 54, 107, cf. 248, 263–65, etc. Clytemnestra's libation diverted: see *Cho.* 23, 42–47, 87, 109. Throwing out *katharmata*: *Cho.* 98.

main reason why after the *Oresteia*, Athens associated Erinyes most tangibly and obsessively with Orestes. It was the shock of it: there, in the city's heart, were the unseen perils of family relationships abroad, shared, visible to all. The watchers, as Erinyes are consistently called, are seen.

ERINYES UNSEEN

> Dostoevski's devils . . . possess a *clinical* reality. He saw the hidden resemblance between evil and infirmity, possession and reflection. His devils . . . tell us: I'm nothing but an obsession. And then: I am the nothing that manifests itself as obsession. I am your obsession. I am your nothing.
> —Octavio Paz, *On Poets and Others*

Tragedy's first Erinyes, in early Aeschylus and in the *Oresteia*'s first two plays, were unseen. Making everyone see them was a *coup de théâtre*. Through stages of his trilogy, Aeschylus brought them closer to being seen, first as hallucinations, private (like the wine-jugs), then public. Making them visible in the third play did not mean they were not there before. On the contrary, it validated the lonely visions of Cassandra and Orestes. Normally, before and after the *Eumenides*, Erinyes are external but unseen.

Modern interpreters have often turned here to modern distinctions, like subjective versus objective.[59] But in the face of Aeschylus's coup, which scrambled Athenian motifs of the "most polluted" day in the lived year, then staged the moment which that day supposedly commemorated, such distinctions are irrelevant. Distinctions that mattered to contemporary imagination were different: the relation, for instance, between the inside and outside of an individual (see Chapter 1), whose immediate visual token is the Erinyes' medium, blood. There is no question of subjective versus objective when Athenian spectators see Erinyes, seeing whom is Orestes' madness. A private darkness is now public, visible in shared daylight. The question is, rather, how will these dark embodiments of what ought to be inside be sent back there? Outside, at large, they are a walking incarnation of the mad blood-guilt that the Choes annually evaded. They embody the horror that this waste-product of a single polluted family may indeed be shared and spread.

The *Oresteia* was a hard act to follow. You can only bring Erinyes onstage for the first time once. Given that annual festival, no power on earth, I think, could have prevented Athenians—or anyway, Euripides—from restaging Orestes' encounter with Erinyes. But where will the Erinyes be

[59] A. L. Brown (1983:13, 19, 22) gives a bibliography for "subjective versus objective Erinyes" in the *Oresteia*.

seen after the *Oresteia*? Outside or inside? What does "inside" mean in that theater, after the *Oresteia*?[60]

Erinyes are outside *and* inside *phrenes*. Sophocles, the only dramatist who does not stage Orestes' encounter with them (in an extant play), points to their dual territory in a single phrase, *Erinus phrenōn*, "Erinys of *phrenes*." Sophocles has a unique power of elision: verbal, theological, grammatical, dramatic. His words locate Erinys as in and belonging to, yet also menacing, *phrenes*. Reading this, as scholars have sometimes done, as "a watered-down 'psychological' Fury, an abstraction," distinguishing "abstraction," "nonliteral," and "psychological" from concrete, is anachronistic.[61] Erinys was all at once: of and in *phrenes*, "psychological" *and* external. Elsewhere, Sophocles gives a strong sense of Erinyes as worshipped daemons, inhabitants of a sacred grove, "daughters of Earth and Darkness," "Erinyes of gods and Hades," blood-drinking, aloft.[62] The phrase does not ignore all this. Rather, it locates the whole lot, terrifyingly, in the mind as well as out of it.

Sophocles' one extant Orestes is markedly pious. He reverences the threshold gods before he enters his family home to kill his mother. He begins by praying to his country's gods. He prays that he not be sent away to exile again. Sophocles plays on the *Choephoroe*, of course. "Hermes, Maia's son," again conducts Clytemnestra's son to his mother in the house. The horror of matricide is not dimmed. Yet the chorus talks as if Erinyes were with Orestes, not against him. "Hounds" pursue Clytemnestra. When the blow is heard, the chorus says,

> The curses are fulfilled. Those lying below earth
> now live. Those who died long ago
> are sucking blood back
> from their killers.

When Orestes comes out with blood on his hands, he says, "What's in the house is well done, if Apollo prophesied well." Apollo commanded murder. The goodness of Orestes' act depends on the goodness of Apollo's word. The only hint of unstoppable future suffering is uttered by Aegisthus:

[60] This question is especially important if (as Taplin 1977:452–59 convincingly argues) the *Oresteia* was the first extant tragedy to use the *skēnē* and the theater now had a new "inside." See Padel 1990:342–65.

[61] *Ant.* 603. Winnington-Ingram (1980:168 n. 46, 211) objects to *Erinus phrenōn*. He thinks it "an abstraction, balancing *logou anoia*," that weakens the personification of other Sophoclean Erinyes. But modern distinctions are no basis (see Chapter 1, n. 19; Chapter 2, nn. 82, 93; Chapter 6, n. 65) for suspecting an MS reading. *Erinus* does not balance *anoia* as another abstract, but makes the thought expressed through the line increasingly concrete and menacing. Sophoclean "elision": see Gould 1978.

[62] *Ant.* 1075, *OC* 40; cf. above, n. 29.

> Must this house see all the evils,
> now and to come, of Pelops's family?

Orestes ignores his words. Aegisthus must die. The play's language keeps Orestes and Erinyes apart. This less polluting murder ends it. Electra calls on Chthonic Hermes, "Lady Curse" (Ara), and "holy Erinyes, children of gods." Erinys utterances surround, not Orestes, but her whose name the play bears.[63]

Sophocles' Erinyes are inside and outside, and also unseen. Euripides' first Erinys-haunted Orestes appears in a play whose cardinal question, apt for Euripides' more sharply self-referential theater, is the truth of dreaming and seeming. Orestes is still pursued by Erinyes. The *Oresteia* has happened, but the cure did not take. "Those of the Erinyes who did not consent to the decree, chased me continuingly." The Choes began, Athenians celebrate their festival, but still Orestes is mad. The *Oresteia* is wound back on itself. Erinyes are again invisible. *Iphigeneia among the Taurians* does not say the Erinyes are not there. But they are there for, visible to, no one but Orestes. We only hear of him seeing them in a messenger-speech. They are what Orestes is reported *seemingly* to see.[64]

Euripides' second Erinys-polluted Orestes is caught at a different moment, frozen between *Choephoroe* and *Eumenides*. The *Orestes* threatens him with death by stoning, death hurled by the indigenous citizens, on account of his pollution, before he ever gets to Athens.

This Orestes, too, "seems to see" Erinyes, to see what is unnameable in family relationships. His uncle Menelaus knows but will not speak of them:

ORESTES: I seemed to see three girls like night.
MENELAUS: I know who you mean. I don't want to name them.
ORESTES: Yes—for they're holy. You're well trained to turn away from talk of them.
MENELAUS: Do they madden you with family blood?

Menelaus's question demonstrates instantly that being "trained" not to talk of Erinyes does not work. This play's truth is that "seeming is stronger," whatever the reality to which "seeming" may or may not correspond.[65]

This is departure from Aeschylus. The *Choephoroe*'s chorus told Orestes that the Erinyes he saw were only *doxai*, "seemings." They rationalized and explained:

---

[63] S. *El.* 1374, 71, 1394 (cf. *Cho.* 811–14), 1387, 1418–20, 1422–25, 1498. Apollo: see 1376–79. Electra: see 110–14, 275.

[64] *IT* 970, 299; Choes: 956. Dreaming and seeming: *IT* 41, 59, 69, 150, 178, 299, 349, 452, 518, 569, 777, 785, 831. The theme belongs with challenges to ordinary conceptions of gods and oracles, see *IT* 388, 570–75.

[65] *Or.* 409–11, 236.

> Blood's fresh on your hands. This is why
> confusion falls on your *phrenes*.

But the same chorus earlier sang, "Earth breeds many horrors." Aeschylus's trilogy knows Erinyes are out there. Orestes recognizes them:

> For me they're no *doxai* of sufferings.
> They're clearly my mother's enraged hounds.

Aeschylus made Orestes' vision come true in *Eumenides*, whose audience saw what Orestes had seen. They were not (or not only) *doxai*. Euripides takes an opposite path. His play seems, at least, to embrace "seeming" as an important truth in itself. Orestes' devil-*doxai* demonstrate the authenticity, and the authentic pain, of seeming. *Doxai* both "seem" and are truly painful. It was simultaneously a spiritual and dramatic solution to Erinys-madness:

> Even if one's not sick but seems to be,
> suffering and impossibility come on human beings.[66]

Aeschylus invalidated the "seeming" status. Erinyes were "clearly" hounds. Euripides' audience, like Pirandello's audiences, must decide for themselves what they are seeming to see. In the final scene, is Pirandello's "Henry IV" a madman pretending to be sane, or a sane man who pretends to have been mad, when he tells the doctor his case is unique in the annals of madness? "I preferred to remain mad . . . to live out this madness of mine, to revenge myself on the brutality of a stone that had bashed my head." At the end of *Six Characters in Search of an Author*, what has the audience seen: a group of actors playing a murder, or a murder performed by a group of actors? Is Euripides' Orestes a madman whose madness is that he thinks he sees Erinyes? Or a man punished by goddesses, visible seemingly only to him, and only when they inflict on him bursts of madness?

Finally, Euripides pinpoints Apollo's relation to Erinyes and to the murder as an area of poignant anxiety. In Aeschylus, Apollo's oracle reminds Orestes of Erinyes that will punish him if he does not avenge his father. Apollo commands the murder, sees the Erinyes off his precinct, and is their chief antagonist. Euripides' *Electra* suggests Apollo may have "spoken unwisely." At the end of Euripides' *Orestes*, Apollo appears in person. Orestes greets him as a true prophet:

> So! you were not a lying seer, but true. And yet fear
> came on me, in case, seeming to hear your voice,
> I heard one of the *alastores* [avenging daemons].[67]

[66] *Cho.* 1051–53, 585; *Or.* 314–15.
[67] E. *El.* 1245, 1302; *Or.* 1667–69.

Orestes' madness is real. So are Erinyes. But the audience's relation to them, always problematic, is newly so. Aeschylus insisted the Erinyes were old, far older than the Olympians: there from the birth of things.[68] For Euripides, the *Eumenides*, with its vision of horrors—hatred, evil, guilt—absorbed constructively into mind and city, was likewise there from birth. But in his intuition, one sacramental hour of facing out evil and anger cannot make them go away forever. Erinyes keep pouring out of human relationships, despite the Choes, despite the *Oresteia*'s momentary stilling. Further, Orestes' story is set up so that Apollo, seemingly against Erinyes, in fact acts with them. Light is in collusion with the dark. Both make Orestes kill his mother. Apollo himself can seem to Orestes, who knows Erinyes at first hand, to sound as "one of them." Is this thought the final signature of Orestes' madness? Or are the spectators mad if they have not worked it out themselves?

WHERE THE TERRIBLE IS GOOD

> . . . he would have us remember most of all
> to be enthusiastic over the night. . . .
> —Auden, "In Memory of Sigmund Freud"

In the *Eumenides*, "There is [a place]," the Erinyes claim, "where the terrible is good." They call themselves "mad mortal-watchers":

> There is [somewhere] where the terrible is good.
> A watcher must stay in *phrenes*. It is worth
> being wise [*sōphronein*, i.e., having a safe *phrēn*] through groaning.
> Who—either city or mortal—would reverence justice,
> unless they nurtured their *kardia* in fear?

The Erinyes' role is "spy in the *phrenes*." Fear, the general principle of Greek approaches to divinity (see Chapter 7), "nurturing the heart" of state and individual, is the Erinyes' point.[69] The *Eumenides* enacts the absorption of this principle into Athens and Athenians. Terror can be good. Let us have spies, monitors of fear, in *kardia* and *phrenes*. They keep down evil and so have power to bless.

Where, then, do the Erinyes belong? Aeschylus's Apollo is clear that they do not belong with him,

> but where there are men cut down and eyes gouged out,
> sentences of throat-cutting, virility annulled
> in seed's destruction, extremities cut off,
> men stoned, impaled with a stake through the spine. . .

---

[68] *Eum.* 778–79, 848; see Gould 1985:28.
[69] *Eum.* 500, 517–25. Cf. above, pp. 132–33 and 156–57.

>Shapes like yours should live in the lair
>of a blood-licking lion.

But Athene offers them

>a seat in a just land, where you'll sit
>on gleaming thrones.

Which does tragedy as a whole endorse, Apollo's or Athene's vision of where Erinyes belong?[70]

Both, maybe. When the Erinyes begin to listen to Athene, the question of where they should "sit" becomes the dynamic for the rest of the play. "What kind of seat do you say we'll have?" In modern performance, it is hard for this question not to get a nervous giggle from audiences. It is the turning point, the trilogy putting its key question: where can fury and foulness bed down bearably in human earth?

Athene says she will install them, these "great daemons, hard to please," among Athenians. This will help Athens, because

>Lady Erinys has great power
>among the immortals and with those below earth.
>Among human beings Erinyes work visibly, perfectly,
>giving song to some, to others life dimmed with tears.

It may not seem to us a caring vision, but it is the way tragic Athene cares. "From these terrible faces," she says, "I see great benefit for these citizens." She organizes Erinyes on their road to "chambers." They go "with holy sacrifices," lit "by the holy light of procession" and "shining torches," "to places below and under earth," "beneath earth."[71]

The play replays the *Choephoroe*'s sense of anger coming up from earth. These daemons, sacramentally changed, are now returning, like dying warriors, to earth whence they came. The play could not say more clearly that it is changing what is dark, inner, deathly, foul, by illuminating this same darkness. Illumination involves calling up violence and returning violence to the dark, giving darkness a home. Erinyes, fauna of the night, in Auden's phrase, take up "home" under and in, the play repeats, our "earth."[72]

These forces threatened Orestes "from the ground." They are the "terrible" now earthed in the city's ground. They "remain." "Remain" is a key word in the Erinyes' own vision of their role.[73] They remain as live forces, in relationships, society, and its ground, in the citizen's *splanchna*, families,

---

[70] Apollo's vision: *Eum.* 185–94; see above, pp. 102–3. Athene's vision: *Eum.* 805–7.

[71] *Eum.* 892, 928, 951–55, 990–91, 1005, 1007, 1023, 1033, 1036.

[72] "Illumination through the dark": Chapter 3, nn. 78–86. "Return to the dark whence they came": Chapter 5, n. 7. "Fauna of the night," see above, p. 76.

[73] See *Eum.* 383, 519, 544, cf. 677, 887.

houses. "All Athenians are Oresteioi." For Athenians who reenact on their most polluted day the principle that the terror of pollution protects from pollution, the "forms" of that terror must go on seeming, as they do to Apollo, themselves polluting and vile.

What and where is this place where the terrible is good? From Apollo's viewpoint, the Erinyes' precinct is foul and fascinatingly appalling. Many words Apollo uses in his image of it are, mercifully, *hapax legomena*, "words spoken once only" in Greek literature. Erinyes, the self-destructive evil that makes self strike other in words or act, and the damaging violence with which other responds, belong in a place of torture and blood.

Innards, of course, are the central place of blood. Apollo's killing-fields are a product of the mind's appalling power to build harm for others. These inhabitants of torture-places are at home in Hades where the wicked are tortured everlastingly. Hesiod's Erinyes forever punish "false oath-makers" in Hades.[74] But they also dwell in the darkness of the mind and house, watching relationships of promises and blood. They are inside the *phrenes*, watchers in the dark. They guarantee fear in the inmost places, the family and the *kardia*. They "sit" where blood is, within. They enact the paradox of belonging inside while remaining outside to say so. Erinyes are both outside and inside, cult divinities but also image and cause of physical and mental damage. Stories that people fainted at the first performance of *Eumenides* mark the shock of "seeing" what is black, repellant, and wrong within: passion, daemon, the nonhuman inside human, the disgusting mad evil of divinity and, inseparably, of self.

The tragic mind or self, then, as tragedy builds it through images, songs, quarrels, and relationships, is "where the terrible is good." This fictional interior of individuals, which audiences construct in their imaginations, is the unseen place to which tragedy most gestures. This imaginary unseen place contains the power to let blood out of others and destruction into others' lives, and responds with violence to other people's words. This "place," the Erinyes' crucial habitat, is parallel to other unseen places they inhabit, to which tragedy also looks: the "house" and the underworld.[75]

The *Oresteia*'s ending does not mitigate the terror of human evil, whether it is innate or an alien guest. The Choes, enacting silence in the face of the polluted stranger, staging in private the competitive separation of people not together while together, "building" (in Euripides' word) an atmosphere of the unspeakable under the Dionysian illusion of connectedness, did not annul the fact that one person's inwardness is dangerously obscure to another, that people connected by blood can betray and shed the blood by which they are bound. But like the Choes, tragedy could

[74] See above, p. 165.
[75] See Padel 1990:352, 364–65.

construct momentarily a place of concerted attention in the center of the city, where people sitting in silence, but together, might see darkness and the polluted horror of what is inside come bearably out. At the end of Choes, something unseen was expelled from the house.[76]

On Dionysus's stage, the seen explains the unseen, the unseen explains the seen.[77] Erinyes, operating unseen in house and mind, explain the violence people do to each other and themselves. Sharing this balance of explanation, seen and unseen, inside and outside, Athenian tragedy accepted horror in the mind and city and turned horror into something it was possible to see as good.

This interpretive principle, explaining seen from unseen, unseen from seen, was articulated at Athens in the fifth century in intellectual circles and, more broadly, was Hermes' share in the audience's response (see Chapter 1). Master of movement into and out of silence, Hades, invisibility, darkness, fiction, his interpreting persona was, if you like, the divinity of the audience's impulse into a play, and also the message they brought out of it. He was a message-daemon, god of inside, outside, and interpretation. His tutelary presence must have helped the spectators be an audience for whom seeing "terrible faces" in silence but together could bring, in Athene's phrase, "great benefit." Athene's city earthed Apollo's vision of the foulness of mind, and made from it the paradox of darkness illumined, the inside brought out. Tragedy, like its own vision of the self, was where the terrible could also, for a while, be good.

[76] See Burkert 1985:238.

[77] Seen and unseen: see Taplin 1978:160; Padel 1990:345. Interpreting seen from unseen: see above, pp. 67 and 114.

WORKS CITED

Many brilliant and powerful relevant studies, especially of individual plays, do not appear here. This is simply a list of secondary works to which I refer for specific points.

Adkins, A.W.H. 1970. *From the Many to the One*. London.

Agulhon, M. 1981. *Marianne into Battle: Republican Imagery and Symbolism in France 1789–1880*. Trans. J. Lloyd. Cambridge.

Alexiou, M. 1974. *The Ritual Lament in the Greek Tradition*. Cambridge.

Argyle, J. M. 1976. *Gaze and Mutual Gaze*. Cambridge.

Austin, N. 1975. *Archery at the Dark of the Moon*. Berkeley.

Bachelard, G. 1969. *The Poetics of Space* [1958]. Trans. M. Jolas [1964]. Boston.

Barnes, J. 1979. *The Presocratic Philosophers*. 2 vols. London, Henley, Boston.

Beard, M., and J. North, eds. 1990. *Pagan Priests*. London.

Beazley, Sir John. 1948. "Hymn to Hermes." *American Journal of Archaeology* 52:336–39.

Becker, O. 1937. "Das Bild des Weges." *Hermes Einzelschriften* 4. Berlin.

Beer, G. 1983. *Darwin's Plots*. London.

Berger E. and R. Lullies. 1979. *Antike Kunstwerke aus der Sammlung Ludwig*. Basle.

Bergson, H. L. 1935. *The Two Sources of Morality and Religion*. Trans. R. A. Audra and C. Brereton. London.

Bion, W. R. 1962. *Learning from Experience*. London.

Blecher, G. 1905. *De extispicio capita tria*. Giessen.

Bleibtreu, J. 1968. *The Parable of the Beast*. London.

Bloch, M. 1954. *The Historian's Craft*. Trans. P. Putnam. Manchester.

Blum, R., and E. Blum. 1970. *The Dangerous Hour: The Lore and Culture of Crisis and Mystery in Rural Greece*. London.

Bodson, L. 1978. *Hiera Zōa: Contribution à l'étude de la place de l'animal dans la religion grècque ancienne*. Brussels.

Böhme, J. 1929. *Die Seele und das Ich im homerischen Epos*. Leipzig and Berlin.

Borthwick, E. K. 1976. "The 'Flower of the Argives' and a Neglected Meaning of *Anthos*." *Journal of Hellenic Studies* 96:1–7.

Bouché-Leclerq, A. 1879–82. *Histoire de la divination dans l'antiquité*. 4 vols. Paris.

Bremmer, J. 1983. *The Early Greek Concept of the Soul*. Princeton.

Breslin, J. N.d. *A Greek Prayer*. Malibu, J. Paul Getty Museum.

Brisson, L. 1976. *Le Mythe de Teirésias*. Leiden.

Brommer, F. 1952. "Herakles und Geras." *Archäologischer Anzeiger* 67:60–73.

Brown, A. L. 1983. "The Erinyes in the *Oresteia*." *Journal of Hellenic Studies* 103:13–34.

Brown, P. 1988. *The Body and Society*. London and Columbia.

Bruchmann, C.F.H. 1893. *Epitheta deorum*. Leipzig.

Buffière, F. 1973. *Les Mythes d' Homère*. Paris.

Bultmann, R. 1948. "Zur Geschichte der Lichtsymbolik im Altertum." *Philologus* 97:1–36.

Burkert, W. 1972. *Lore and Science in Ancient Pythagoreanism*. Trans. E. Minar. Cambridge, Mass.

———. 1977. "Air-Imprints or *Eidola*: Democritus' Aitiology of Vision." *Illinois Classical Studies* 2:97–109.

———. 1979. *Structure and History in Greek Mythology and Ritual*. Berkeley.

———. 1983. *Homo necans* [1972]. Trans. P. Bing. Berkeley.

———. 1985. *Greek Religion* [1977]. Trans. J. Raffan. Oxford.

Burnyeat, M. F. 1976. "Plato on the Grammar of Perceiving." *Classical Quarterly* 26:29–51.

———. 1977. "Socratic Midwifery, Platonic Inspiration." *Bulletin of the Institute of Classical Studies* 24:7–16.

———. 1980a. "Aristotle on Learning to Be Good." In A. Rorty, ed., *Essays on Aristotle's Ethics*, pp. 69–92. Berkeley and Los Angeles.

———. 1980b. "Tranquillity without a Stop: Timon fr. 68." *Classical Quarterly* 30:86–93.

Burton, R.W.B. 1980. *The Chorus in Sophocles' Tragedies*. Oxford.

Buxton, R. 1980. "Blindness and Limits: Sophocles and the Logic of Myth." *Journal of Hellenic Studies* 100:22–37.

———. 1982. *Persuasion in Greek Tragedy: A Study of Peitho*. Cambridge.

Cameron, A., and A. Kuhrt, eds. 1983. *Images of Women in Antiquity*. London.

Carden, R. 1974. *The Papyrus Fragments of Sophocles*. Berlin and New York.

Cassirer, E. 1946. *Language and Myth* [1925]. Trans. S. K. Langer. New York.

Caswell, C. P. 1990. *A Study of THUMOS in Early Greek Epic*. *Mnemosyne*, special issue. Leiden and New York.

Chadwick, N. K. 1942. *Poetry and Prophecy*. Cambridge.

Classen, C. J. 1965. "Licht und Dunkel in der frühgriechischen Philosophie." *Studium Generale* 18:97–116.

Claus, D. B. 1981. *Towards the Soul: An Inquiry into the Meaning of Psyche before Plato*. Yale.

Collinge, N. E. 1962. "Medical Terms and Clinical Attitudes in the Tragedians." *Bulletin of the Institute of Classical Studies* 9:43–55.

Cook, A. B. 1914–40. *Zeus*. 3 vols. Cambridge.

Cook, R. M. 1952. "Dogs in Battle." In T. Dohrn, ed., *Festschrift für A. Rumpf*, pp. 38–42. Krefeld.

———. 1972. *Greek Painted Pottery*. 2d ed. London.

Courtois, J. C. 1969. "La Maison du prêtre aux modèles de poumon et de foies d' Ugarit." In *Mission de Ras Shamra*, tome 17, *Ugaritica* 6, pp. 91–119. Paris.

Darcus, S. M. 1979. "A Person's Relation to *Phren* in Homer, Hesiod, and the Greek Lyric Poets." *Glotta* 57:159–73.

———. 1980. "How a Person Relates to *Thumos* in Homer." *Indogermanische Forschungen* 85:138–50.

———. 1981. "The Function of *Thumos* in Hesiod and the Greek Lyric Poets." *Glotta* 59:147–55.

Dawe, R. 1966. "The Place of the 'Hymn to Zeus' in Aeschylus' *Agamemnon*." *Eranos* 64:1–21.

——. 1968. "Some Reflections on *Ate* and *Hamartia*." *Harvard Studies in Classical Philology* 72:89–124.

Delcourt, M. 1961. *Hermaphrodite: Myths and Rites of the Bisexual Figure in Classical Antiquity*. Trans. J. Nicholson. London.

Déonna, E. 1965. *Le Symbolisme de l'oeil*. Paris.

De Romilly, J. 1958. *La Crainte et l'angoisse dans le théatre d'Eschyle*. Paris.

Derrida, J. 1972. "La Pharmacie de Platon." In *La Dissemination*, pp. 71–197. Paris.

Detienne, M. 1977. *The Gardens of Adonis*. Trans. J. Lloyd. Hassocks.

——. 1981a. "Between Beasts and Gods." In Gordon 1981:215–28.

——. 1981b. "The Sea-Crow." In Gordon 1981:16–42.

——. 1989. *Dionysus at Large*. Trans. A. Goldhammer. Cambridge, Mass. and London.

Detienne, M., and J-P. Vernant. 1978. *Cunning Intelligence in Greek Culture and Society*. Trans. J. Lloyd. Sussex.

Deubner, L. 1899. *De incubatione*. Leipzig.

Dierauer, U. 1977. *Tier und Mensch im Denken der Antike*. Amsterdam.

Dietrich, B. C. 1965. *Death, Fate and the Gods*. London.

——. 1974. *The Origins of Greek Religion*. Berlin.

Dilthey, W. 1972. "The Rise of Hermeneutics." Trans. F. Jameson. *New Literary History* 3:229–245.

Dodds, E. R. 1951. *The Greeks and the Irrational*. Berkeley.

——. 1973. *The Ancient Concept of Progress*. Oxford.

Douglas, M. 1970. *Natural Symbols*. London.

——. 1975. *Implicit Meanings*. London.

Douglas, N. 1928. *Birds and Beasts of the Greek Anthology*. London.

Dover, Sir K. 1974. *Greek Popular Morality in the Time of Plato and Aristotle*. Oxford.

Dowden, K. 1989. *Death and the Maiden: Girls' Initiation Rites in Greek Mythology*. London and New York.

Doyle, R. E. 1984. *ATĒ: Its Use and Meaning*. New York.

DuBois, P. 1982. *Centaurs and Amazons*. Ann Arbor, Mich.

——. 1988. *Sowing the Body: Psychoanalysis and Ancient Representations of Women*. Chicago.

Du Boulay, J. 1974. *Portrait of a Greek Mountain Village*. Oxford.

Durand, J. L., and F. Lissarague. 1979. "Les Entrailles de la cité." *Hephaistos* 1:92–108.

Earp, F. R. 1948. *Aeschylus in His Style*. Cambridge.

Edelstein, E. J., and L. Edelstein. 1945. *Asclepius*. 2 vols. Baltimore.

Eitrem, S. 1953. "The Pindaric *Phthonos*." In Mylonas 1953, 2:531–36.

Ellinger, I. 1953. "Winged Figures." In Mylonas 1953, 2:1185–90.

Evans-Pritchard, E. E. 1962. *Essays in Social Anthropology*. London.

——. 1972. *Social Anthropology* [1951]. London.

Farnell, L. R. 1896–1909. *Cults of the Greek States*. 5 vols. Oxford.

Fascher, E. 1927. *PROPHETĒS*. Giessen.

Firth, R. 1973. *Symbols, Public and Private*. London.

Flashar, H. 1966. *Melancholie und Melancholiker in den medizinischen Theorien der Antike*. Berlin.

Fletcher, A. 1970. *Allegory: The Theory of a Symbolic Mode* [1964]. Ithaca.

Fontenrose, J. 1959. *Python: A Study of Delphic Myth and Its Origins*. Berkeley.

Foucault, M. 1970. *The Order of Things* [1966]. Trans. Alan Sheridan. London.

———. 1971. *Madness and Civilization* [1961]. Trans. R. Howard. London.

Fraenkel, E. 1931. "Der Zeushymnus im *Agamemnon* des Aischylos." *Philologus* 86:1–17.

Fränkel, H. 1921. *Die homerischen Gleichnisse*. Göttingen.

———. 1975. *Early Greek Poetry and Philosophy* [1962]. Trans. M. Hadas and J. Willis. Oxford.

Frame, D. 1978. *The Myth of Return in Early Greek Epic*. New Haven.

Freud, S. [1931] 1932. "The Acquisition and Control of Fire." In *The Standard Edition of the Complete Psychological Works of Sigmund Freud*, ed. and trans. J. Strachey, with A. Freud, assisted by A. Strachey and A. Tyson, 22:187–96. London 1964.

———. [1932] 1933. "New Introductory Lectures on Psychoanalysis." In *The Standard Edition of the Complete Psychological Works of Sigmund Freud*, ed. and trans. J. Strachey, with A. Freud, assisted by A. Strachey and A. Tyson, 22:7–184. London 1964.

Garland, R. 1981. "The Causation of Death in the *Iliad*: A Theological and Biological Investigation." *Bulletin of the Institute of Classical Studies* 28:43–60.

———. 1985. *The Greek Way of Death*. London.

Giglioli, G. 1953. "Herakles e Geras." In Mylonas 1953, 2:111–13.

Giglioli, P. P., ed. 1972. *Language and Social Context*. London.

Goheen, R. F. 1951. *The Imagery of Sophocles' Antigone*. Princeton.

Goldhill, S. 1986. *Reading Greek Tragedy*. Cambridge.

Gordon, R. L., ed. 1981. *Myth Religion and Society*. Cambridge and Paris.

Gould, J. P. 1978. "Dramatic Character and 'Human Intelligibility.' " *Proceedings of the Cambridge Philological Society* 204:43–67.

———. 1980. "Law, Custom, and Myth: Aspects of the Social Position of Women in Classical Athens." *Journal of Hellenic Studies* 100:38–59.

———. 1985. "On Making Sense of Greek Religion." In P. E. Easterling and J. V. Muir, eds., *Greek Religion and Society*, pp. 1–33. Cambridge.

Gow, A.S.F. 1934. "*Iunx, Rhombos, Rhombus, Turbo*." *Journal of Hellenic Studies* 54:1–13.

Halliday, W. R. 1913. *Greek Divination*. London.

Hamdorf, F. W. 1964. *Griechische Kultpersonifikationen der vorhellenistishen Zeit*. Mainz.

Hamilton, M. 1906. *Incubation or the Cure of Disease in Pagan Temples and Christian Churches*. St. Andrews and London.

Handley, E. 1956. "Words for 'Soul,' 'Heart,' and 'Mind' in Aristophanes." *Rheinisches Museum für Philologie* 99:205–25.

Harries, K. 1979. "Metaphor and Transcendence." In Sacks 1979:71–88.

Harris, C.R.S. 1973. *The Heart and Vascular System in Ancient Greek Medicine from Alcmaeon to Galen*. Oxford.

Harrison, J. 1927. *Themis*. 2d ed. Cambridge.

————. 1922. *Prolegomena to the Study of Greek Religion*. 3rd ed. Cambridge.

Henderson, J. 1975. *The Maculate Muse: Obscene Language in Attic Comedy*. New Haven.

Henrichs, A. 1978. "Greek Maenadism from Olympias to Messalina." *Harvard Studies in Classical Philology* 88:121–60.

Herter, H. 1976. "Hermes, Ursprung und Wesen eines griechischen Gottes." *Rheinisches Museum für Philologie* 119:193–241.

Herzog, R. 1931. "Die Wunderheilungen von Epidaurus." *Philologus* 22, 3:1–164.

Hess, E. 1965. "Attitude and Pupil Size." *Scientific American* 212:46–54.

Hill, B. H. 1965. "The Grain and the Spirit in Mediaeval Anatomy." *Speculum* 40:63–73.

Horton, R., and R. Finnegan, eds. 1973. *Modes of Thought*. London.

Huizinga, J. 1955. *The Waning of the Middle Ages* [1924]. Trans. F. Hopman. Harmondsworth.

Humphreys, S. C. 1983. *The Family, Women and Death*. London.

Hunter, G. K. 1978. *Dramatic Identities and Cultural Tradition*. Liverpool.

Irwin, E. 1974. *Colour Terms in Greek Poetry*. Toronto.

James, W. 1952. *The Varieties of Religious Experience* [1902]. London.

Jaynes, J. 1976. *The Origin of Consciousness in the Breakdown of the Bicameral Mind*. Boston.

Jucquois, G., and B. Devlamminck. 1977. *Compléments aux dictionnaires étymologiques du grec ancien*. Tome 1. Louvain.

Jung, E., and M-L. von Kranz. 1971. *The Grail Legend*. Trans. A. Dykes. London.

Just, R. 1989. *Women in Athenian Law and Life*. London and New York.

Kahn, C. H. 1979. *The Art and Thought of Heraclitus*. Cambridge.

Kahn, L. 1978. *Hermès passe*. Paris.

Kamerbeek, J. C. 1948. "On the Conception of *Theomachos* in Relation with Greek Tragedy." *Mnemosyne* 4, 1:271–83.

Kassel, R. 1983. "Dialoge mit Statuen." *Zeitschrift für Papyrologie und Epigraphik* 51:1–10.

Keller, O. 1913. *Die Antike Tierwelt*. Leipzig.

Kelly, L. G. 1979. *The True Interpreter*. Oxford.

Kenny, A. 1973. *The Anatomy of the Soul*. Oxford.

King, H. 1983. "Bound to Bleed: Artemis and Greek Women." In Cameron and Kuhrt 1983:109–27.

Kirk, G. 1970. *Myth: Its Meaning and Functions in Ancient and Other Cultures*. Berkeley.

Klibansky, R., E. Panofsky, and F. Saxl. 1964. *Saturn and Melancholy*. London.

Körte, G. 1874. *Über Personificationen psychologischer Affekte in der späteren Vasenmalerei*. Berlin.

————. 1905. "Über die bronze Leber von Piacenza." *Mitteilungen des Deutschen Archäologischen Instituts Athenische Abteilung*. Pp. 348–79.

Kouretas, D. 1960. "Aspects modernes des cures psychotherapiques appliquées dans les sanctuaires de la Grèce antique." *Commentaires au XVIIe Congrès International d'histoire de la médicine.*

Kranz, W. 1938. "Kosmos und Mensch in der Vorstellung frühen Griechentums." *Nachrichten von der Gesellschaft der Wissenschaft zu Göttingen* I, 2, 7:121–61.

Kraus, T. 1960. *Hekate, Studien zu Wesen und Bild der Göttin in Kleinasien und Griechenland.* Heidelberg.

Kristeva, J. 1989. *Black Sun: Depression and Melancholia.* Trans. L. S. Roudiez. New York and Oxford.

Ladner, G. 1979. "Mediaeval and Modern Symbolism, A Comparison." *Speculum* 54:223–56.

Laing, R. 1965. *The Divided Self* [1960]. Harmondsworth.

Laplanche, J., and J-B. Pontalis. 1973. *The Language of Psychoanalysis.* London.

Lattimore, R. 1962. *Themes in Greek and Latin Epitaphs* [1942]. Urbana, Ill.

Lawson, J. C. 1910. *Modern Greek Folklore and Ancient Greek Religion.* Cambridge.

Lebeck, A. 1971. *The Oresteia.* Washington, D.C.

———. 1973. "The Central Myth of Plato's *Phaedrus.*" *Greek, Roman and Byzantine Studies* 14:267–90.

Levi, C. 1947. *Christ Stopped at Eboli.* Trans. F. Frenaye. Harmondsworth.

Lienhardt, G. 1961. *Divinity and Experience.* Oxford.

———. 1980. "Self, Public and Private: Some African Representations." *Journal of the Anthropological Society of Oxford* 11:69–82.

Lincoln, B. 1975. "Homeric *Lussa*: 'Wolfish Rage.'" *Indogermanische Forschungen* 80:98–105.

Lindsay, J. 1965. *The Clashing Rocks.* London.

Lloyd, G.E.R. 1966. *Polarity and Analogy.* Cambridge.

———. 1973. "Right and Left in Greek Philosophy." In Needham 1973:167–86.

———. 1975. "Alcmaeon and the Early History of Dissection." *Sudhoffs Archiv* 59:113–47.

———. 1979. *Magic, Reason, and Experience.* Cambridge.

———. 1983. *Science, Folklore and Ideology.* Cambridge.

———. 1987. *The Revolutions of Wisdom.* Berkeley, Los Angeles, London.

———. 1990. *Demystifying Mentalities.* Cambridge.

Lloyd-Jones, Sir Hugh, 1975. *Females of the Species.* London.

———. 1983. *The Justice of Zeus.* 2d ed. Berkeley.

———. 1990. *Academic Papers* i (*Greek Comedy, Lyric and Tragedy*) and ii (*Greek Comedy, Hellenistic Literature, Greek Religion and Miscellanea*). Oxford.

——— and Wilson, N. G., 1990. *Sophoclea: Studies on the Text of Sophocles.* Oxford.

Löffler, I. 1963. "Die Melampodie." *Beiträge zur klassischen Philologie* 7 (Meisenheim).

Long, A. A. 1966. "Thinking and Sense-Perception in Empedocles: Mysticism or Materialism?" *Classical Quarterly* 16:256–76.

————. 1967. "Poisonous Growths in the *Trachiniae.*" *Greek, Roman and Byzantine Studies* 8:275–78.

————. 1968. *Language and Thought in Sophocles.* London.

————. 1978. "Timon of Phlius: Pyrrhonist and Satirist." *Proceedings of the Cambridge Philological Society* 204:68–91.

Lonie, I. M. 1965. "Medical Theory in Heraclides of Pontus." *Mnemosyne* 18:125–43.

Loraux, N. 1978. "Sur la race des femmes et quelques-unes de ses tribus." *Arethusa* 11:43–87.

Lullies, R. 1931. *Die Typen der griechischen Herme.* Königsberg.

Majno, G. 1975. *The Healing Hand.* Cambridge, Mass.

Malten, L. 1961. *Die Sprache des menschlichen Antlitzes im frühen Griechentum.* Berlin.

Maritain, J. 1943. *Redeeming the Time.* Trans. H. L. Binsse. London.

Martines, L. 1983. *Power and Imagination: City States in Renaissance Italy* [1979]. Harmondsworth.

Masson, O. 1962. *Les Fragments du poète Hipponax.* Paris.

Meissner, B. 1951. "Mythisches und Rationales in der Psychologie der euripideischen Tragödie." Diss. Göttingen.

Miller, H. W. 1944. "Medical Terminology in Tragedy." *Transactions of the American Philological Association* 75:156–67.

Milner, M. 1952. "Aspects of Symbolism in Comprehension of the Not-Self." *International Journal of Psychoanalysis* 33:181–95.

Mitropoulos, E. 1978. *Deities and Heroes in the Form of Snakes.* Athens.

Moke, D. 1984. *Eroticism in the Greek Magical Papyri: Selected Studies.* Ann Arbor.

Müller, G. 1967. "Das zweite Stasimon des *König Ödipus.*" *Hermes* 95:269–91.

Murdoch, I. 1953. *Sartre, Romantic Rationalist.* Cambridge.

Murray, P. 1981. "Poetic Inspiration in Early Greece." *Journal of Hellenic Studies* 101:87–100.

Mylonas, G., ed. 1953. *Studies Presented to D. M. Robinson.* 2 vols. St. Louis.

Nagy, G. 1980. "Patroklos, Concepts of Afterlife, and the Indic Triple Fire." *Arethusa* 13, 2:161–95.

Napoli, H. 1970. *La Tomba del tuffatore.* Bari.

Needham, R., ed. 1973. *Right and Left: Essays on Dual Symbolic Classification.* Chicago.

————. 1978. *Primordial Characters.* Charlottesville, Va.

Nilsson, M. 1906. *Griechische Feste von religiöser Bedeutung.* Leipzig.

————. 1940. *Greek Popular Religion* [1925]. New York.

————. 1955. *Geschichte der griechischen Religion.* 2d ed. Munich.

Nitze, W. A., ed. 1927. *Robert de Boron, le roman de l'estoire dou Graal.* Paris.

Norden, E. 1956. *Agnostos theos* [1913]. Stuttgart.

Nussbaum, M. 1972. "*Psuchē* in Heraclitus." *Phronesis* 17:1–15, 153–70.

————, ed. 1978. *Aristotle, "De motu animalium."* Princeton.

O'Brien, D. 1968. "The Relation of Anaxagoras and Empedocles." *Journal of Hellenic Studies* 88:93–113.

O'Brien, D. 1970. "The Effect of a Simile: Empedocles' Theories of Seeing and Breathing." *Journal of Hellenic Studies* 90:140–79.

Onians, R. B. 1954. *The Origins of European Thought.* 2d ed. Cambridge.

Oosten, J. G. 1973. "The Examination of Religious Concepts in Religious Anthropology." In T. P. van Baaren and H.J.W. Drijvers, eds., *Religion, Culture and Methodology*, pp. 99–108. The Hague and Paris.

Osborne, R. 1985. "The Erection and Mutilation of the Hermai." *Proceedings of the Cambridge Philological Society* 211:47–73.

Owens, E. J. 1983. "The *Koprologoi* at Athens in the Fifth Century and Fourth Century B.C." *Classical Quarterly* 33:44–50.

Padel, R. 1981. "Madness in Fifth-Century Athenian Tragedy." In P. Heelas and A. Lock, eds., *Indigenous Psychologies*, pp. 105–31. London.

———. 1983. "Women: Model for Possession by Greek Daemons." In Cameron and Kuhrt 1983:3–19.

———. 1990. "Making Space Speak." In Winkler and Zeitlin 1990:336–65.

———. Forthcoming. *Connexions: Mapping and Divinity in the Greek Tragic Self.* Princeton.

Pagel, W. 1981. "The Smiling Spleen." In H. Lloyd-Jones, V. Pearl, and B. Worden, eds., *History and Imagination: Essays in Honour of H. R. Trevor-Roper*, pp. 81–87. London.

Papathanassiou, D. 1935. *L'Oracle de Trophonios.* Athens.

Parke, H. W. 1967. *Greek Oracles.* London.

Parker, R. 1983. *Miasma.* Oxford.

Pearson, A. C. 1910. "Phrixus and Demodice." *Classical Review* 23:255–57.

———, ed. 1917. *The Fragments of Sophocles.* 3 vols. Cambridge.

Pfeiffer, R. 1966. "Sophoclea." *Wiener Studien* 79:63–66.

Pickard-Cambridge, A. 1946. *The Theatre of Dionysus in Athens.* Oxford.

Pigeaud, J. 1981. *La Maladie de l'âme.* Paris.

Pley, H. 1911. *De lanae in antiquorum ritibus usu.* Giessen.

Pollard, J. 1948. "Birds in Aeschylus." *Greece and Rome* 17:116–26.

———. 1965. *Seers, Shrines and Sirens.* London.

———. 1977. *Birds in Greek Life and Myth.* London.

Prag, A.J.N.W. 1985. *The Oresteia.* Warminster.

Preller, L. 1887–94. *Griechische Mythologie.* 4 vols. Berlin.

Rahn, H. 1967. "Das Tier in der homerischen Dichtung." *Studium Generale* 20:90–105.

Redfield, J. M. 1975. *Nature and Culture in the Iliad: The Tragedy of Hector.* Chicago and London.

Reinhardt, K. 1926. *Kosmos und Sympathie.* Munich.

Richter, G. 1930. *Animals in Greek Sculpture.* Oxford.

Robertson, M. 1981. *A Shorter History of Greek Art.* Cambridge.

Rohde, E. 1925. *Psyche.* Trans. W. B. Hillis. London.

Rosaldo, M. Z. 1980. *Knowledge and Passion: Ilongot Notions of Self and Social Life.* Cambridge.

Rosaldo, M. Z., and L. Lamphere, eds. 1974. *Women, Culture and Society.* Stanford.

Rycroft, C. 1968. *Imagination and Reality*. London.

————. 1979. *The Innocence of Dreams*. London.

Sacks, S., ed. 1979. *On Metaphor*. Chicago.

Sansone, D. 1975. "Aeschylean Metaphors for Intellectual Activity." *Hermes Einzelschriften* 35. Wiesbaden.

Schaps, D. 1979. *Economic Rights of Women in Ancient Greece*. Edinburgh.

Schneider, L. M. 1968. "Compositional and Psychological Use of the Spear in Two Vase-Paintings by Exekias: A Note on Style." *American Journal of Archaeology* 72:385–86.

Scholz, H. H. 1937. *Der Hund in der griechisch-römischen Magie und Religion*. Berlin.

Schouten, J. 1967. *The Rod and Serpent of Asklepios*. Amsterdam.

Sharpe, E. 1978. "Psycho-Physical Problems Revealed in Language: An Examination of Metaphor" [1940]. In E. Sharpe, *Collected Papers on Psychoanalysis*, pp. 155–69. London.

Sifakis, G. M. 1971. *Parabasis and Animal Choruses*. London.

Silk, M. 1974. *Interaction in Poetic Imagery*. Cambridge.

Simon, B. 1978. *Mind and Madness in Ancient Greece*. Ithaca, N.Y.

Six, J. 1885. *De gorgone*. Amsterdam.

Slater, W. J. 1976. "Symposium at Sea." *Harvard Studies in Classical Philology* 80:161–70.

Snell, B. 1931. Review of Böhme 1929. *Gnomon* 7:74–86.

————. 1953. *The Discovery of the Mind*. Trans. T. G. Rosenmeyer. Oxford.

————. 1978. "Der Weg zum Denken und zur Wahrheit: Studien zur frühgriechischen Sprache." *Hypomnemata* 57. Göttingen.

Snodgrass, A. 1967. *Arms and Armour of the Greeks*. London.

————. 1974. "An Historical Homeric Society?" *Journal of Hellenic Studies* 94:114–25.

Sontag, S. 1979. *Illness as Metaphor* [1978]. New York.

Sourvinou-Inwood, C. 1979. "The Myth of the First Temple at Delphi." *Classical Quarterly* 29:231–51.

————. 1981. "To Die and Enter the House of Hades: Homer, Before, and After." In J. Whaley, ed., *Mirrors of Mortality*, pp. 15–39. London.

Southern, R. 1967. *The Making of the Middle Ages*. [1953]. London.

Stallmach, J. 1968. "*Atē*: zur Frage des Selbst- und Weltverständnisses des frühgriechischen Menschen." *Beiträge zur klassischen Philologie* 18. Meisenheim.

Stanford, W. B. 1939. *Ambiguity in Greek Literature*. Oxford.

————. 1983. *Greek Tragedy and the Emotions*. London.

Steiner, G. 1972. *Extraterritorial: Papers on Literature and the Language Revolution*. London.

————. 1975. *After Babel*. London.

————. 1984. *Antigones*. Oxford.

————. 1990. "A Note on Absolute Tragedy." *Journal of Literature and Theology* 4, no. 2:147–56.

Stinton, T.C.W. 1990. *Collected Papers on Greek Tragedy*. Oxford.

Sullivan, S. D. 1988. *Psychological Activity in Homer*. Ottawa.

Sutton, D. 1979. "Sophocles' *Inachus*." *Beiträge zur klassischen Philologie* 29. Meisenheim.

Svenbro, J. 1990. "The 'Interior" Voice: On the Invention of Silent Reading." In Winkler and Zeitlin 1990:366–84.

Taillardat, J. 1965. *Les Images d'Aristophane*. Paris.

Tambiah, S. J. 1969. "Animals Are Good to Think and Good to Prohibit." *Ethnology* 8, 4 (Oct.):424–59.

———. 1973. "Form and Meaning of Magical Acts: A Point of View." In Horton and Finnegan 1973:199–229.

Taplin, O. 1977. *The Stagecraft of Aeschylus*. Oxford.

———. 1978. *Greek Tragedy in Action*. London.

———. 1982. "Sophocles in His Theatre." In *Sophocle*, Entretiens Hardt 29, pp. 155–83. Geneva.

Taylor, A. E. 1962. *A Commentary on Plato's Timaeus* [1928]. Oxford.

Thomas, K. 1973. *Religion and the Decline of Magic* [1971]. Harmondsworth.

———. 1984. *Man and the Natural World*. Harmondsworth.

Thompson, H. A., and R. E. Wycherley. 1972. "The Agora of Athens." In *The Athenian Agora*, vol. 14. Princeton.

Tolstoy, N. 1985. *The Quest for Merlin*. London.

Totman, R. 1979. *Social Causes of Illness*. London.

Toynbee, J.M.C. 1973. *Animals in Roman Life and Art*. London.

Trendall, T., and T.B.L. Webster. 1971. *Illustrations of Greek Drama*. London.

Usener, H. 1948. *Götternamen* [1895]. 3d ed. Frankfurt.

Van Gennep, A. 1977. *The Rites of Passage* [1909]. Trans. M. Vizedom and G. Caffee [1960]. London.

Vernant, J-P. 1980. *Myth and Society in Ancient Greece*. Trans. J. Lloyd. London.

———. 1983. *Myth and Thought among the Greeks* [1965]. Trans. J. Lloyd. London.

———. 1985. *La Mort dans les yeux*. Paris.

Vernant, J-P., and P. Vidal-Naquet. 1981. *Tragedy and Myth in Ancient Greece* [1972]. Trans. J. Lloyd. Sussex.

Vidal-Naquet, P. 1975. "Bêtes, hommes et dieux chez les Grecs." In L. Poliakov, ed., *Hommes et bêtes: entretiens sur le racisme*, pp. 129–42. Paris and The Hague.

———. 1981. "Sophocles' *Philoctetes* and the Athenian *ephēbeia*." In Vernant and Vidal-Naquet 1981:175–99.

———. 1986. *The Black Hunter*. Trans. A. Szegedy-Maszak. Baltimore and London.

Vlastos, G. 1947. "Equality and Justice in Early Greek Cosmologies." *Classical Philology* 42:156–78.

———. 1965. "The Theory of Recollection in Plato's *Meno*." *Dialogue* 4:143–67.

Von Fritz, K. 1943. "*Noos, noein* in the Homeric Poems." *Classical Philology* 38:79–125.

———. 1945. "*Nous, noein*, and Their Derivatives in Presocratic Philosophy (Excluding Anaxagoras), Part I." *Classical Philology* 40:223–42.

———. 1946. "*Nous, noein,* and Their Derivatives in Presocratic Philosophy (Excluding Anaxagoras), Part II." *Classical Philology* 41:12–34.

Walcot, P. 1978. *Envy and the Greeks.* London.

———. 1979. "Cattle-raiding, Heroic Tradition, and Ritual: The Greek Evidence." *History of Religions* 18:326–51.

Warner, M. 1985. *Monuments and Maidens: The Allegory of the Female Form.* London.

Webster, T.B.L. 1954. "Personification as a Mode of Greek Thought." *Journal of the Warburg and Courtauld Institutes* 17:10–21.

———. 1957. "Some Psychological Metaphors in Greek Tragedy." *Journal of Hellenic Studies* 77:149–54.

West, D. A. 1967. *Reading Horace.* Edinburgh.

West, M. L. 1983. *The Orphic Poems.* Oxford.

Whorf, Benjamin Lee. 1956. *Language, Thought and Reality.* Ed. John B. Carroll. Cambridge, Mass.

Wicker, B. 1975. *The Story-Shaped World.* London.

Wilamowitz-Moellendorff, U. von. 1931–32. *Der Glaube der Hellenen.* 2 vols. Berlin.

Winkler, John J. 1990. *The Constraints of Desire.* New York and London.

Winkler, John J., and Froma I. Zeitlin, eds. 1990. *Nothing to Do with Dionysos?* Princeton.

Winnington-Ingram, R. P. 1980. *Sophocles: An Interpretation.* Cambridge.

———. 1983. *Studies in Aeschylus.* Cambridge.

Wollheim, R. A. 1974. "The Mind and the Mind's Image of Itself." In R. Wollheim, *On Art and the Mind,* pp. 31–53. Cambridge, Mass.

Wright, M. R., ed. 1981. *Empedocles: The Extant Fragments.* New Haven and London.

Zelliot, A., and M. Berntsen, eds. 1988. *The Experience of Hinduism.* New York.

INDEX

Achilles, 13, 19–20, 23–24, 30, 47, 54, 62, 75, 86, 120, 162, 164, 166–68, 170; horses of, 166, 168

Aeschines, 177–78

Aeschylus, 5, 17, 30, 35, 37, 64, 70, 74, 83, 90–93, 107, 109, 116, 124, 135, 142, 153, 155, 158, 163, 165–66, 171–73, 176, 179, 188–89; *Ag.*, 35, 73–74, 83, 91–95, 119, 126; *Cho.*, 50–51, 82, 84, 91, 96, 105–6, 108, 124, 170, 184–88; *Eum.*, 74, 80, 103, 107–8, 123, 176–91; *Oresteia*, 74–75, 80, 104, 123, 156, 169–92; *Pers.*, 125, 162–63; *PV*, 17, 82; *Sept.*, 83, 154–55; *Supp.*, 130, 135

Agamemnon, 19, 28, 64, 68, 75, 92–95, 118, 156, 164, 166–67, 173, 184

Ajax, 13, 62, 91–92, 97, 118–19, 129, 140, 151, 173

Alcmaeon, 56–59

Anaxagoras, 32, 41, 57, 66, 68, 109

Anaximenes, 43

Antigone, 87, 91–92, 116, 124

Aphrodite, 8, 57, 59–60, 70, 116, 118, 122, 126–27, 145, 154, 156–57, 159, 168

apokrisis, 56–59

Apollo, 3, 17, 28, 71–72, 98, 107–9, 116, 153, 155–56, 178, 181, 188–89, 190–92

apoplexy, 51, 55, 57, 67, 92

Archilochus, 19, 43

Ares, 90–91, 116–17, 125, 146, 154–55, 157

Aristophanes, 5, 13, 19, 22, 28–30, 32, 40–41, 87, 89, 124, 127, 147–48

Aristotle, 9, 13, 28, 34, 41, 44, 48, 58, 65–66, 69, 81, 83, 89, 135, 145, 149–50, 163

Artemis, 7, 94, 121, 141, 152–53, 155–56, 163

Asclepius, 69, 72, 115, 125, 145–46

Ate. See *atē*

atē, 25, 27, 87, 96, 101, 118, 120, 125–26, 129–30, 132–34, 156, 162–64, 166–77, 180

Athene, 80, 97, 104, 114–15, 120, 129, 146, 151, 154–55, 166, 190–92

atomists, 42, 58, 60–61, 102

Augustine, 131, 158

Bacchus. *See* Dionysus

birds, 43, 47, 97, 130–31, 143, 145–47; bird omens, 15, 122, 147

blackness: of blood, 25, 174; of dreams, 80–91; of earth and underworld, 78, 180; of Erinyes, 104, 179, 191; of evil, 71; of hellebore, 55, 69; of house-doors, 182–84; of innards and inner liquids, 23–25, 68, 175; of madness, 69, 104, 174–75; of *menos* and anger, 25, 62, 81, 174; of Night, 101, 181; of passion, 69; of sea, 69, 86; of sun, 24. *See also* darkness

blindness, 72, 79; mental, 162, 168. See also *atē*

blood, 13, 23, 25–27, 30, 37, 41–43, 54, 57–58, 61, 67–68, 74, 78, 81, 84, 86, 88–89, 90, 123–24, 134–35, 141, 144, 148, 153, 155, 163, 165, 172–76, 178, 180–81, 183–91; bloodletting, 55, 82; bloodshed, 81, 170, 173–76, 184

brain, 12–13, 20, 25, 30, 40, 46, 58–59, 81–82, 133

breath, 26, 29, 30, 31, 37, 39, 44, 50, 54–55, 57–58, 60–61, 67, 86, 88–99, 116–17, 142, 174, 176

bulls, 17, 59, 142–43, 151, 170

Calchas, 72, 75

Cassandra, 75, 83, 90, 97, 119, 147, 173, 181

cattle. *See* bulls; cows

caves, 72–75, 100, 136; cave-entrance, 74

Cerberus, 125, 151

changes, 52–53, 68, 81; of breath, 92–93

Chimaera, 90

Choes, 181–84, 187–89, 191–92

cholē, 19, 23–24, 39, 69, 82, 84, 116

cholos, 23–24, 27–29, 39, 68, 81, 83–85, 116–17